Making Literacy Magic Happen

Edited, with commentary, by

Mark Gura and Rose Reissman

The Best of

Learning & Leading with

Technology

on Language Arts

International Society for Technology in Education
EUGENE, OREGON

Making Literacy Magic Happen

The Best of *Learning & Leading with Technology* on Language Arts

Edited by Mark Gura and Rose Reissman

Director of Publishing
Jean Marie Hall

Acquisitions Editors
Mathew Manweller
Scott Harter

Production Editor
Tracy Cozzens

Production Coordinator
Amy Miller

Copy Editor
Ron Renchler,
The Electronic Page

Cover Design
Katherine Getta,
Katherine Getta Graphic Design

Layout and Production
Learning and Leading with Technology staff
Tracy Cozzens
Signe Landin

International Society for Technology in Education (ISTE)

Washington, D.C., Office
1710 Rhode Island Ave. NW, Suite 900, Washington, DC 20036

Eugene, Oregon, Office
175 West Broadway, Suite 300, Eugene, OR 97401-3003
Order Desk: 1.800.336.5191
Order Fax: 1.541.302.3778
Customer Service: orders@iste.org
Books and Courseware: books@iste.org
Permissions: permissions@iste.org
Web site: www.iste.org

First Edition
ISBN 10: 1-56484-175-8
ISBN 13: 978-1-56484-175-9

ABOUT ISTE

The International Society for Technology in Education (ISTE) is the premier membership organization for educators engaged in improving teaching and learning through the effective use of technology. ISTE is the trusted source for professional development, knowledge generation, advocacy, and leadership in education technology innovation.

ISTE Book Publishing works with experienced educators to develop and produce practical resources for classroom teachers, teacher educators, and technology leaders. Every manuscript we select for publication is peer-reviewed and professionally edited. We look for content that emphasizes the effective use of technology where it can make a difference—increasing the productivity of teachers and administrators; helping students with unique learning styles, abilities, or backgrounds; collecting and using data for decision making at the school and district levels; and creating dynamic, project-based learning environments that engage 21st-century learners. We value your feedback on this book and other ISTE products. E-mail us at **books@iste.org**.

ISTE is home of the National Educational Technology Standards (NETS) Project, the National Educational Computing Conference (NECC), and the National Center for Preparing Tomorrow's Teachers to Use Technology (NCPT^3). To find out more about these and other ISTE initiatives and to view our complete book list or request a print catalog, visit our Web site at **www.iste.org**. You'll find information about

- ISTE, our mission, and our members;
- membership opportunities and services;
- online communities and special interest groups (SIGS);
- professional development services;
- research and evaluation services;
- educator resources;
- ISTE's National Educational Technology Standards (NETS) for Students, Teachers and Administrators;
- *Learning & Leading with Technology* magazine; and
- the *Journal of Research on Technology in Education*.

Contents

Making Magic Happen
Technology Links to Literacy—
How Did it Begin?

Over the past few years Rose Reissman has been actively involved with *Learning &
Leading with Technology (L&L)*. She has noticed that many new teachers and teachers new to technology are eager for strategies and projects that will support
them in using technology as a tool for teaching literacy. Indeed, readers of *L&L's*
Language Arts section often comment on how well a particular article's strategy
fits with the literacy curriculum they are already teaching in language arts and
social studies. They often ask authors for more ideas.

Rose suggested to *L&L* Editor Anita McAnear that it would be a terrific idea to
review the last few years of the magazine and collect the best literacy articles into
a single volume of ready-to-use strategies, projects, performances, and portfolios.
Compiling such a compendium of technology-driven literacy resources complete
with Web sites, annotated software listings, and suggested readings would be a
wonderful service to the growing audience of literacy educators who are more
than eager to tap into technology's infinite capacity to support, engage, and excite
students and teachers in lifelong reading and writing online communities.

As a 30-year veteran teacher educator in the language arts field, Rose can testify
to the ways in which her use of technology has transformed and invigorated her
literacy teaching and learning. Her inner-city public school residencies, nationwide
projects, unique graduate courses for language arts teachers, and consulting for
cultural institutions have all been greatly enriched by the use of the computer.

When Anita encouraged the compilation of this volume, Rose thought it would be
wonderful to draw on the talents of Mark Gura, her colleague and award-winning
veteran teacher educator, who is currently the director of instructional technology for the New York City Board of Education. Both Mark and Rose are content
experts in areas other than technology. Rose is the author of *The Evolving
Multicultural Classroom* and also authors social studies curriculum. Mark has won
numerous awards, fellowships, and distinctions for authoring curriculum and
creating projects in fine arts, science, social studies, and cultural studies.

All of this introductory biography information is a way of saying that in addition to their excitement over technology, Rose and Mark are teachers through and through—in reading, writing, language arts, and social studies. Together, they decided that the key mission of this book would be to share the magic they had seen created by technology in our own teacher educator lives with a broader audience of new teachers and teachers new to technology. Ultimately, the hope is that the projects, performances, portfolios, and resources described in this book will inspire readers to contribute additional ideas to the world of education.

This book is divided into the following chapters:

- **Begin with the Basics**—Reading through Writing
  Word processing as transformed by technology integration

- **Painting Performances**—Drawing on Technology to Foster Literacy
  Using art and graphics in the literacy curriculum

- **The Computer as Catalyst for Critical Thinking**—Technology Tools for Constructivist Learning
  Examples of constructivist projects

- **Oh, the Places You'll Go**—From the Classroom to the World
  Using the Internet to explore the world

- **Beyond the Basics**—Products, Performances, and Projects That Keep Building
  Multimedia scrapbooks, electronic books, online quilts, and more

- **Inquiring Minds**—Student-Centered Inquiry
  Using your Web wizard talents to design your own Web site and Internet-based projects

Each chapter features selected articles published in *L&L* introduced by running conversations between Mark and Rose. At the end of the chapters sections called Theory into Practice and Insights connect the articles to specific teaching and learning theories.

The appendixes constitute a kind of cyberspace bookshelf. In Appendix 1, the "voices" of teacher educators provide comments on favorite Web sites, technology teaching strategies, and software. Appendix 2 describes a technology-based approach for preparing students to take standardized tests.

The teacher-to-teacher conversations and the descriptions of technology-centered projects that focus on the development of literacy among students are meant to inspire readers to get involved in using technology to improve literacy instruction for students of all ages. See you in cyberspace!

Rose Reissmann and Mark Gura

Technology Integration
What's It All About?

By Mark Gura

"Technology Integration." It's a popular phrase that often eludes precise definition. Of the two roads taken by schools with computers—teaching *about* computers or teaching *with* computers—integration, the use of computers to extend instruction's capabilities, is the more desirable.

In an earlier era of classroom computer use, teachers identified "technology extensions" for their noncomputer-driven lessons and pointed proudly to their accomplishments in finding ways to connect them to technology. At that time, the computer was seen as a wonderful add-on, something beyond the scope of the ordinary minute-to-minute business of teaching and learning. Lessons were complete without computers but were enriched with some flashy technology function or computer product as icing on the cake.

In the current era of full technology integration, the computer assumes much more of the limelight in a leading role.

To integrate technology into the instructional program effectively, several important factors must be addressed. First, and most important, is curriculum. Technology activities must present an opportunity for teaching and learning that which is central to the content area. No matter how exciting or impressive computer use may be, it proves its worth most strongly when it brings to fruition learning objectives that hold a prominent position on the learning community's radar screen.

It is important to acknowledge that some parts of the curriculum may be handled better without the computer, while others can be facilitated immeasurably better with it. Know which is which, but be prepared to change your opinion about this as applications, perceptions, and instructional objectives change. Accordingly, use computers where and when they can add the most.

The computer does have the potential to push the envelope in the classroom in some wonderful ways. The "bells and whistles" factor, if used wisely, will help teachers motivate the hard to reach and ensure that learning activities address a broad base of intelligences and learning styles. Additionally, the computer enables youngsters to produce learning products, which, incidentally, are another source of intense motivation. Learning products capture learning and the processes that lie beneath it.

In a portfolio approach to student work and its assessment, computers are particularly valuable in that they permit the student to produce impressive, easily read learning products that can be readily reproduced, stored, disseminated, and expanded upon as the work progresses and skills grow.

For teachers looking for opportunities to create authentic activities, technology is especially valuable. Having students interface with real audiences dictates that some form of publishing takes place. The computer is perfect for that. Everything from the acquisition of stock graphics to the generation of original images to the selection of type faces and layout of pages is made possible and easy with the computer. Creating a Web site may be the ultimate opportunity for "everyclass" to find its voice and have it heard. All these activities can be accomplished with free, easy-to-use Web authoring software. And now, with the advent of free hosting services, student projects can easily culminate with an uploading to the Web, where students can gain access to the attention of the worldwide online family.

CHAPTER I

Begin with the Basics
Reading through Writing

The Conversation Begins

Rose: My very first experience with technology was word processing. Even though I was a lifelong writer, I had lousy penmanship. Fortunately, I have excellent typing skills. Seeing my words emerge on the screen and in hard copy bearing beautiful fonts was exciting and inspiring.

Mark: In my case, I always wanted to be a writer, but until I stumbled on word processing this just wasn't possible for me. Word processing was a break-through experience for me, and once I found my way it continued to support me in every growth stage I've gone through as a writer, from producing those first pieces that I felt were at all presentable, through the thrill of the first time I was published, to the way I rely on writing to help me get my job done and express my ideas to the world on a daily basis.

Rose: As a teacher I always tried to nurture and support those students who had learning styles and strengths in areas other than the linguistic. These students desperately wanted to demonstrate that they could, indeed, be writers, even if they told stories through spoken words, pictures, or gestures. Word processing literally provided a screen on which they could project their stories for an audience. The transformative power of word processing for these story tellers who had never experienced their stories presented in a format that could be shared and respected by others was apparent to me.

Mark: I was not a language arts teacher. However, including text in art-driven learning projects was something I often did. When the word processor was made available to me, the inclusion of text became effortless. My students and I gravitated toward it more and more as an important expressive resource.

Rose: I remember watching some students who had the kernels of wonderful story ideas and the beginnings of plays struggle manually with the task of organizing their ideas and revising them as they worked toward a finished piece. This was a problem I myself had as a writer. I often limited or shortened my ideas because of the time it would take for me to manually revise and organize details. As I was teaching my first seventh-grade basic word-processing class in the mid-1980s, I watched with amazement as my students effortlessly revised their developing stories. As a teacher-researcher I watched how students who used to write the fewest words possible so that they could complete a writing task or prompt were suddenly "writing themselves out" in wordy detail, with alacrity and energy.

Mark: You've put your finger on it. Word processing takes the drudgery out of the process, freeing minds up to express and develop the craft of writing.

Melissa's Year in SixthGrade

A Technology Integration Vignette

In 1995, Texas allowed school districts to integrate technology skills into their curricula rather than require them to institute seventh-grade computer-literacy classes. Instructional technology pioneers soon began working with subject-area teachers to facilitate this integration. Our author, Jeanie Hemmer, begins here with the first of three vignettes, this for the sixth grade; those for the seventh and eighth grades will appear in upcoming issues. These vignettes were written to help educators visualize what subject-area technology integration might look like. You can use them yourself to help set a vision for your own middle or junior high school. You can also use the summary and integration ideas for specific subject areas.

By Jeanie Hemmer

Before this school year even started, curriculum coordinators for junior high schools met with subject-area technology committee members and campus instructional technologists (CITs) to complete the state-mandated technology curriculum units for the 1997–98 school year. The CITs and committee members then returned to their campuses to plan with their subject-area teachers. We chose to integrate technology into regular subject areas in our district's junior high schools rather than simply teach a separate computer literacy class. In this series of articles I describe how this change will affect the progress of three fictional students—Melissa, Eduardo, and Lakeisha—through junior high.

By the time Melissa has begun her sixth-grade year, her teachers had met with the CIT many times, and the new units had been fully planned. Teachers attended technology training in August to prepare for the units using spreadsheets, databases, multimedia, reference CD-ROMs, and Internet tools. The teachers continued to meet with the CIT each week during the year to develop new ideas.

Fall: The New Curriculum Begins

 September: Social Studies and Math. By the fourth week of school, Melissa was able to choose the country she would research for her class on world cultures. She decided to study about Peru, and she learned about its geography during the first six weeks.

Mrs. Perkins, the CIT, joined the teacher in the multipurpose lab as Melissa's class began to study using CD-ROM encyclopedias. Mrs. Perkins demonstrated how to search for information, and the teacher posed questions to the class, allowing students to brainstorm ways to answer the questions using the encyclopedias. As Melissa used her computer to study Peru, the teacher and the CIT helped students think of possible ways to investigate their countries. Melissa took notes as she studied.

Over the next three days, the CIT and Melissa's teacher helped the students organize and store their information in a database. The teacher helped Melissa find an Internet-connected classroom in Lima, Peru, and Melissa sent questions to the Peruvian students about their country's geography. She then added the information they sent back to her database.

After six weeks, Melissa created a poster-sized map of Peru and labeled the different geographical areas. She included personal comments from her classroom friends in Lima. She was excited about telling her own class about the country she had chosen. The entire class, working in small groups, then spent several days comparing the geography of each country. Many parents who visited during an open house said that they have never seen their children so excited about learning.

In September, Melissa's sixth-grade math class began a unit on decimals using Olympic diving. Mrs. Perkins and Melissa's math teacher brought the students into the multipurpose lab to begin a spreadsheet unit that covered rounding decimals. The CIT demonstrated ways in which the students could use the spreadsheet program to do calculations. The teacher then asked them to think of ways in which they might organize a spreadsheet to calculate the rounding of decimals.

Next, Mrs. Perkins demonstrated Olympic scoring. Students were assigned Olympic divers and asked to create a spreadsheet that could calculate the statistics or scores for each dive. During the culminating activity, students ranked their divers and were awarded medals. In advisement, the students continued to follow diving meets, and a competition developed among several advisement classes as they followed diver statistics. The advisement classes also visited the multipurpose lab so that students could update their spreadsheets.

By now, Melissa could see the benefits of the keyboarding class she had started at the beginning of the school year. The keyboarding instruction that fall was part of her fine arts rotation of art, music, and speech.

 October: Social Studies, Language Arts, and World Cultures. During October, sixth-grade classes in world cultures began a unit on Europe. As the classes studied the Middle Ages, students gathered and entered data into a database in the multipurpose lab. They consulted the CD-ROM encyclopedias when they had questions.

Mrs. Perkins again helped Melissa's class as students used the Internet to network with other world cultures classes in the district and developed more intensive areas of study. As interest groups developed, students continued their research and added to their databases. Melissa's class worked on HyperStudio class presentations. As the unit on Europe continued, students began to study World Wars I and II.

In October, language arts classes began a unit on the Holocaust. During each six-week period, Melissa's class worked on thematic projects in small groups. Students used word-processing software in the classroom minilab.

Melissa had just completed an extensive study of World War II in her world cultures class, so the activities in language arts tied in well with what she had already learned. As her class read *Number the Stars,* the students worked on creative-writing projects in small groups. Mrs. Perkins again helped the teachers as their classes worked on activities at several stations. Students also participated in group discussions, presentations, and debates about cause and effect. Teachers said that they had never before seen such enthusiasm for reading.

World cultures classes visited the multipurpose lab to write to other Internet-connected classes that were also reading *Number the Stars.* Melissa's own class created HyperStudio presentations that were related to the students' studies of the Holocaust. Stimulated by the resulting interest, language arts teachers in the district and campus CITs met and developed a Holocaust symposium. The production was arranged and conducted by students and attended by a large number of students and parents. Melissa was very proud that her group's HyperStudio presentation was chosen for display.

 November: Science. In November, Melissa's science class began to study the classification of organisms. Melissa was given several groups of organisms to classify, and she stored the information she found in a database in the multipurpose lab. The sixth-grade students also used the CD-ROM encyclopedias when they needed answers to questions they had about their topics.

Mrs. Perkins and the students also created an Internet newsgroup that they called "Mystery Organism." They posted several mystery descriptions and were excited when they received guesses from students around the world. As the students finished organizing their databases, they created projects that showed how they classified the organisms.

Melissa's science teacher was thrilled with the students' enthusiasm toward the unit. They then visited the multipurpose lab to begin a simulation unit using Amazon Trail simulation software.

 December: Math and Science. In December, the sixth-grade math classes began a unit on "The 12 Days of Christmas" that included work on statistics and calculating interest. The students divided into groups and gathered newspaper clippings on the prices of all the items identified in the song: partridges, geese, gold rings, pear trees, and so forth. With help from Mrs. Perkins and Melissa's math teacher, the students used the multipurpose lab to create spreadsheets using these prices. The students then posted questions to the Kidcafe site (**http://www.kidlink.org**) that asked children from around the world their opinions about the costs of "eight maids a milking" and "10 pipers piping."

The students were given $100 in play money to spend on the items. Because the total was far more than that—several thousand dollars—Mrs. Perkins helped the students look for various types of loans in the newspaper. Using the information they found, the students then created a spreadsheet that showed the interest rates available. The research group that developed a shopping unit and spent the least amount of money was given special recognition. Many parents complimented Melissa's math teacher on the shopping unit. Several also explained that their children were now comparing prices on Christmas gifts they wanted so that their parents could save money and get them more presents!

Winter: The New Curriculum Continues

January: Social Studies. In January, the world cultures students used the multipurpose lab to continue studying the countries they were researching, including food, clothing, music, and religion. Melissa added new information on Peru to her database. Her teacher also demonstrated more ways to search for data. Students looked at the CD-ROM encyclopedias for information on the various cultures. After the students finished entering data into their databases, the teacher matched each of them with a partner, and they sat together to compare their two countries. Melissa was surprised at the occupational differences between Peru and France, her partner's country. They excitedly talked together and composed a compare-and-contrast article to share with their class.

February: Language Arts, Science, and Teacher Evaluations. In February, the sixth-grade language arts classes began reading *Mr. Popper's Penguins.* As they worked on several activities, students took turns writing in the classroom minilab. Melissa's teacher was very pleased with the students' descriptive writings during their study of figurative language.

Because of the class's interest in research, the teacher and Mrs. Perkins planned a research unit using the multipurpose room. There the students selected different varieties of penguins and began doing their research in the CD-ROM encyclopedias. Several students suggested that they begin databases to store their penguin information. The teacher and Mrs. Perkins helped them as they created their databases. Students

were grouped by the characteristics of their penguins. They used information in their databases to create generalizations and make HyperStudio presentations to share with the class.

Because of the sixth graders' heightened interest in penguins and their habitat, Melissa's science teacher met with Mrs. Perkins to work on the Antarctica unit. The CIT helped the class connect with the "Live from Antarctica" newsgroup on the Internet (**http://passporttoknowledge.com/antarctica**). Students attended the multipurpose lab several times each week to read the newest bulletins from Antarctica and to pose questions to the scientists.

The teachers attended an inservice training in February. The CIT met with each subject-area team to refine plans for the new semester. During an all-school meeting, many teachers said that they had never before seen students as excited about learning. Because of the students' interest in multimedia demonstrations and the Internet, Mrs. Perkins decided to offer additional classes on newsgroups and importing digitized images into HyperStudio. Subject-area curriculum training was offered in multipurpose labs around the district. Coordinators, CITs, and teachers worked on new study units using word processors, spreadsheets, databases, and multimedia.

March: Science. In March, science classes began a unit on temperature, light, and motion. Mrs. Perkins taught the children how to use the temperature and light probes in the multipurpose lab. As the students worked on their assigned lab experiments using the probes, they stored their results in databases. The students then plotted their results in charts and created their own experiments to continue their investigations. The students connected with other science classes on the Internet and compared their study results.

Spring: The New Curriculum Crosses the Finish Line

April: Social Studies, Language Arts, and Math. In April, the world cultures classes began studying the Asian continent. In assigned research groups, the students investigated individual subjects and reported to the whole class. Melissa's class visited the multipurpose lab for several days as the students used the CD-ROM encyclopedias and added information to their databases. Melissa's own group studied the Great Wall of China, while her friend's group learned about the Himalayas. The class also searched the Internet for material on the various topics. As the students created HyperStudio presentations, Mrs. Perkins helped students use the Internet to find graphic images from Asia.

The language arts students read and enjoyed *Summer of the Swans* as they continued to study Asia in world cultures. Mrs. Perkins assisted the students as they wrote poems in their classroom minilab and later shared the poetry on the Internet with other classes in the district.

Math classes visited the multipurpose lab in April to learn about calculating probability using spreadsheet programs. Students searched newspapers and magazines for probability examples that they could use in their spreadsheets. After many requests from parents, Mrs. Perkins offered a "parent inservice" on spreadsheets and allowed students to teach their parents how to use Lotus 123. Melissa's parents were pleased with her growing enthusiasm for math.

 May: Social Studies, Language Arts, and Math. In May, world cultures students collected all of their previous research on their individual countries to prepare for a culminating report. They busily worked in the multipurpose lab using the CD-ROM encyclopedias, creating HyperStudio presentations, using e-mail to correspond with penpals from their countries, and adding new facts to their databases.

Finally, during the last few weeks of school, the students took turns teaching the world cultures class about their countries. Melissa was quite proud of her HyperStudio presentation on Peru. After she showed it in the multipurpose lab, she helped her class write to her Peruvian penpals. The students then hosted an international festival and invited their parents to visit. The principal commented that he had never received so many compliments from parents for their children's enthusiasm for school.

The New Curriculum in Review

Over the summer, Mrs. Perkins, the CIT, offered technology classes to subject-area teachers. Because of the students' demonstrated interest, the math teachers worked on new study units using spreadsheets. Language arts teachers wanted to capitalize on the year's reading successes, so they worked on more student-directed, small-group thematic projects. World cultures teachers refined their use of databases for research and searched the Internet for new activities that they could use. Science teachers requested workshops on the Internet and new units that used CD-ROM encyclopedias.

The use of technology during the previous school year had engaged students from the beginning, and their enthusiasm made teaching both more rewarding and more challenging. And parents were able to see their children thrive in ways they had never seen before. It made them also want to learn. Everyone agreed that it had been a wonderful year.

Resources
Amazon Trail is available for $29.95 from MECC, 6160 Summit Drive North, Minneapolis, MN 55430; http://www.mecc.com.

Lotus 123 can be purchased for $293.44 from Lotus Development Corporation, 55 Cambridge Parkway, Cambridge, MA 02142; http://www.lotus.com.

Technology Integration Ideas by Sixth-Grade Subject Areas

World Cultures

"Countries of the World" Database Unit. For this unit, students are assigned individual countries to research. They gather information on their countries using library books, CD-ROM encyclopedias, magazines, Internet resources, and other reference materials. The classes set up a database to store information on each country, and the students add their information to it. Working in small groups, the students analyze and solve problems using the database. Students then create HyperStudio presentations on their countries for their classmates.

For each six-week period, students are given a different topic on their countries. They begin with geography and then study government, history, culture, and economics. Students continue to add information to the database during the year and compare and contrast the country information. In the final six weeks, students complete their final country HyperStudio projects and include all of their research. The projects are presented at an international festival held by the school.

"World War II: Holocaust" Thematic Unit. As students in world cultures complete a unit on World War II and the Holocaust, language arts classes read books such as *Number the Stars* and *Anne Frank: The Diary of a Young Girl.* Classes are paired with Internet penpals to discuss the books. Individual classes, for example, might be encouraged to become or represent a character from a book; their language arts penpals might then e-mail questions for the character: "Why did you decide to trust the couple next door?" "Did you feel safe?" Students can also pair up with classes as they read the book and discuss their feelings about it. "Would you have wanted to leave your home? I would have been afraid."

Math

"Olympic Diving" Decimal Unit. This unit can be completed as students learn to calculate and round with decimals. These are the very skills needed to maintain team statistics. Students "adopt" a sports team (for example, an Olympic diving team or a baseball or football team) and create a spreadsheet that calculates player averages, team scores, and so on. As an extension, individual classes can keep records on competitive teams and use the spreadsheet's graphing function to compare teams during the year.

"The 12 Days of Christmas" Interest Unit. Students look for the current costs of "The 12 Days of Christmas" by using newspapers, Internet surveys, and other sources. They might, for example, create an Internet survey to answer the question, "How much does a 'piper piping' cost?" Students are loaned $100 of play money and then gather information on bank loans from the newspaper or the Internet. After totaling the costs for all items in "The 12 Days of Christmas," they create a spreadsheet that demonstrates five methods of financing. The group with the best financing scheme wins.

"Probability" Spreadsheet Unit. Students search for examples of probability in newspapers and magazines. They create a spreadsheet that calculates, for example, the probability of winning a lottery or buying winning scratch-off tickets, using the lottery's own statistics.

Parents can be invited for an after-school spreadsheet session, where students can teach their parents how to calculate probability using spreadsheets.

Language Arts

"World War II: The Holocaust" Thematic Unit. Language arts students read books such as *Number the Stars* or *Anne Frank: The Diary of a Young Girl.* Working in groups of five or six, the students discuss the books and create writing projects on such topics as "What I Would Do After Chapter Two" or "A Different Ending for *Number the Stars.*" Writing projects are shared and discussed in class.

Mr. Popper's Penguins Unit. As language arts students read *Mr. Popper's Penguins,* they can learn about Antarctica and penguins. The students also can read the "Live from Antarctica" reports on the Internet and create classroom newsletters. Information such as penguin and Antarctica facts can be collected in a database and shared in class through HyperStudio projects.

Summer of the Swans Unit. As students read *Summer of the Swans,* they work on writing projects or poems about characters in the book. Class creative writing can be collected and shared on the Internet with other classes reading the book.

Science

"Organism Classification" Unit. Working in small groups, students gather information and characteristics of various organisms using CD-ROM encyclopedias and the Internet. Information is organized and added to a database. Students create and post "Mystery Organism" puzzles on the Internet for other classes to solve. They describe an organism's characteristics and allow other classes to find the solution using their classroom databases. Paired classes can take turns posing "Mystery Organism" puzzles, and HyperStudio projects can be created that share "Mystery Organism" puzzles in class.

"Amazon Trail" Unit. Students use the simulation program Amazon Trail in small groups. They use their classification skills from the previous unit to study, create hypotheses, and analyze options as they complete the simulation.

"Antarctica" Unit. Students gather daily weather and temperature information from Antarctica using the "Live from Antarctica" Web site. Students e-mail questions to the scientists, such as what the scientists predict for future weather patterns or what the Antarctic living conditions are.

"Temperature, Light, and Motion" Unit. Students use temperature and light probes to collect data on various materials and enter the information into a database. For example, they can gather temperatures for dry ice, ice, ice water, ice with salt, and other compounds. Students can identify new compounds with which they can experiment. Students then sort the information in the database and create tables to show to the class. If several classes are completing the same unit, then shared data can be included in the database. Students can also publish data on the Internet for other science classes to use.

Eduardo's Year in Seventh Grade

A Technology Integration Vignette • Part 2

This month we continue our look at a hypothetical curriculum-development plan developed for Texas schools. As noted in last month's article, in 1995 the state encouraged school districts to integrate technology skills into their curricula rather than require seventh-grade computer-literacy classes. Similar to last month's vignette, this one was written to help educators see what technology integration would look like for the seventh grade.

By Jeanie Hemmer

In the summer before he entered seventh grade, Eduardo's teachers were busy with technology training. Mrs. Perkins, the school's campus instructional technologist (CIT), worked with each subject-area group to improve the previous year's technology integration units. The teachers had found that students who used the word-processing programs, spreadsheets, databases, multimedia, CD-ROM references, and Internet materials were far more motivated and worked at a much higher cognitive level. Because of this, the teachers wanted to increase their own knowledge of these tools so that they could continue to help the students in their individual studies.

Fall: The Students Begin Their Studies

August: History, Mathematics, Language Arts, and Science. In August, Eduardo's class in Texas history visited the multipurpose lab to begin its study of the state's different regions. Students were assigned to research groups to study specific regions. Eduardo's group began using the CD-ROM encyclopedias to gather information on the state's central plains region. Each student specialized in a specific geographical subject. As they gathered information, the students created a database on the central plains that included information about its major rivers, elevations, vegetation areas, and so on. Mrs. Perkins, the CIT, visited the students when their information was organized and helped each one work on individual pages of a HyperStudio presentation. Mrs. Perkins helped the groups as they combined their individual regional presentations and displayed them for the rest of the class. Eduardo's Texas history teacher then divided the class into new groups, and each was assigned two regions to compare and contrast. She was extremely pleased with the detailed information each group found.

During the first six weeks of school, Eduardo's math class began a unit on the stock market. Mrs. Perkins and Eduardo's math teacher brought the class to the multipurpose lab to begin a spreadsheet lesson on adding, subtracting, multiplying, and dividing decimals. Mrs. Perkins demonstrated how to calculate the profits and losses of stocks using a spreadsheet and comparing prices from older and more recent newspapers. The students were each given $500 in pretend money and a week to decide which stocks they wished to purchase. Eduardo used his time wisely. He went home and asked his father. They spent an enjoyable week contacting his father's stockbroker and calling Eduardo's grandfather. Eduardo cautiously invested in IBM, AT&T, and General Electric. His class attended the multipurpose lab each week to calculate its profits and losses. Although other students' stocks rose dramatically at different times, Eduardo's choices proved to be good investments by the end of the unit.

Eduardo's language arts class read *Where the Red Fern Grows*. The students worked on writing activities using the classroom minilab, and Eduardo practiced writing poetry. As they continued the unit, the students worked in small groups on different parts of the writing process. They shared their stories on the Internet with other classes in the district that were reading the same book. The language arts teacher noticed that the students were writing much longer and more detailed stories as they shared them with other classes.

Eduardo's science class attended its multipurpose lab during the first six weeks to work with the SimAnt simulation program. Eduardo really enjoyed using this program, and he was surprised by how much the outcomes changed as he changed the variables in his ant colony. He developed several theories about the best conditions and worked hard to improve his colony.

September and October: Science, History, and Math. During the second six-week period, Eduardo's science class began a unit on living organisms. His experience with SimAnt had helped him understand how different conditions affect living things. His class also used a CD-ROM encyclopedia to research the characteristics of living organisms. To classify the living organisms that he studied, Eduardo created and maintained a database. His teacher heard many compliments about the science units from parents during the school's open house later in October.

In history in September and October, the students continued to research the various regions of Texas. The class was divided into research groups to study the cities of Texas. Mrs. Perkins helped the students search the Internet for information about their cities. When working on a report on El Paso, Eduardo and his group found a World Wide Web page on the city. He was able to read the El Paso newspaper and see information about El Paso's tourism. Mrs. Perkins helped the groups find children in the cities they were studying, and they were able to correspond through Tenet's e-mail programs. Eduardo was able to write to a class in El Paso, and his group made a HyperStudio presentation and reported to Eduardo's class on El Paso. Eduardo was surprised to see how different El Paso was from Houston. He hoped to visit the city one day.

Eduardo's math class visited the multipurpose lab in October to begin a unit on expressions, equations, and integers. Mrs. Perkins helped the students as they learned to write the expressions and equations needed to use the spreadsheet that would solve the various problems. The students enjoyed changing the variables in the equations and watching the results.

November and December: Language Arts and Science. During the third six-week period, Eduardo's language arts class began a unit on comprehension strategies and parts of speech. Eduardo practiced writing in his classroom minilab each week. He noticed that it was easier for him to write after each week. His class read many good stories in the literature book. He began keeping a journal to record his story ideas so that he would have plenty to write about during his time at the computer.

Eduardo's science class began a unit on environmental issues in December, and Eduardo began to study different areas in the world with environmental problems. He and his classmates investigated these areas through the CD-ROM encyclopedias. Students organized their information in databases and created HyperStudio presentations. Later, their parents were able to see the students' work during an evening PTO program. The students were quite knowledgeable about their topics, and the parents were impressed by their work. In the next few weeks, the students continued their research with an environmental-simulation program, and their science classes participated in a unit using an ecosystems-simulation program.

Winter: The Students Expand Their Understanding of Technology

January and February: History and Teacher Inservice Training. In January, the teachers attended curriculum inservice training. The CITs from different schools assisted the curriculum coordinators in offering technology training in each area. Texas history teachers requested more training on using the Internet, so they were given the task of searching the Internet with

Netscape to find new sites to visit with their classes. Science teachers asked to work with simulation software, language arts teachers planned small-group units that could be done using the classroom minilab, and math teachers practiced new units using spreadsheets.

In the first two months of the new calendar year, history classes began an intensive study of the history of Texas. The students attended the multipurpose lab to do research using the CD-ROM encyclopedias. Mrs. Perkins helped the students store their information in a Texas history database. The students then used their information to create a timeline of Texas history and a HyperStudio presentation. Students e-mailed their classroom friends in other Texas cities and shared research information over the Internet with other Texas history classes.

Eduardo's math class attended the multipurpose lab in February to begin a unit on ratios, proportions, and percentages. Mrs. Perkins assisted the students as they created spreadsheets to solve equations given to them by their math teacher. As they became more proficient in creating spreadsheets, the students were given more detailed situations that required them to develop their own formulas. For individual projects, Eduardo's math teacher assigned them to find a real-world ratio or proportion problem for the class to solve. They enjoyed trading problems and creating spreadsheets to solve them.

Spring: The Year Ends on a High Note

March and April: Science and Language Arts. Eduardo's science class began a unit on the human body during March and April. The students researched several assigned subjects using the CD-ROM encyclopedias in the multipurpose lab. As they continued their study, Mrs. Perkins helped them send e-mail questions to the "Ask the Doctor" Internet site (**http://www.parentsplace.com**), which is staffed by physicians at several national hospitals. Students developed many individual areas of interest and enjoyed the help they received from the doctors. Eduardo's project was on the respiratory system, and the doctors referred him to several other research sites on the Internet. Eduardo's science teacher found that several extra days were needed in the multipurpose lab so that students could search through the information available on the Internet. When they were done with their research, they created HyperStudio presentations to share in class.

Eduardo's language arts class began reading folk tales and short stories in April. Eduardo continued writing in his journal as he thought of new writing ideas. He looked forward to working with his notes at the minilab computer. His class wrote some wonderful stories, and they decided to share them on the Internet with other seventh-grade classes in the district. Mrs. Perkins helped Eduardo's class as the students visited the multipurpose lab every few days to send and receive stories. During the final six weeks of the school year, the students enthusiastically worked on a figurative language unit. Eduardo's language arts teacher found that the students worked many times harder to write well when they were sending their work to other classes over the Internet! She was also pleased with the wonderful stories that came from other schools.

The students in Texas history finished the year by preparing projects for the history fair. They used the CD-ROM encyclopedias to reference historical information and added it to their databases. Eduardo's project involved the Battle of San Jacinto. He enjoyed creating his project for the history fair and even persuaded his parents to visit the San Jacinto Monument and several other historical sites. By the time the school year ended, the principal again received many compliments from parents on the students' heightened passion for learning. The principal noted improvement in three areas for the second year in a row: attendance, TAAS scores, and discipline problems.

Resources
HyperStudio is available for $199.95 (single-user set) from Roger Wagner Publishing Inc., 1050 Pioneer Way, Suite P, El Cajon, CA 92020; http://www.hyperstudio.com.

Technology Integration Ideas: Seventh-Grade Subject Areas

Texas History

"Regions of Texas" Unit. Students divide into research groups to study specific geographic regions of Texas. The students do their research using the library, CD-ROM references, and the Internet. The information they gather on major rivers, elevations, vegetation areas, and so on is stored in a database. Students create HyperStudio presentations to share in class. After dividing into new groups, they use the information to compare and contrast the geographic regions.

"Cities of Texas" Unit. Students divide into groups to research individual cities in Texas; again they use the library, CD-ROM references, and the Internet, including various cities' tourism Web sites. The students also advertise for e-mail penpals so that they can share information about their cities with one another. Students in Houston, for example, can e-mail a classroom in El Paso and ask students about that city. The students then create HyperStudio presentations to share what they have learned.

"Texas History" Unit. Students form groups to study specific subjects related to Texas history and begin their research with the library, CD-ROM encyclopedias, and the Internet. Typical examples of their research subjects include Juan Seguin, Lorenzo de Zavala, James Fannin, and the Battle of San Jacinto. The students share their information and create a Texas history database and timeline. They then present their information in HyperStudio projects in class. Group projects are published on the Internet and thus shared with other students.

"History Fair" Unit. Students select history topics to investigate for a history fair. Again, they gather their information through the library, CD-ROM reference software, field trips, and the Internet. The students then create projects to share at the history fair by using word processors for the research papers and multimedia software for the projects.

Math

"Stock Market and Spreadsheet" Unit. Students practice calculating profits and losses in stocks using newspapers to find stock pricing information and quotes. The students are then given $500 of play money to invest in the stock market. The students are encouraged to research stocks of their interest by consulting family members, newspapers, and the Internet. The students then "invest" their play money and calculate profits and losses for several weeks. High-dollar winners are announced at the end of the unit.

"Expressions, Integers, and Equations Spreadsheet" Unit. After being introduced to expressions, integers, and equations, the students create spreadsheets to solve problems using the processes they have learned in class.

Language Arts

"Thematic Creative Writing" Units. Students compose creative-writing assignments as they read novels in class. For example, as they read *Where the Red Fern Grows,* the students can read a newspaper of the period (as if they lived during that time) and then write articles in which they predict events to come in the book. The students' creative writing can be shared with other classes reading the book and even over the Internet. This encourages debate as other students express their opinions.

"Journal Writing" Unit. Students create a journal file that can be used throughout the year. In it, they can include comments about books they are reading, creative writing, and ideas for future writing activities.

Science

"SimAnt" Unit. Students work with SimAnt simulation software as they begin a unit on living organisms and learn their characteristics. The unit continues periodically for six weeks as the students complete a database on living organisms.

"Living Organisms Database" Unit. Students use the library and CD-ROM reference materials such as "CD-ROM Science Classroom" to research living organisms. They create a database of the characteristics of living organisms and then use it to compare, analyze, and predict additional characteristics. Excellent examples can be found at http://phylogeny.arizona.edu/tree/phylogeny.html.

"Environmental Problems" Unit. Students divide into groups to investigate environmental problems in various areas of the world; they do their research by using "CD-ROM Multimedia Science Classroom," CD-ROM encyclopedias, the library, and the Internet. The groups compile statistics and data about each environmental problem in a database and use the information to create a HyperStudio presentation to share in class.

"Human Body" Unit. Students select research topics that are related to the human body and use the library, CD-ROM reference materials, and the Internet to find information. As students investigate their subjects, they can send questions to several Internet sites, such as "Ask the Doctor" (http://www.parentsplace.com). When research is complete, the students create HyperStudio projects to share in class.

Lakeisha's Year in Eighth Grade

A Technology Integration Vignette • Part 3

In this third and final article, we look at the hypothetical Texas curriculum-development plan developed for the eighth grade. As noted early in this series, in 1995 the state encouraged school districts to integrate technology skills into their curricula rather than require computer-literacy classes. Similar to the previous two months' vignettes, this one was written to help educators see what technology integration would look like for the eighth grade. Teachers in Jeanie Hemmer's school district have begun to apply this model to their curricula.

By Jeanie Hemmer

As in the previous two years, the summer before Lakeisha's eighth-grade year was a busy one for her teachers. They attended technology workshops taught by Mrs. Perkins, the school's campus instructional technologist (CIT). Mrs. Perkins tailored each workshop to the needs of the teachers at her school. The math teachers requested more training on algebra spreadsheets, the language arts teachers searched for interesting Internet sites, and the science and American history teachers spent time organizing database projects and looking for new CD-ROM reference programs. The teachers had seen a great improvement in the quality of student work during the past two years, and they wished to be prepared for the new eighth graders, who would already have had two years of experience using databases, spreadsheets, multimedia programs, CD-ROM reference programs, and the Internet.

Fall: A New Curriculum Begins

 September and October: Language Arts, Math, Social Studies, and Science. Lakeisha's language arts class began the year learning organizational strategies for improving writing. Lakeisha practiced making outlines, Venn diagrams, and charts during prewriting activities. She also continued to write ideas in her journal, just as she had the year before. When she used the computer in her classroom minilab, she practiced using the strategies she was learning and found that they helped her keep her writing ordered.

Lakeisha's algebra class began working in the multipurpose lab using spreadsheets. Mrs. Perkins assisted the students as they learned to solve quadratic equations by using a spreadsheet. The math teacher introduced application problems, and Lakeisha's class made spreadsheets to solve them. She found it much easier to understand math concepts after she had used a spreadsheet to break them down.

In American history, Lakeisha's class began studying Native

Americans and early explorers to the New World. Her teacher assigned a subject for each student to research and share with the rest of the class. Lakeisha was assigned to report on explorer Samuel de Champlain. In the multipurpose lab, the class used the CD-ROM encyclopedias to create databases. After Lakeisha and the other students had organized their information, Mrs. Perkins assisted them in creating HyperStudio presentations and making their individual reports to the class.

Lakeisha's science class began studying laboratory safety and the metric system. A few weeks later the class began a chemistry unit. Lakeisha's science teacher brought the students to the multipurpose lab to begin a database on chemistry elements and terms. Lakeisha found that she could remember her information more easily if she organized it with a database. She continued adding to her database during the next six weeks as the class performed its chemistry experiments. The students even e-mailed other science classes in the district with results of their labs, including detailed notes about chemical reactions in the experiments.

 November: Interdisciplinary Projects. As the fall progressed, language arts and American history classes worked together on a Revolutionary War unit. Students were divided into two groups: colonists and English government officials. As language arts students learned about persuasive writing, they composed newsletters that supported the viewpoints of their respective groups. Lakeisha's American history class added to the project by researching the Revolutionary War period using the CD-ROM encyclopedias and creating databases for use with a HyperStudio presentation and a newsletter that supported the colonists.

 December: Math and Language Arts. Lakeisha's algebra class then began a unit on linear functions and inequalities. Mrs. Perkins assisted the students as they learned to solve equations using a spreadsheet in the multipurpose lab. Later, Lakeisha's algebra teacher gave each student an individualized set of equations to solve. With some help, Lakeisha was able to complete her assignment and understand the math concepts involved. Lakeisha's parents mentioned during open house that she was really enjoying math this year.

In December, students in Lakeisha's language arts class worked in small groups to write prose, poetry, and nonfiction. Lakeisha found that making charts in her word-processing programs helped her organize her thinking and write with more purpose. Her language arts teacher was quite pleased with the class's progress.

Winter: Student Technology Use Continues to Grow

 January and February: Science and Social Studies. Eighth-grade science classes began a unit on rocks and minerals during the third six-week period. Lakeisha and her classmates explored topics using the CD-ROM encyclopedias and stored both the information they found and results from their laboratory sessions, including a week-long rock-simulation program, in their databases. When their studies were complete, Mrs. Perkins helped the students create HyperStudio presentations to share with the class. She also found an Internet site called "Ask a Geologist"; Lakeisha and her classmates were then able to e-mail questions about rocks and minerals to the geologists who were sponsoring the site. Lakeisha and her friends were fascinated with the information they received on rocks and minerals in the Houston area. Lakeisha's science teacher organized a local geologic dig to help students begin their own rock and mineral collections.

Lakeisha's American history class studied a unit on the federal government and the U.S. Constitution in January. Students looked at individual topics using the CD-ROM encyclopedias. Mrs. Perkins helped them find individual Internet sites for various agencies and people in the federal government. Lakeisha e-mailed the U.S. senators from Texas, who then mailed her several documents about the federal government. Lakeisha presented the information to her class.

During the fourth six weeks, Lakeisha's algebra class learned about exponents and operations with exponents. Mrs. Perkins assisted the students as they created spreadsheets to solve equations using exponents. Lakeisha's algebra teacher was amazed at how quickly the class was learning concepts during the year.

 March: Language Arts and Science. As language arts classes wrote in their classroom minilabs, they worked with small group projects on parts of speech and revisions. Students wrote stories and articles using science and American history topics: the environment and the Constitution. Students continued to improve their writing during the fourth and fifth six weeks.

During the second semester, Lakeisha's science class began studying earth science. She herself studied environmental issues and stored information in a database in the multipurpose lab. Mrs. Perkins found many Internet sites on environmental issues, and the class sent questions to several of them. Lakeisha's teacher asked the students to write a report in which they compared the environmental issues they had studied. Because she had been using the database, Lakeisha found that her information was already well organized, and she was able to complete her report quickly. The class worked on the SimEarth simulation program during the last week of the six-week period. Because of her studies of the environment, Lakeisha's SimEarth project was successful for many days.

Spring: Eighth Graders Wrap Up Their Year

 March and April: Social Studies and Science. Lakeisha's American history class began a unit titled "People of Conscience." The students learned about slavery and other nineteenth-century social issues in American culture. Lakeisha's teacher assigned a subject to each student, and they visited the multipurpose lab to investigate their topics using the CD-ROM encyclopedias. Mrs. Perkins assisted the students as they stored information in their databases. Lakeisha created a HyperStudio presentation on antislavery crusades, which was her topic. The class members shared their presentations and continued reading about social issues from the 1800s.

Lakeisha's science class studied the earth's eternal processes, mapping, and oceanography during the fifth six-week period. Students worked on individual assignments using the CD-ROM encyclopedias. Later in the six-week period, Mrs. Perkins helped the class use the "Plate Tectonics" simulation program in the multipurpose lab. As they continued their study of earth science during the last six weeks, the students learned about astronomy and meteorology. They contacted NASA's Web site and "The Weather Underground" Internet site to learn about astronomy and meteorology. The class divided into small groups and worked on individual projects. The students stored their research in a database and created their own HyperStudio presentation for the rest of the class. Finally, at the end of the year, the science students presented an astronomy and meteorology fair.

 May: Language Arts and Social Studies. The language arts classes finished a unit on proofreading. Students practiced editing each other's stories using the classroom minilab. Lakeisha's teacher saw vast improvement in her class's writing assignments because the students were doing extra reading and writing while using the CD-ROM encyclopedias, databases, and the Internet. Their stories were longer, more descriptive, and contained fewer errors than she had ever seen in this sort of class.

Lakeisha's American history class studied a unit on the Civil War and Reconstruction during the final six-week period. Lakeisha selected Atlanta's postwar reconstruction as her final research project. She studied her subject using the CD-ROM encyclopedias and created a database to organize her information. After importing several digitized images of Atlanta over the Internet, Lakeisha created a HyperStudio presentation for her final project.

Lakeisha enjoyed her eighth-grade year. She hoped that she would be able to use computers again in high school—just as she had in sixth, seventh, and eighth grade.

Looking Ahead

Over the following summer, Mrs. Perkins taught several technology workshops to interested teachers. She offered workshops on small-group minilabs, Internet activities, and simulation programs. Because parents were so interested in learning about databases and spreadsheets, Mrs. Perkins offered workshops for parent volunteers. The principal heard many compliments from parents about their children's enthusiasm for learning. Once again, everyone agreed that it had been a great year.

Resources

HyperStudio costs $199.95 and can be ordered from Roger Wagner Publishing, 1050 Pioneer Way, Suite P, El Cajon, CA 92020; http://www.hyperstudio.com.

Technology Integration Ideas: Eighth-Grade Subject Areas

American History

"Native Americans and Early Explorers" Unit. Students are given individual subjects for topic-related research such as Francisco Vásquez de Coronado, the Native American region known as Quivera, Álvar Núñez Cabeza de Vaca, and so on. Students research their topic using the Internet, the library, CD-ROM references, and other sources. Students create a database to collect explorer and Indian information and to problem solve and to create hypotheses. Students create a HyperStudio presentation about their topic and share their projects in class.

"American Revolution" Unit. Students are divided into two groups: colonists and English government officials. As language arts classes prepare to write persuasive newsletters in the style of the American Revolution, students in American history are given topics on either the colonists or English government officials. The students do their research using CD-ROM encyclopedias, the Internet, and the library, and they gather their information into a database for use in creating generalizations and hypotheses about their topics. When they're done, they create HyperStudio projects to share in class.

"Federal Government and U.S. Constitution" Unit. Students are assigned individual topics related to the federal government or the Constitution. They do their research using Internet sites, gather information directly from federal agencies, and correspond with government officials through e-mail. The students then create HyperStudio presentations to share in class.

"People of Conscience" Unit. Students are assigned individual topics on slavery and other 19th-century issues. They use the Internet, CD-ROM encyclopedias, and other sources to gather and store information in a database for use in analyzing their topics. Students create HyperStudio presentations and share them in class.

"Civil War and Reconstruction" Unit. Students select topics that are related to the American Civil War and the period known as Reconstruction. They do their research using CD-ROM reference materials, the Internet, and other sources. They then create HyperStudio presentations to be shared in class.

Algebra

"Quadratic Equations" Unit. Students work on spreadsheet models to solve quadratic equations. Given application problems, they use a spreadsheet to solve them.

"Linear Functions and Inequalities" Unit. After being introduced to linear functions and inequalities, pairs of students are given individual sets of equations or problems to be solved using a spreadsheet. The students share their problem-solving methods in class.

"Exponents and Operations with Exponents" Unit. Students learn about exponents in class. They pair up or join small groups to solve given problems using exponents. The groups also explore ways to solve the problems by using spreadsheets. All solutions are shared in class.

Language Arts

"Organizational Strategies" Unit. Using a word processor and concept-webbing software, students practice prewriting using outlines, Venn diagrams, and charts. They thus learn to organize their ideas for writing assignments. The students' writing products can be shared in class or published over the Internet.

"American History and Persuasive Writing" Thematic Unit. As American History classes begin studying the Revolutionary War, language arts students divide into two groups: colonists and English government officials. Students create persuasive newsletters for each point of view using the persuasive writing techniques they learn in class. Newsletters are shared and published over the Internet.

"Prose, Poetry, and Nonfiction Writing" Unit. Working in pairs and small groups, the students use organizational strategies to write creatively, including prose, poetry, and nonfiction. The students use word processors and concept-webbing software to plan and create their writing assignments.

"Group Projects" Unit. Students learn about parts of speech and revisions as they create stories and articles in class. They learn to select topics that are related to their study units in science or social studies, and they use word processors to create projects for classroom sharing. They continue the group projects model in May while completing a unit on proofreading. They create stories and then practice proofreading each other's stories. The stories also can be shared with other classes over the Internet.

Science

"Chemistry" Unit. Students research elements and terms in class and organize the information into a database. As they continue working with compounds, they add new information to the database. Students solve problems, make predictions, and make hypotheses by using the "sort" function as they analyze the database information. As they work on chemical reactions and other experiments, the students e-mail other classes and share their own notes and observations.

"Rocks and Minerals" Unit. Students learn about rocks and minerals in class. As they explore new areas, they use CD-ROM reference materials, lab experiments, and other sources to gather information. From their own database information, they create generalizations about rock and mineral groups. The students also send e-mail messages to the "Ask a Geologist" Web site (http://walrus.wr.usgs.gov/ask-a-geologist/).

"Earth Science" Unit. Students research environmental issues in class using the Internet and other reference materials. They send questions to Web sites related to their topics of interest. As specific environmental areas are studied, the students create a database for individual locations and then sort the collected information to make predictions and generalizations. The students write reports that include their generalizations and predictions about specific environmental issues. They also work on the SimEarth simulation program to practice applying the information learned in this unit.

"Earth's Eternal Processes" Unit. Students learn about the earth's "eternal" processes as well as mapping and oceanography. The students are divided into small groups to research individual topics and then use a "plate tectonics" simulation program to apply the information they have learned.

"Astronomy and Meteorology" Unit. As the students learn about astronomy and meteorology, they send questions to "The Weather Underground" (http://www.wunderground.com) or to NASA (http://www.nasa.gov/). Students select individual topics of interest and create HyperStudio presentations for classroom sharing. Finally, the students display their projects at an astronomy and meteorology fair.

SCAMPER-CR

A Framework to Integrate Technology into the Curriculum

No, it's not the latest toy that kids will be asking for this Christmas. And it's not high-tech equipment that your school and district can't afford. This strategy to improve literacy at all educational levels will actually do more for your students than any toy, and it uses the technology you already have.

By Janet M. Beyersdorfer

Planning for Innovation and Technology Integration

Teachers want their students to use technology efficiently and appropriately in their literacy activities, but this is often a challenging task. This goal might be easier to reach through the use of a thinking frame based on cognitive-processing work. Using Eberle's (1984) theories, Martin, Cramond, and Safter (see Noyce & Christie, 1989) developed a prewriting strategy called SCAMPER—for "substitute, combine, adapt, modify/magnify, put to use, eliminate/streamline, and rearrange/reverse." This strategy promotes original thinking by having students link and combine existing ideas; flexibility and divergent thinking skills are essential elements.

When SCAMPER is used as a prewriting activity, students alter the elements of a story (characters, setting, and conflict) using the verbs of the acronym. Consider these alterations to the fairy tale "Snow White." For the poisoned apple, substitute a pizza ordered from a favorite shop. Combine Cinderella's three stepsisters with Snow White's family. Adapt the tale to take place in another setting such as the Arctic, and include snowshoes, icebergs, and igloos. Modify the story by telling it from the Prince's point of view, or magnify it by describing the Prince's encounter with a dragon who defends Snow White. Have Snow White or the Prince (instead of the Wicked Queen) use the magic mirror. Eliminate the role of the Prince and describe how Snow White might have been awakened by the dwarves. Or streamline the description of the Prince's search. Rearrange or reverse the story by having

the Prince fall asleep and having Snow White search for and awaken him. These ideas might also be discussed or incorporated into original stories.

Using SCAMPER-CR to Revise Lessons

I have adapted this strategy for curriculum review, hence the name SCAMPER-CR. The adaptation systematically guides the teacher through integrating technology into an existing curriculum plan. SCAMPER-CR is just one component of curriculum revision, and it is not intended to replace the comprehensive review process. The five-step SCAMPER-CR process is detailed in the following paragraphs. Use the SCAMPER-CR Template accompanying this article.

Step 1: Select a unit for revision. The selected unit can be well or poorly designed, or perhaps a favorite or a troublesome teaching experience. Study the unit's goals, objectives, activities, and assessments to identify its strengths and weaknesses. This study helps pinpoint areas in which technology might prove beneficial.

Step 2: Assess your access to technology. Determine the number of available computer workstations and software, the schedule for workstation use, and the parameters of the school's Internet access. This initial survey helps determine how much access students have to technological resources and services. After the unit is revised, you can schedule the time and resources.

Step 3: Locate your resources. Begin with the familiar approach to curriculum design and survey the print materials that are available and suitable for student use. Consider what type of additional information or which electronic formats might expand student understanding of a topic. Collaborate with your library media technology specialists to identify useful laserdiscs, CD-ROMs, and software programs.

Find and bookmark appropriate Web sites, and consult texts (e.g., Blachowicz & Fisher, 1996) and journals like *Learning & Leading with Technology* that discuss specific software programs concerned with literacy or that describe valuable technology projects. Be prepared to recommend resource purchases (e.g., Web site handbooks, CD-ROM programs, magazine indexes) to those who administer budgets; they may be able to allocate funds to address your needs.

Step 4: Complete the SCAMPER-CR process. With your unit materials and list of technology resources in hand, complete each action in the SCAMPER-CR process.

- Substitute. Replace a midpoint or final project that relies on traditional delivery with one that has a technological format. Examples: Teach students to display information using a database or spreadsheet rather than to produce a paper-and-pencil chart. Instead of using cardboard and markers to create signs and posters, demonstrate a desktop-publishing or drawing program so that students can explore relationships between graphic design and communication.
- Combine. Use electronic resources and formats as well as print-based materials. Examples: Require students to use CD-ROM references such as encyclopedias, atlases, and yearbooks. Direct students to specific Web sites or to laserdiscs that contain pertinent information. Teach, construct, and use templates and reading guides that help students locate information using electronic media.
- Adapt. Identify and eliminate inaccurate and unnecessarily detailed information and update the content. Examples: Compare and contrast emerging and traditional communi-

SCAMPER-CR Template

Teacher: _____

Title of the Unit: _____

Available Technology Resources

    Laserdiscs: _____

    CD-ROM: _____

    Software Programs
        Word Processing: _____
        Desktop Publishing/Graphics: _____
        Spreadsheet: _____
        Database: _____
        Commercial Programs: _____

    Web or Internet Sites: _____

Substitute: _____

Combine: _____

Adapt: _____

Modify or magnify: _____

Put to use: _____

Eliminate or streamline: _____

Rearrange or reverse: _____

An ISTE Copy-Me Page

cation formats. Introduce e-mail writing styles while also reviewing such traditional formats as business and friendly letters. Introduce presentation software during lessons on public speaking.
- Modify or magnify. Alter or expand a project, discussion topic, story, or writing assignment that does not meet your expectations for student involvement and learning. Examples: Demonstrate how a laserdisc, multimedia presentation, or electronic slide show will bolster enthusiasm and understanding of a topic. Teach students how to prepare a report using one or more of these technologies.
- Put to use. Use available resources to become more familiar

with technology, and continue to experiment with new software applications. Examples: Collaborate with colleagues or use the expertise of other professionals within or beyond the district boundaries to help your students' projects. Develop collaborative student work groups with roles related to specific technology uses (e.g., graphic artist or layout designer, proofreader, and video or audio technician). Share and discuss information gathered at conferences and from professional journals.

- Eliminate or streamline topics for review. Evaluate the quality and quantity of your instructional material. Identify and emphasize essential learning ideas while minimizing details. Use the time for technology use. Examples: Assign one fewer essay, task, or project that elaborates on a topic already presented or reviewed. Streamline assignments by eliminating one activity in a series or by scaling down the requirements of a culminating project. Assign an essay or oral presentation.

- Rearrange or reverse. Prioritize unit activities and allocate time to assignments that reflect these changing priorities. Examples: Review the students' daily and weekly procedures and tasks. Incorporate technology into these activities. Shorten, eliminate, and alternate these tasks.

Step 5: Rewrite the unit plan. Revise the unit's goals, objectives, and activities to reflect your proposed changes. Prepare a list of resources that are specific to the unit's content.

Step 6: Prepare the unit materials. Develop the instructional materials, student handouts, and assessments needed for the unit activities. Establish a schedule that maximizes student access to technology.

Committing to Technology Integration

Teachers commit to technology integration because they are aware of the changing definition of literacy, the growing necessity for literate individuals to have technological skills, and the research findings of the education community. The SCAMPER-CR strategy offers a frame in which to review and revise existing units and unite literacy and technology.

References

Barba, R. H. (1993). The effects of embedding an instructional map in hypermedia courseware. *Journal of Research on Computing in Education,* 25, 405–412.

Blachowicz, C., & Fisher, P. (1996). *Teaching vocabulary in all classrooms.* Englewood Cliffs, NJ: Prentice-Hall.

Bolter, J. D. (1991). *Writing space: The computer, hypertext, and the history of writing.* Hillsdale, NJ: Lawrence Erlbaum.

Calfee, R. (1994). Critical literacy: Reading and writing for a new millennium. In N. J. Ellsworth, C. N. Hedley, & A. N. Baratta (Eds.), *Literacy: A redefinition* (pp. 19–38). Hillsdale, NJ: Lawrence Erlbaum.

Daniel, D. B., & Reinking, D. (1987). Construct of legibility in electronic reading environments. In D. Reinking (Ed.), *Reading and computers: Issues for theory and research* (pp. 24–39). New York: Teachers College Press.

Eberle, R. F. (1984). *Scamper on.* Buffalo: D.O.K. Publishers.

Haas, C. (1996). *Writing technology: Studies on the materiality of literacy.* Mahwah, NJ: Lawrence.

Noyce, R. M., & Christie, J. F. (1989). *Integrating reading and writing instruction in grades K–8.* Boston: Allyn & Bacon.

Zigler, E., & Gilman, E. (1994). Literacy and the school of the 21st century. In N. J. Ellsworth, C. N. Hedley, & A. N. Baratta (Eds.), *Literacy: A redefinition* (pp. 3–17). Hillsdale, NJ: Lawrence Erlbaum.

My Writing Teacher

By Mark Gura

My writing teacher sits on my desk 24 hours a day. Although it's only 12 years old but already in semi-retirement, I'll never forget what this teacher has done for me. I am referring to my first computer, a little beige box that truly taught me to write. Although I've acquired several more modern and powerful computers since I bought that first one, I'll never throw it away. It simply means too much to me.

I was not much of a student. I had a good but undisciplined mind. It always seemed to me that the world going on outside the window was more compelling than the tasks my teachers assigned. I often escaped what I considered classroom drudgery by reading a book that I would keep hidden under the desk. Because of this, I developed a voracious appetite for reading and, of course, along with that came a powerful admiration for the art of writing and those who wrote.

Unfortunately, this led to intense frustration as I developed a strong desire to be published myself but understood that my writing skills were simply not up to the task. I could see no way that this would ever change.

Fast forward to my adult life. I was almost 40, a teacher for 16 years, when out of the blue my wife, a language arts teacher, came home with an announcement. Her new colleagues were all using the school's computers and purchasing computers to use at home as well. Maria insisted that we pool our money and buy a Macintosh for our home. I won't go into the details of the long battle Maria and I waged. In the end, and fortunately for me, she won. Furthermore, when the computer arrived she turned to me and said, "Why don't you learn how to use it and teach me?" Happily, I did!

Experimenting with the word-processing program, I made discoveries that profoundly impacted my weaknesses in writing. Most importantly, the extraordinary drudgery that resulted from my nemesis, Revision, disappeared. Magically, I could have as many copies or versions of my evolving text as I wanted. The ordering of sentences became a joy as I cut and pasted with abandon, trying out one combination after another. Incredibly, some of the things my ex-teachers taught me actually began to make sense. For the first time I was starting with an outline and not hating it. How exciting it was to work on a bulleted outline, go back to the document and flesh out each of the bullets as a paragraph or two, and then delete the bullets, transforming the outline into a finished piece! There seemed to be no end to the ways that the little beige machine made everything doable, easy, and fun.

There were some other serendipities that nourished my starved writing skills as I embraced the computer. My handwriting had always been so miserable that I was loath to share my work with others, regardless of its quality. The computer enabled me to turn out polished items of which I was proud. With the power to import graphics and choose fonts, sizes, and styles, my need for self-expression was also well satisfied. Most important, my poor spelling and imperfect grammar improved as I used the spelling and grammar checkers. Unlike the way I resented being corrected by my teachers as a youngster, my reaction to the nonjudgmental and relentlessly consistent computer was very positive. By dint of ceaseless repetition, slowly but surely my spelling and grammar improved greatly—something I never thought possible.

Just a year after my wife and I got that first computer, a very supportive colleague suggested that I submit a piece to the New York State Department of Education, which had put out a call for essays and articles for a publication entitled *Possibilities Catalog: The Quest for Excellence and Equity in Education.*

I must have disturbed the neighbors terribly some months later when I came home one evening, unwrapped a mystery package, and found inside the finished book with my very first published piece. I let out a series of screaming cheers of self-satisfaction. Imagine that, the kid who hated school and was convinced that he would never get what he most desperately wanted—to be a published writer— had a piece in the State Department of Education's new book. That editor will never know the extraordinary irony of running my first piece in the *Possibilities Catalog.*

We have come to a point when virtually every professional writer uses a computer as the tool of choice to do his or her work. Technology has so positively transformed the writing process that it would be very foolish to deny youngsters the benefits it can offer them as they grow into literate members of the community. My experience is one clear example of the potential the computer offers those struggling to learn to write. By the way, for old time's sake I've written this piece with the help of my writing teacher, my first computer.

The Classroom as Book
Living and Learning in a Print-Rich Environment

By Mark Gura

Of the many ways computers improve learning and literacy, no aspect highlights their wizardry more than their power to transform the classroom environment. In a good classroom students have access to books and learn to appreciate and read them. In a successful computer-supported learning environment students "write" their classroom as a book. In such fertile ground, their literacy skills grow and blossom as the classroom undergoes endless revisions and drafts.

In an exciting classroom the computer is the energy of the "literary ecosystem." Ideas may be germinated through online research, just plain follow-your-nose surfing, or bursts of creative inspiration. These initial concepts are nourished with project templates, autoformat outlines, and graphic organizer software. Maturing themes gain mass and strength as they become completed first drafts. With the aid of cut, paste, copy, insert, and delete functions, the drafts are pruned, grafted, trimmed, and polished as they are brought to a state of completion. Completed works are published in a wide variety of formats dictated by subject and the author's interest and taste. The process swings full circle as the spirit of published works is absorbed by residents of the classroom, triggering within them new ideas waiting to come to life. As in any other environment that teems with life, evidence of the struggle and glory of each stage is present and conspicuous in profusion.

The computer-and-printer combination can produce such a wide range of student products that it is unlikely two classrooms will look much alike; instead, each classroom will evolve over a period of time, as do the chrysalis, caterpillar, and butterfly.

All traditional student writing assignments can produce better products with the aid of the computer. Essays, compositions, haiku, and reports radiate with the taste and personality of their authors. Students can use styles, fonts, type sizes, and other standard word-processing functions. Add a color printer and the results are even more startling. No color printer? Colored pencil, watercolor marker, and other basic art materials harmonize easily with basic 8.5x11-inch black-and-white printouts to produce personal and marvelous results.

Standard-size paper need not produce an insurmountable barrier either. While access to a copy machine with advanced features such as a sizing function can yield products in a larger format, a simpler solution is to produce the product in sections and then join them together to yield projects of unlimited size. Thus, students may produce not only books, flyers, and newspapers but also posters, billboards, and full-size wall murals.

Nor do classroom bulletin boards and walls have to be the only medium that carries the ever-increasing biomass of print that students generate. Student publications can be bound and placed on bookshelves and magazine racks as they become part of a library of resources that blurs the line between the roles of reader and writer. Text and accompanying images can be printed out on transfer paper that, with the aid of a hot iron, can be "printed" on fabric. By producing T-shirts and other similar items, students can wear what they write.

Finally, classroom computers themselves can become part of the environment, and in their passive phases may be pressed into service to make the classroom a mosaic of message-bearing surfaces. For example, customized screen savers can be created for conveying off-line messages, and when the computer is online, personalized message-bearing home pages can be developed.

When a "book" is no longer a discreet thing but an ongoing, evolving process, "reading" is transformed from an activity into a basic function of living and growing. Finally, we have the technology to make this happen.

Constructing Literacy
Technology Makes It Happen

By Rose Reissman

Scenario 1: Students are seated in small groups using word processing and graphics to design a brochure, poster, invitation, feedback form, ticket, and exhibit texts for a city museum.

Scenario 2: Individual readers are stretched out on a rug in a reading center. They are working with storyboards to plan a multimedia retelling of an independently selected literature text from a perspective other than the one printed. In the text, one student uses a multimedia program to combine text, graphics, sound, animation, and video into a captivating presentation of Elli Weisel's *Night*.

Scenario 3: Inner-city Philadelphia students debate homework and social promotion policies online with students from an independent school in Palm Beach. They e-mail questions to noted theorists in the field.

Scenario 4: Students design their own board games using information from a unit on the environment. They use desktop-publishing applications to create game cards. Scanners are used to reproduce plots of the environment that have appeared in newspapers. Photographs of the environmental site are also scanned. The students produce playing pieces and design the playing board using a template.

Scenario 5: A digital quilt of community and family images comprising the Ordinary People's Hall of Fame is created as digital photos of student and adult nominees to the hall of fame are taken. Student explanations of their nominees' heroic qualities are directly uploaded to the Web site and recorded in English and other languages.

What do all these diverse, student-centered creative learning snapshots have in common?

Each of these dynamic products demonstrates how the use of literacy-focused basic technology skills—word processing, graphics, multimedia, and telecommunications—can realize constructivist education theory.

The development of technology-driven and technology-infused interactive products—museums, multimedia storytelling, online debates and exchanges, board games, halls of fame, photo galleries—engages students in authentic literacy activities that are key elements of constructivist theory. These elements include:

- Supporting learners in complex environments
- Engaging collaborative peer groups for testing student views
- Adapting curriculum to address student questions
- Providing ideas and centering learning around larger tasks

In addition, the use of technology as an instrument for constructivist learning provides the teacher and the student with actual products for assessment in the context of literacy, personal, and civic goals.

Given these proactive, readily accessible, engaging outcomes, you are motivated to filter your own class and curriculum goals through a technology-enhanced lens. Make constructive learning happen!

CHAPTER 2

Painting Performances
Drawing on Technology
to Foster Literacy

The Conversation Continues

Mark: The computer is a powerful tool for making art. In many respects it extends the image-making capabilities of those who are natural artists. Perhaps more importantly, it can make an artist out of the nonartist. The computer can help both kinds of students. Most important, for teachers who are committed to fostering literacy skills in a powerful way, computers can not only give youngsters a lift in their art making, they can also be a powerful tool for making the connection between words and images. Once this is done, stand back. They are ready to fly!

Rose: It is appropriate, Mark, that you use the word "fly." I have seen students "take off" on descriptions, stories, and narratives from illustrations, graphics, and online animations. The very existence of multimedia programs effortlessly envelopes, engages, and enthralls student authors and artists in an easily accessible, fluid medium through which they can become both participants and creators! Multimedia opens a portal to a world of artistic forms, images, and words, which I spent years as a teacher and learner trying to access for my students. With the arrival of the computer, one click made this world available to them. They could take books and add sounds, video, animation, and canned photos to literally become part of an electronic circle of readers, authors, and illustrators.

Mark: It has always impressed me how similar writing and making art are when you consider that the crux of both involve expressing ideas, telling stories, and communicating feelings. How unfortunate that students, indeed all of us, have seen this as an either/or talent. Now it is so much easier and more powerful to have students employ both as they reach for something that goes far beyond mere technique in a multimedia world.

Flights of Fancy
Capturing Viewpoint with Technology

By Rose Reissman

Several years ago, I joyously shared Faith Ringgold's *Tar Beach* (1991) with a group of first graders. As I read to them, I thought of Akira Kurosawa's *Rashomon* (1950). In that classic film, the same story is told by different narrative characters from their own unique perspectives. In the midst of reading *Tar Beach* to my eager young audience, I decided to adapt Kurosawa's cinematic approach to nurturing this emerging literacy. I asked the students who else was in the story besides third grader Cassie Louise Lightfoot (the eight-year-old narrator who flies over the city). They quickly listed Cassie's father, her mother, Mr. and Mrs. Honey, and BeBe, the baby brother. Then I asked the children if there were any other important characters or objects in the story.

Subject: Language arts

Grade Level: K–5 (ages 5–10)

Software/Hardware: Creative Artist and Plus for KIDS (Microsoft), Kid Pix (Brøderbund, a division of The Learning Company), Storybook Weaver (The Learning Company)

Turning young students into active story listeners and storytellers is one of the most exciting experiences an early childhood and preschool teacher can have. The biggest challenge, however, may be finding ways for educators to use technology to get K–12 readers to present stories in their own words. Fortunately, as Rose Reissman describes in this article, children's desktop-publishing programs such as Kid Pix can support these young readers and authors as they develop literacy habits and skills.

The students didn't respond immediately, so I went through the picture book page by page with them, and they were able to identify other key characters and objects. Among them were the George Washington Bridge, Grandpa, the Union Building, the Ice Cream Factory, Tar Beach, and the Stars.

Role-Playing Characters

We were able to use Microsoft's Creative Artist and Brøderbund's Kid Pix, so I asked the students to become illustrators and help Faith Ringgold create a new edition of her book. They could use the programs to create their own characters and objects. When they were done, we printed their color illustrations. The professional "look" of their own real artwork brought actual applause.

After displaying the students' illustrations, I asked for volunteers to play-act the various characters in each student's story. One volunteered to fly as Cassie, while others portrayed other people, objects, and landmarks. Each volunteer stood and presented the plot of *Tar Beach* from the perspective of his or her individual character. As each child spoke, I transcribed the story, saved the text using Microsoft Plus for KIDS, and then printed it using Storybook Weaver.

The following are some sample perspectives.

TAR BEACH
BY FAITH RINGGOLD

AS TOLD BY
BE BE

Created by Elizabeth Gil

Oh, I think Cassie's flyin' again! She likes to look over the bridge and fly around the whole city. She does that whenever we sit on the roof and watch the stars while Mommy and Daddy play cards with Mr. and Mrs. Honey.

She told me how she can see the Union Building and she even flies over our building. I think she does it to be sure we're safe at home.

Cassie knows how much I love ice cream. She loves it, too. She said she's going to own the Ice Cream Factory so we can have ice cream all of the time!

Cassie says it's easy to fly. I'm not afraid to try. I want to feel the freedom Cassie says she gets and I want Some Buildings and other stuff, too.

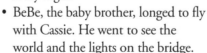

I told Cassie, if she doesn't take me flying with her, I'll tell Mommy and Daddy about her flying adventures. I think they'll get worried that she'll hit a star and fall, so they might try to make her stop. She wouldn't like that. I like flying with the stars with Cassie and I am glad she taught me how to fly.

- The George Washington Bridge told how Cassie always flies over. The bridge loved the stars and the night. It was proud to be so big and beautiful.
- Mommy explained that she had so much fun playing cards with Mr. and Mrs. Honey and Daddy that she didn't notice where Cassie went. Mommy told how she cried during winter when Daddy couldn't find work.
- Mrs. Honey said she slept late, and

she and her husband had ice cream every night.
- BeBe, the baby brother, longed to fly with Cassie. He went to see the world and the lights on the bridge.
- The Ice Cream Factory told how children loved it, and the ice cream was at tables every night.
- Tar Beach told how it loved the families who came up at night to play. It also loved the smell of peanuts and frying chicken, but it hated the watermelon seeds on its tar.

As each "character" retold the story, I asked the other students to hand draw the character using the picture in the book. We used large white sheets, such as from an artist's oversize sketchbook, that could contain several students' work. Because we had three computers in the room, I gave students the option of drawing using the computer.

Using the Results for More Learning
When the volunteers had all finished their stories, the pictures from each

character's story were hung side by side on a wall. Then I posted the *Tar Beach* character stories I had printed next to the hand-drawn illustrations and the computer graphics; I had to reenter some of the stories after several children told me I got them wrong.

Together we counted and recorded more than 10 character stories in *Tar Beach.* Finally, we talked about how every story really contained more than one perspective. Each character watches from his or her own set of eyes, such as the way BeBe in *Tar Beach* watches his older sister fly through the sky.

In our next shared story reading, the students listened for and volunteered to be character storytellers. Student artists drew the characters by hand or with the draw programs. I again recorded and printed their stories. At the end of the story hour, we had another galaxy of character viewpoint stories from the larger story. Although my young readers had never seen Kurosawa's *Rashomon,* they were acting out or role-playing his cinematic multiperspective storytelling style.

As they began writing on their own late in Grade 1 and continued in Grades 2 and 3, these emerging readers, writers, and illustrators have been examining illustrations and redrawing them through their own artistic perspectives. By refocusing their attention on the illustrations, the students have become adept at retelling the story from the viewpoints of various characters.

Emerging Literacy Brings Personal Understanding

This approach not only connects oral, pictorial imagery and the written word but also promotes critical, reflective, and empathetic reading. For instance, in Mavis Jukes's *I'll See You in My Dreams* (1993), which is told from the perspective of a young girl saying goodbye to her dying uncle, the technique allows students to focus on Aunt Hannah, the uncle, his adult sister, the hospital nurse, and other characters in the hospital setting. In this way, young students can explore different empathetic perspectives in this tragic but inevitable bereavement in a child's life.

In Rene Escudie's *Paul and Sebastian* (1988), the lessons of friendship beyond or despite economic, social, and housing backgrounds are enriched and made concrete as students retell the story by playing the mothers of the title characters. Exploring the mothers' initial antagonistic perspectives helped the students embrace Paul's and Sebastian's stories of shared fears, adventures, and friendship. Indeed, Paul's and Sebastian's role-plays were applauded, while the mothers' role-plays of initial dislike were booed. The printed stories and illustrations made these lessons in tolerance and cooperation more apparent.

We also used Katherine Orr's *My Grandpa and the Sea* (1990). The author's words and illustrations show how a traditional fisherman in St. Lucia loses his livelihood because technology has depleted his island's fish population. This story generated many different but logical storyline illustrations, role-plays, and retellings. As the young readers played and told the pictured relationship between Grandpa and his granddaughter, Lila, the students did not match the exact particulars of Grandpa's dilemma over the paucity of fish in the sea. Nor did they include Grandpa's sadness, his closeness with Lila, or his beached boat, Fancy Lady, and the sea crop garden (actually, a sea moss farm). Instead, the children were describing their own personal stories of relationships with their grandparents, using Orr's book as a starting point.

A book such as Irene Smalls-Hector's *Jonathan and His Mommy* (1992), vibrantly illustrated by Michael Hays, is also a good choice for encouraging role-plays. The physical activities described in the work provide lots of opportunities for students to render, role-play, and retell the story from the mother's or son's perspective. Students can graphically detail such movements and animations as racing, taking giant and little steps, executing ballet movements, and dancing to reggae music. The slideshow or small movie features available in many children's drawing and publishing programs can also help students show connections between words and images.

Teachers can use easily affordable software to apply the approach described here. Families themselves also can integrate it into their own story reading, writing, and reflecting.

Technology is now helping young children join the circle of readers, writers, and illustrators before they even need to write their own stories down. That's a wonderful and rich realm for early childhood educators and parents, one quite reminiscent of *Rashomon.*

References

Escudie, R. (1988). *Paul and Sebastian.* Brooklyn, NY: Kane/Miller Book Publishers.

Jukes, M. (1993). *I'll see you in my dreams.* New York: Alfred A. Knopf.

Orr, K. (1990). *Grandpa and the sea.* Minneapolis, MN: Carolahoda Books.

Rashomon. (1950). Kurosawa, A. (Director). Tokyo: Daiei Production Co.

Ringgold, F. (1991). *Tar beach.* New York: Crown Publishers.

Smalls-Hector, I. (1992). *Jonathan and his mommy.* Boston: Little, Brown, & Co.

Stoking Creative Fires

YOUNG AUTHORS USE SOFTWARE FOR WRITING AND ILLUSTRATING

Various ways first- and fourth-grade students used electronic paint and word-processing programs to produce creative-writing and creative-drawing projects.

By Marilyn H. Catchings and Kim MacGregor

The past few years have seen a dramatic increase in the number and features of electronic paint programs for children. Many of them provide word-processing and even publishing capabilities along with their paint and draw features. Children exhibit delight and enthusiasm when using these programs, but teachers wonder whether they hinder or enhance creativity and literacy. In fact, the ability of computer technology to support a broad array of visual forms—illustrations, graphs, animations, and video—makes it a valuable tool for developing visual literacy.

In early childhood, visual thought and communication are closely related. As developmental psychologists such as L. S. Vygotsky (1974) have shown, images play an important part in children's attempts to understand and think about the world. The early written communication attempts of young children make extensive use of both verbal and visual symbols (Blackstock & Miller, 1992; Schickendanz, 1986). Computer programs can be rich promoters of visual thinking skills and can provide a visual springboard for writing (Rezabek & Ragan, 1988). An exploration of the use of computer graphic programs by young children in their "symbol weaving attempts" supports this view (Blackstock & Miller, 1992).

Beginning Our Project

Our project was designed to study first- and fourth-grade children as they used a paint program that provided them with an easel on which they painted pictures as well as a writing tablet on which they entered and edited text. We chose 100 first- and fourth-grade children to study because we were interested in learning what effect the features of a paint program would have on young authors and illustrators at different developmental levels. The program used was EasyBook because it provides children with assorted paint and draw tools and also allows students to write below the picture or on a following page. Each story appears on the screen as pages in a book; together, they can be printed in the correct sequence and bound.

We discussed the basic principles of graphic design and expression so that we could establish a baseline of information for all of the children. We engaged students in a lively conversation about how illustrations and color can be used to create mood. We showed them examples from several Caldecott Award–winning books: *The Polar Express,* written and illustrated by Chris Van Allsburg; *Lon Po Po* (A "Red Riding Hood Story" from China), translated and illustrated by Ed Young; and *Owl Moon*, written by Jane Yolen and illustrated by John Schoenherr. All of them were available to students in their library.

Half the students in each class were

randomly assigned to a "Crayon/ Marker" (Crayon) group and the other half to an "Electronic Paint" (Paint) group. The Crayon groups could use crayons, markers, or both. We worked with each small group of 10 to 14 students for 30 minutes once a week for 12 weeks in a computer lab. Students in the Crayon group drew their pictures at tables in the middle of the room before moving to the computers to write their stories. All groups wrote at the computer using the word-processing portion of the program, thus ensuring that no differences in the quality or length of the stories would occur solely because a word processor was used. Paint groups worked at the computers to draw their pictures and write their stories. To provide a record of the creation process, we videotaped several students in each session.

Collaboration and Creativity

Differences in both the creative process and product were documented. The nature of the interactions among the students in the two groups was noticeably different. In the Paint groups, peer collaboration was extensive, vocal, and boisterous. Students helped not only their next-door neighbors but also others across the lab. Many questions, answers, comments, and exclamations bounced back and forth across the room. Students in the Crayon groups also talked, commenting on what they were drawing or asking for help finding particular colors, but their conversations were more subdued and less frequent. Most of the interactions between these students focused on finding a missing color or replacing a broken crayon or dry marker. While they were drawing, they often talked about things other than the task at hand.

A higher degree of collaboration among children in the Paint groups was also evident during the writing stage of the authoring process. Students sitting next to each other would lean over to ask the spelling of words or what something should be called. Some even used each other's names in their stories. We did not record this much verbal exchange among the Crayon group's writers. The latter would ask the researchers about the spelling of a word, but they did not seem to talk among themselves about the stories they were writing. Because all of the groups used EasyBook's word-processing function, we could only surmise that the collaboration begun during the drawing portion continued into the writing session.

Visual–Verbal Literacy and Creativity

Observations of the Paint students and analysis of the videos revealed interesting facets in the way the paint program was used. Some students started over several times. Some changed elements of their pictures, background color, and minor objects, all of which served as a setting for the main characters; the students were de-

termined to get the surroundings just right. One student remarked that he loved drawing with the paint program because "you can change mistakes and it doesn't show." Unusual colors, patterns, and effects were part of the experimentation that most of the children did. Often a child was pleased with some whimsical color and adapted the story to fit the resulting strange visual effects. One first grader drew a bedroom with dark red walls. When asked if it was the color of her bedroom, she replied that it was not but that she liked the color and wanted to see how it would look. When we checked back with her later, the walls were still dark red and in her story a fairy godmother had changed her blue walls to that luscious red.

The Paint students' freehand drawing with the mouse was often not as precise as they would have liked; this was particularly true for the first graders. Frequently, less adept students combined stamps with freehand drawings to illustrate their stories. For example, one student did a nice freehand drawing of a road winding through a meadow of green grass with flowers along the road. Walking down the road are a boy and a dog (both stamps); a

Figure 1. A student has combined the use of paint tools and stamps.

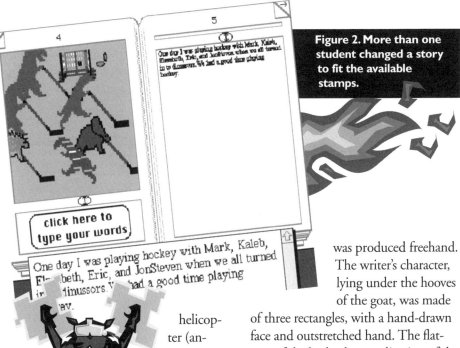

Figure 2. More than one student changed a story to fit the available stamps.

helicopter (another stamp) is getting ready to land in the meadow by the road. In this story, the helicopter stops to ask the little boy for directions.

In another example, a fourth grader had drawn himself and several of his pets. Using an eyeglass stamp, he put glasses on himself (which he wears) *and* his pets. He did not mention this whimsical treatment in his story, which was about a delightful adventure they shared.

Some students embellished the stamps to fit their needs. In one picture, for example, a fourth-grade student added horns to a deer stamp to make it a goat. Her delightful picture was a curious mix of stamps, freehand drawing, the rectangle tool, and the paint bucket tool (Figure 1). In the story a man driving a goat cart ran into a person (the story writer), who ended up under the goat. The blue sky and green grass of the background were hand-drawn but filled in with the paint bucket. The wagon was created with the rectangle tool; the wheels were drawn by hand. The driver's body was one rectangle disappearing into the cart, the arms were formed by two rectangles, and the head

was produced freehand. The writer's character, lying under the hooves of the goat, was made of three rectangles, with a hand-drawn face and outstretched hand. The flatness of the body, the supplication of the outstretched hand, and the nose pointing skyward are quite expressive. The character looks as if she has been crushed into the ground. The total effect conveys the writer's feelings to the reader.

Observations of the children indicated that the younger and less creative children were likely to search for stamps to express their ideas. If they could not find one that represented their original idea, then they might select an existing stamp and change their story to fit it (Figure 2). The more artistic fourth graders did not use the stamps at all; they used all of the paint box tools to render more creative and vividly colored drawings (Figure 3). One student remarked about the paint program, "I love these colors. It's easier to pick up colors. Crayons get broken and lost."

In addition, first graders needed more time to complete their stories than did the older students. In this case, they were able to represent ideas through their illustrations, but they had more difficulty writing the story in text form.

Observations

So what were the advantages and disadvantages of the electronic paint programs? Their limitations, in fact, seem

few in number. One drawback may be that children have some trouble using a mouse to draw after they have learned to draw with a pencil. This was confirmed by one fourth grader who is particularly adept: "[I]t's easier to draw with a pencil." Another hurdle for children is the discrepancy between the drawing and the visual planes; a mouse pad on which the child draws requires her to create on a horizontal surface an image that will appear on a vertical plane. Some children seemed disoriented because they could not see what they were drawing under the mouse, thus throwing off their eye–hand coordination. This seemingly affects some children more than others, but it did not deter them from drawing. Most of them soon became adept at manipulating the mouse.

One feature that may also inhibit task completion is the ease with which a student can erase a drawing with one simple mouse click. A few children were observed repeatedly "wiping out" their pictures with abandon and starting over. Erasing and moving tools are almost too attractive and fun! This may contribute to some impulsiveness and perhaps inhibit reflection and purposeful planning.

Despite the few limitations we observed, electronic paint programs seem to have significant advantages over paper-based drawing. We discovered that the Paint pictures were more creative and the stories accompanying them longer and more interesting. The pictures were evaluated using criteria developed for the Torrance Tests of Creative Thinking (Torrance, 1974). The criteria included the number of colors used, elaboration, and creative strength; the latter is recognized by emotional expressiveness, movement, humor, unusual visualization, richness of imagery, and fantasy.

In addition, the picture's correlation to the story was assessed by identifying the number of picture elements that were included in the story and whether use of both words and graphic images created a richer story than either one alone. The Paint pictures were analyzed and found to have more elaborations and a greater number of colors than the Crayon pictures. More picture elements were mentioned in the Paint stories than in the Crayon stories, and the Paint stories were found to be longer. This could have been because the children were so conscious of adding elaborations to the Paint pictures that they tried hard to include them in the stories. This helped with background description and action details.

In one story, for example, the main character was walking through woods; instead of using this simple statement, the author included descriptions of beautiful red, yellow, and brown leaves on the trees, the flowers growing on the path, and the birds flying overhead, all of which set the mood for the happy story that followed. In general, among all groups, the more intricate the picture, the more detailed and complete the story.

Using Paint Programs in Your Own Classroom

We believe teachers should try these electronic paint programs because of their capabilities to produce books with students of all ages. Spend a short time demonstrating how to use the main tools and then provide a couple of sessions in which you encourage your students to experiment with many of the program's features. Letting each student tell the group about her or his favorite effect and how to achieve it provides a great way for them to learn more about the program and it encourages the collaborative tendencies that are paramount to the successful use of this medium. Print student masterpieces (in color, if possible) and display them on a bulletin board so everyone can admire the special effects and visual representations.

Students can add pictures on each page of the story as it continues, and the end product can be printed as a finished book. Easy Book, for example, makes this especially easy. If students want to present their stories to the class or to visitors, then they can use the simple slide-making capabilities of a paint program such as Kid Pix II to accompany their presentation. In addition, some of the paint programs have sound-recording capabilities; these will allow a child to speak the story directly into the microphone. The narration is subsequently attached to the illustration. (See "Choosing a Paint Program" for more information about the different features in common pieces of software.)

Publishing activities engage students because they are interesting, challenging, and creative. By adding technology to these activities, you can make the projects even more exciting by providing them with professional end products.

Acknowledgement
A special thanks to Wedgewood Elementary School in Baton Rouge, Louisiana.

References
Allsburg, C. Van. (1985). *The polar express.* Boston: Houghton Mifflin.

Blackstock, J., & Miller, L. (1992). The impact of new information technology on young children's symbol-weaving efforts. *Computers in Education, 18,* 209–221.

Rezabek, L. L., & Ragan, T. J. (1988). Using computers to facilitate visual thinking: An analogy between visual and verbal processing. *Reading Psychology, 9*(4), 455–467.

Schickendanz, J. A. (1986). *More than the ABC's: The early stages of reading and writing.* Washington, DC: National Association for the Education of Young Children.

Torrance, P. E. (1976). *Guiding creative talent.* Huntington, NY: Robert E. Drieger.

Vygotsky, L. (1978). *Mind in society.* Cambridge, MA: Harvard University Press.

Yolen, J. (1987). *Owl moon.* New York: Philomel Books.

Young, E. (1989). *Lon Po Po.* New York: Philomel Books.

Figure 3. Highly artistic fourth graders produced the most creative drawings using only the paint box tools.

Choosing a Paint Program

Many electronic paint programs are available for classroom use, but we have examined 13 here. Several of them have broader multimedia tools that allow students, for example, to animate parts of the picture and use recorded sound (see Table 1). Most of them contain large clip art libraries, backgrounds, stamps, or stickers; a few even incorporate QuickTime movies. Some have broader text-manipulation features (see Table 2). All of them make writing a pleasure.

TABLE 1

	ANIMATION	SOUND	MOVIE CLIPS	CREATES SLIDESHOWS	ELECTRONIC PLAYBACK
Kid Works Deluxe	x	x			x
Kid Pix Studio	x	x	x	x	
EasyBook; EasyBook Deluxe					x
The Amazing Writing Machine					
Kid's Media Magic		x	x		x
Storybook Maker Deluxe		x			
The Ultimate Writing & Creativity Center	x	x		x	
Make-A-Book		x			
Creative Writer 2		x			
Magic Media Slate	x	x	x		
Storybook Weaver Deluxe		x			
Super Young Authors		x			x
ClarisWorks for Kids		x	x	x	

TABLE 2

	TEXT-TO-SPEECH	SPELL CHECKER	REBUS TOOL	GUIDES PROCESS WRITING	PRINTS IN BOOK FORMAT
Kid Works Deluxe			x		
Kid Pix Studio					
EasyBook; EasyBook Deluxe	x	x			x
The Amazing Writing Machine			x	x	
Kid's Media Magic	x		x		
Storybook Maker Deluxe					
The Ultimate Writing & Creativity Center	x	x		x	x
Make-A-Book					x
Creative Writer 2					
Magic Media Slate					
Storybook Weaver Deluxe	x	x		x	
Super Young Authors					x
ClarisWorks for Kids	x	x			

Try one or more of these programs with your students and watch the enthusiasm, collaboration, and creativity flow!

Students can use PowerPoint or other presentation software to create "electronic books," a concept Bob Hodges developed in response to his district's five-year plan to integrate technology into the learning process.

Electronic Books
Presentation Software Makes Writing More Fun

By Bob Hodges

Subject: Language arts

Grade Levels: 3 and up (Ages 8 and up)

Technology: PowerPoint (Microsoft) or other presentation software, scanner, digital camera, CD-ROM, microphones

Standards: *NETS* 3 & 4. (See http://cnets.iste.org for more information on the NETS project.) *NCTE/IRA* 3, 4, 6, & 9. (See www.ncte.org for more information on these language arts standards.)

Online Supplement: www.iste.org/L&L

Worksheet samples included.

Microsoft's PowerPoint is an electronic slideshow and presentation application that uses text, photos, clip art, sound, animation, and video. It was originally designed as a business application for adults but can easily be adapted for children. I use it with third, fourth, and fifth graders in a public school in Issaquah, Washington. By learning a few basic skills, a child can create a story that is more fun, more motivating, more creative, and more sophisticated than anything he or she might ever do on paper. I call these stories Electronic Books.

Electronic Books are stories that are created using PowerPoint (or any other presentation application) as the storytelling medium instead of pencil and paper or word processor. Electronic Books use features we often associate with cartoons, comic strips, videos, and slideshows. The writer creates and presents a story using a combination of text, audio, and graphics. The audience might be one reader sitting alone at a computer or 100 readers sitting in an auditorium with the author. Electronic Books also can be e-mailed. The only skills necessary to read an electronic book are the ability to open a file (which can be as easy as double-clicking on the story's icon on the desktop) and the ability to press the <Enter> key to advance the story—that is, turn the page. The Electronic Books unit has four fundamental parts.

1. Introducing the concept
2. Planning the story
3. Creating the story
4. Sharing the story

1. Introducing the Concept

To prepare and motivate my students, I tell them we're beginning a long-term computer project, and I show them several Electronic Books. I always include an Electronic Book I've made that is light and funny and includes many names from our class. (I save time by using the same story year after year with the names updated.) I also show several Electronic Books created by students from previous years. For many, this is the first time they've experienced an electronic slideshow or presentation. My students enjoy watching them and are excited to know they'll be creating their own.

2. Planning the Story

I insist my students sit down and plan their stories using paper and pencil. I provide a worksheet roadmap that forces them to think about where they're going, what they're doing, how to start, and how to finish. This roadmap is called the Beginning/Middle/End Worksheet (see sample), and it must be completed and approved before access to a computer is granted.

Skills Checklist

In my electronic book, I used the following:
- [ ] Sounds from PowerPoint
- [ ] Sounds from a disk
- [ ] Sounds from a microphone
- [ ] Builds or Animations (how an object comes on the screen)
- [ ] Transitions (how an entire slide comes on the screen)
- [ ] Clip art from PowerPoint's Clip Gallery
- [ ] Clip art from a disk
- [ ] Clip art from any source—recolored
- [ ] Digital photos
- [ ] Scanned objects that were photos
- [ ] Scanned objects that were personal drawings
- [ ] Background or Design changes
- [ ] WordArt

iste | copy me

Each entry on the worksheet is only a sentence or two, and I stress that anything can be changed once the story is under construction. The worksheet is a map that points the writer in the general direction, not a recipe that mandates a certain result.

The planning that is most crucial to the success of the story takes place in the "Things that happen" and the "What problems or conflicts get resolved?" sections. The "Things that happen" questions force the author to figure out the flow and logic of the story. The "What problems or conflicts get resolved?" section is critical. All good fiction features characters who have problems to solve or conflicts to overcome. This section forces the author to understand his or her own story and say what it is really about. Once the writer understands and focuses on this, he or she has made significant progress. I do allow writers to create nonfiction Electronic Books. They follow a modified worksheet.

3. Creating the Story

After receiving teacher advice and approval concerning the Beginning/Middle/End Worksheet, a student is assigned to a computer for the duration of the project. When it is time to work, the student simply goes to the assigned computer and double-clicks on his or her story icon on the desktop. At the end of daily work sessions, each student is required to save his or her file to the desktop. Students are also encouraged to save files to a disk as a backup.

As the student uses the worksheet to begin building an electronic book, he or she also must focus on demonstrating certain PowerPoint skills. These skills include modifying text, inserting photos and clip art, adding sound, and animating objects (see the Skills Checklist.) Modifying text includes sizing text, changing fonts, coloring text, and creating WordArt. Inserting photos and clip art includes using PowerPoint's Clip Gallery, second-party software, and

scanning personal drawings and photos from another source. Adding sounds and animating objects includes using PowerPoint's sound files, using second-party software, creating sounds using a microphone, and animating objects and text in various ways.

These skills are taught in several ways: minilessons, teacher tutoring, and peer tutoring. I use minilessons to teach large groups. I announce to the class that I am going to demonstrate a particular skill and anyone who wants to learn that skill should pay attention.

The best and most frequent way PowerPoint skills are taught in my classroom is through peer tutoring. Peer tutoring happens when one student does something cool with his or her electronic book and all the other students want to know how it was done so they can do it too. There is nothing more powerful or effective than this student-to-student teaching, and it leaves me free to help in other ways.

In addition to demonstrating their PowerPoint skills, my students also use and teach what we call "Cool Tools." Whenever someone figures out how to do something cool—something the teacher does not appear to know about—it becomes a Cool Tool, and the discoverer gets to demonstrate and tell everyone about it. (See the sample list of Cool Tools.)

For this assignment I require a title page that includes the book's title, author's name, publication date, and a credits page that includes the author's name and a digital photo. I set a minimum presentation length for fifth graders at 25 slides, for fourth graders at 20 slides, and for third graders at 15 slides, but I never have to enforce them!

4. Sharing the Story

Sharing stories is one of the best and most enjoyable parts of creating Electronic Books. We share stories and parts of stories informally within our own classroom on a regular basis. We also share more formally when we invite K–2 students to read our Electronic Books. By sharing the books in this way, not only do the authors get the "recognition of publication" but they get the opportunity to teach literacy and computer skills to younger students at the same time.

Formal sharing works like this: A younger reader is assigned to an author, and the two students read the book together according to the literacy skills of the reader. Readers can choose to read the book themselves, have the book read to them, or share the reading. Readers always drive, which means they animate the objects and advance the pages at their own speed. When finished, readers move to another Electronic Book and repeat the process.

Benefits to Students

The Electronic Book project benefits writers in many ways because they exercise an extraordinary variety of skills when creating these books. Students learn the fundamentals of the presentation application. They also expand general computer literacy skills, especially concerning the operating system and peripherals such as digital cameras, microphones, CD-ROMs, and scanners. They learn to collaborate and tutor. They learn to tell a story from beginning to middle to end, and they learn how to assess the flow and logic in a story. Students also learn how to present their work and how to help others increase literacy skills. Perhaps best of all, as electronic writers, the students discover the satisfaction and joy of using computers to create books of their own.

Resource

PowerPoint is available separately or as part of Microsoft's Office suite. See www.microsoft.com/office/powerpoint/ for more information.

Beginning/Middle/End Roadmap Worksheet

The title of my story is: _____

The main characters are: _____

In general my story is about: _____

_____

A problem that gets solved or a conflict that is resolved: _____

_____

My first slide will include: _____

_____

Things that happen in the beginning: _____

_____

Things that happen in the middle: _____

_____

Things that happen at the end: _____

_____

My last slide will include: _____

_____

iste copy me — "Electronic Books: Presentation Software Makes Writing More Fun" by Bob Hodges. *Learning & Leading with Technology*, Sept. 1999, volume 27, number 1. ©1999, International Society for Technology in Education, 800.336.5191; cust_svc@iste.org; www.iste.org. Freely reproducible.

Cool PowerPoint Tools

File Menu/Pack and Go: When your Electronic Book gets too big for one disk, this is what you use to save it to several disks. (For Windows version.)

Edit Menu/Find: Use this tool when you want to go directly to a specific word in your book.

View Menu/Slide Sorter: Go in here to see all your slides at once in miniature. You can pick them up and move them around here, too.

Insert Menu/Duplicate Slide: Make an exact copy of a cool slide (then make whatever changes you need for the new slide).

Insert Menu/Organization Chart: One student noted, "The organization charts are stupid," but you can make cool insects or aliens out of them. (For Windows version.)

Tools Menu/AutoClipart: If you get tired of finding your own clip art, this tool will do it for you. (For Windows version.)

Slide Show Menu/Custom Animation/Timing: Tell the computer which objects to animate and in what order.

Interactive Multimedia Storybooks

Integrating Technology into the Language Arts Curriculum

Technology doesn't always seem to fit in well with the language arts curriculum. Students can word process their reports and papers, but that has always been peripheral to the actual curriculum. With the advent of interactive storybooks, however, learners at all levels can use the computer to read. This article describes a project that brings technology even further into the language arts curriculum: Middle school students designing interactive storybooks for first and second graders.

By Scott Frederickson

Finding appropriate, interesting, and useful ways to integrate technology into language arts can be a challenge. Including multiage and multigrade components adds an additional degree of difficulty or interest, depending on your perspective. Don Kosmicki of Phelps County R7 School District in Holdrege, Nebraska, has accomplished both with the following project.

R7 is a rural, K–8 school district in central Nebraska with approximately 95 students. Don is the technology coordinator for the district and also teaches computer applications for the seventh- and eighth-grade classes. While watching the first- and second-grade teachers use commercially produced interactive CD-ROM storybooks with their students, Don was impressed by the enthusiasm the students demonstrated when they used the programs. Because he was in the process of selecting new projects for his multimedia class for the following semester, he thought a language arts project focusing

on interactive storybooks seemed only natural. Why not have the eighth-grade students create interactive storybooks for the first and second graders? After consultations with the language arts teachers, Don began to plan the project.

Planning the Project

Before Don turned his students loose with this project, he had to decide what skills they would need to learn before beginning—in addition to listing what skills he could expect them to learn in the process of carrying it out. To begin, the students needed to have a basic understanding of the multimedia program, be able to tell an interesting story, and be willing to put in a lot of time revising the project. At the end of this project, he anticipated that all of these skills would be directly enhanced, as well as students' problem-solving, instructional-design, and group skills.

In addition, Don had to plan how students should tackle the project. He decided to have them work as "developmental teams" rather than as individuals, similar to the way multimedia product teams operate in the "real world." As soon as he had finished planning and listing the expectations he had for the project, he was ready to get started.

Five Phases

Don divided the nine-week project into five phases: preproduction, story creation, interactive design, construction, and assessment. Each phase would have its own objectives and a timeline for accomplishing those objectives.

Preproduction. The preproduction phase was almost three weeks long. The students spent this time learning to use basic HyperStudio commands and tools, including the drawing, animation, audio, navigation, and text tools. All class sessions in this and all subsequent phases were 40 minutes per day, five days per week. Don assigned several minor projects to teach students to use the program. For example, students used the drawing tools to create a map of their school that showed locations such as the library, offices, classrooms, cafeteria, and so on. They learned how to use the navigation buttons by typing short reports on several cards and connecting the cards with buttons such as Previous Page and Next Page. Students used New Button Actions to move various objects across the screen, thereby learning animation skills. After becoming competent with the basic skills needed to create HyperStudio projects, students were ready to move on to the story creation phase.

Story Creation. The story creation phase took five class sessions, where students were introduced to the instructional goal of the project—creating interactive multimedia storybooks for the primary grades to help teach beginning reading. The eighth-grade students viewed and worked with the CD-ROM storybooks *Just Grandma and Me* and *Arthur's Teacher Trouble* (both from Living Books) to get a feel for the genre. Students were divided into small groups to critique the two examples and to discuss issues they would need to be concerned with as they created their interactive books. The small groups then combined to discuss all of their ideas.

Students decided that two factors made the Living Books exceptional. First, the programs were not too sophisticated for young students. They were simple, attractive, and straightforward. Second, the books were internally consistent. For example, the buttons for turning the pages were in the same place on each page. The students also noted that the colors were attractive, the sounds were not overused or distracting, and the programs did not have a lot of different actions taking place simultaneously on the screen, which might have confused younger students. These were points the students would need to consider when they developed their own projects.

After gaining a complete understanding of good ideas and pitfalls to avoid, each student team developed its own creative story using ClarisWorks. The students had two major things to keep in mind throughout the project: (a) the audience consisted of first and second graders and (b) the stories needed to be interesting and fun. By keeping the audience in mind, the students would use vocabulary that was appropriate for first- and second-grade students, rather than for their

The three screenshots on this page were created for first and second graders by Don Kosmicki's eighth-grade language arts students.

The illustrations on this page come from the electronic "bookshelf" of multimedia storybooks created by the eighth-grade multimedia design teams at Phelps County R7 School District. As a supplemental activity, eighth graders paired up with the first and second graders to create storybooks based on the younger students' stories. The sample shots on the left side of the page are from storybooks designed by the younger students, and those on the right side of the page are from stories created and designed by the older students. In each multimedia stack, students can click on each sentence to listen to it read aloud, or they can click on individual words to have them pronounced.

usual audience of teachers and eighth-grade peers. It was interesting to note that the students initially did not understand why they were writing in the "technology" class because they thought that writing was the domain of English class. The students were told they would have to use skills from all of their classes and perhaps even some things they had learned outside of school. With all this in mind, the storytellers began their task of creating, proofing, editing, rewriting, and completing their stories.

Interactive Design. After developing their stories, students began the interactive design phase: the transition from written story text to interactive electronic storybooks. Students broke down their stories into electronic "pages" that would be displayed onscreen. Each page was drawn on a 4" x 6" note card. Text, graphics, and other items for each page were either drawn or written on the note cards, or an annotation was made indicating the action that would take place on a particular card. Students used the note cards to develop their initial storyboards, and the index cards made it easier for students to rearrange items to make the story and its components flow better. Students discussed their storyboards and offered each other suggestions, advice, and comments. By the end of the week, students were eager to begin the process of converting their storyboards into interactive computer-based stories.

Construction. The construction phase took the longest, lasting three five-day weeks. Using their knowledge of HyperStudio, students transcribed the information from their storyboards into cards. After creating the initial file, students would decide to add to their project, adding scanned images and photographs, voice recordings, and a variety of sounds. These additions would occasionally take students deeper into their assignments and require them to use more elaborate HyperStudio features than they had been taught. Students would pull out their manuals and begin asking Don questions, and he would encourage them to consult the manuals and work together. This helped them develop better problem-solving and teamwork skills. Students gathered in small groups to discuss problems and share solutions. During these sessions, students shared new ideas with each other. Although almost completed, the projects were not quite ready to be shared with the first- and second-grade students.

Assessment. The assessment phase took one week to complete. Before turning the younger students loose with the electronic storybooks, class members viewed and evaluated each other's projects. Students gave detailed critiques for each project, focusing on accuracy, continuity, interest, and creativity. They then modified their projects as needed. The eighth graders were overflowing with excitement when the first graders came in to read and interact with their stories. Eyes were bright and shiny and smiles were abundant as the first and second graders eagerly read and interacted with each story. Because many of the stories had a "local flavor" to them, it seemed the younger students enjoyed them even more than the Brøderbund storybooks! The assessment was not quite complete until the eighth-grade students probed the younger students for questions or suggestions they might have for the programs.

When all the stacks were finished, they were placed into an electronic "bookshelf" shell that Don created. The bookshelf showed the various titles of the storybooks (and had room for future additions) and allowed users to select and interact with each book. The bookshelf of storybooks was installed on the computers in the first- and second-grade classrooms to be used by future classes.

Follow-Up Project

The following semester, Don's eighth graders did a follow-up project. This time, the second graders dictated the stories, and the eighth graders turned them into interactive books. It was an interesting sight to watch second graders explaining to the older students what should belong on the screen and how things should look. Neither group was used to working in that way, but they both seemed to enjoy the process.

For both groups of students, bringing in skills and experiences from other areas and classes while using problem-solving and evaluative and reflexive skills was a challenging and interesting way to integrate technology into their language arts curricula.

Resources

Arthur's Teacher Trouble, by Marc Brown, and Just Grandma and Me, by Mercer Mayer, are published by Living Books: A Random House/Brøderbund Company. These and many other CD-ROM storybooks are available from Brøderbund Software Inc., 500 Redwood Boulevard, Novato, CA 94948; 800/354-9706 or 415/382-4400; fax 415/382-4419.

HyperStudio is available from Roger Wagner Publishing Inc., 1050 Pioneer Way, Suite P, El Cajon, CA 92020; 800/hyperstudio or 619/442-0522; fax 619/442-0525; www.hyperstudio.com.

THEORY INTO PRACTICE

"MI" Kind of Learning
Using Media Technology to Foster Multiple Intelligences

By Rose Reissman

Think of the student who is not drawn into the richness of experiences, language, and narratives of printed texts. Consider the student who in response to a writing prompt stares into space and aimlessly shifts back and forth on a seat without putting pencil to paper. Reflect on the student who during a live student performance, screening, audio recording, or listening session "fools around," squirms, and pays no attention to the text.

Howard Gardner (2000) has articulated, in a compelling and cogent fashion, an evolving framework for a theory of multiple intelligences. Gardner conceives of drawing on the strengths of students' multiple intelligences as a means for engaging them in literacy activities as "entry points" to traditional literacy habits of mind, behaviors, and activities. Teachers who want to use this framework to individualize, motivate, engage, and empower students who demonstrate strengths in multiple intelligences should literally tap the magic of technology.

Gardner's theoretical framework for multiple intelligences as translated through multimedia technology skills, software, and products can offer teachers an educational tool that transforms unengaged students into enthralled and active participants who can carry out an infinite string of literacy enterprises.

Literacy Entry Points—Windows on Writing and Reading

The eight multiple intelligences Gardner describes are:

1. LINGUISTIC—dealing with language, text, speaking, writing

2. AUDITORY/MUSICAL—dealing with sound recordings, music

3. MATHEMATICAL/PROBLEM SOLVING—Focusing on problem constructs, mathematical operations, and interdisciplinary problem solving, as well as using interdisciplinary logic/critical-thinking skills

4. SPATIAL—Referencing drawing, graphics, illustration, and design capacity (used for engineering and architectural design capacities)

5. INTRAPERSONAL—Reflecting, responding, and reacting to events, texts, and experiences; having leadership capacities

6. INTERPERSONAL—Collaborating and working with small groups or teams

7. KINESTHETIC—Focusing on movement, dance, and other actions

8. NATURALIST—Classifying and categorizing living things, particularly in the sciences (botany, zoology, geology, earth science)

The accompanying chart provides some additional details on multiple intelligences.

While the literacy educator in the classroom can use the strengths and under-standings inherent in multiple intelligences to motivate students who do not immediately and enthusiastically respond to traditional literacy instruction, the success made possible by technology immediately elicits the students' various talents and perspectives on literacy. Create your own multimedia strategies, procedures, and projects that strengthen your students' capacities for multiple intelligences. Use the password "multiple intelligences" to observe technology make a successful classroom happen.

Reference

Gardner, H. (2000). *Framing and reframing intelligence: Multiple intelligence reconisdered.* NY: Basic Books.

Finding an Entry Point

Multiple Intelligences	Media-Mediated Process	Technology Transformation
LINGUISTIC KINESTHETIC SPATIAL	*Word Processing:* graphics, text flow, scrolling, editing. *Desktop Publishing:* font choices, point size selection, graphics, text block manipulation. Word processing and graphics allow students to use illustrations, create visual layouts, manipulate icons, use clip art, scan print materials, import digital images, and design maps.	Enables and enhances qualitative writing capabilities of linguistic and kinesthetic learners through the flow of text on the screen, supported by keyboarding and mouse-clicking. Students can effortlessly create covers, crossword puzzles, indexes, pagination, tables of contents, charts, tables, and other material. Empowers artistic and inventive storytellers to infuse their artistic and graphic ideas into reports, stories, and other work.
KINESTHETIC SPATIAL LINGUISTIC INTRAPERSONAL AUDITORY/MUSICAL MATHEMATICAL	Multimedia presentations offer text, animation, sounds, and video.	Enthralls, engages, and energizes individual and group presentations; provides a polished, immediately viewable product; and offers peer and adult feedback, with immediate editing possible.
NATURALIST LINGUISTIC INTRAPERSONAL INTERPERSONAL MATHEMATICAL SPATIAL	Databases help organize and sort categories of things.	Energizes and engages students in performing sorts and using filters. Enhances, facilitates, and expands students' capacity to create reports and other documents.

INSIGHTS

Art, Computers, and Literacy

By Mark Gura

Cro-Magnon hominids used charred wood to draw the images of animals on cave walls as graphic accompaniment to oral recountings of their hunts. Fast forward to today and we would be hard pressed to find a Web site without both words and graphics. Those seeking to invest words with additional power have always sought to marry them to images. In fact, not only do pictures go with words but in many pre-alphabet cultures, pictures were words. The tradition of enhancing writing with graphics is a great one that can be applied beneficially to youngsters who are in the process of learning to write.

Using classroom computers for this purpose creates tremendous educational possibilities. The computer offers a number of unique opportunities for young illustrators. It can be used to locate an endless variety of previously created images found in clip art or digital photo collections, some of which comes as part of the word-processing or desktop-publishing software. With appropriate permission and copyright acknowledgements, images from most digital sources, including encyclopedias and Web sites, can be copied and used, making the possibilities truly endless.

Creating original images is even more satisfying. Most youngsters find representational drawing to be challenging even with materials designed for making art. The mouse makes line rendering even more difficult. Fortunately, with the addition of a drawing tablet, a computer can simulate a real pencil, crayon, or paint brush. Of course, if the artist's intention is to produce something more abstract or in the nature of mechanical drawing, standard drawing programs can easily be used to create wonderful work. Once the drawing hurdle is surmounted, paint programs with paint bucket or spray can functions can be used to generate startling effects almost effortlessly.

A couple of other low-cost peripherals can make the classroom computer art program much richer. Scanners are inexpensive and easy to use. They enable students to rework conventional drawings made with markers and pens by scanning them and reopening them in image-editing software. Some scanners now come with an onboard processor so that valuable computer time need not be sacrificed in order to operate them. Students simply save their scanned work to a disk that they insert into the computer when necessary.

While photographs can be scanned as well, a digital camera makes a very useful addition to the classroom. Not only does it free up the scanner for other jobs, but it can also be taken outside the classroom to record images that can be uploaded to the computer. For some purposes, such as newspapers and year-books, no other type of image but a good photograph will do.

Reworking and transforming images is an area where the computer can make a startling contribution. In the nondigital world, this aspect of producing images requires finely honed skills. With the computer, however, even the artistically challenged can express the dictates of their hearts and imaginations with little fear of failure. Drawings and photos can be resized, recolored, transformed into sepia-toned antiques, or broken up into a multifaceted view of the world. Images can morph into one another or come to life with animation. Two-dimensional images can be instantly plotted as three-dimensional wire-frame drawings, and three-dimensional views of solid forms can be put into the virtual reality of four-dimensional "sculptural" space. In short, the computer is the genie that grants "everykid" his or her wish to be an artist.

The digitized image—however it is acquired, created, or transformed—can, with the aid of the computer, be easily and seamlessly joined to the words it is intended to accompany. By pressing the mouse button, moving the cursor along a pull-down menu, and lifting the finger to activate the Insert function, the student can import the image into the word-processing or desktop-publishing document. Words and pictures, pictures and words—together they create something far greater than the sum of their parts: student publishing!

CHAPTER 3

The Computer as Catalyst for Critical Thinking
Technology Tools for Constructivist Learning

The Conversation Continues

Mark: Does the computer make your vision real enough to work on? Or is it that computers enable you to evolve a vision?

Rose: The answer to both of those pertinent questions is yes! It depends on the student's particular entry point (MI theory) in the constructing and learning process. For students who are designing a potential playground or garden for their school, the nonartists can use the drawing function of the software to realize their various visions of the item to be created. Therefore, technology enables the vision to evolve. For students whose strengths are critiquing, reconfiguring, and realizing the vision, technology makes the vision real enough to work on. Whatever the student problem-solver's strength, multimedia provides an extensive toolkit from which the teacher and the student may select those items appropriate to their construct needs.

Mark: So, what you're saying is that if I were to challenge my students to come up with a plan for a space station, some of them might use a design program to easily establish a model from which ideas can be generated and reflected on. Some of them might use the technology to get past the difficulties of getting started, and others might get more benefit during the refinement stages of the project.

Rose: Whatever step of the problem-solving process, be it identifying problems or strategizing for solutions, access to technology empowers and broadens the feedback potential for the constructivist learner. What is wonderful here—and is truly multiple intelligence magic—is the access to technology and its tinker-toy–like, construct-building components.

An Epic Adventure in Problem Solving

As most of us know, getting students interested in problem solving is half the battle in getting them to think critically. Fortunately, the authors of this article have found and tested a new software program that actively engages students in solving problems in math and science. Along with many other teachers around the United States, our contributors implemented My Make-Believe Castle in kindergarten through third-grade classes and shared their observations and experiences on a listserv.

By Donna Bearden and Kathleen Martin

In January 1997, we embarked on a grand adventure with teachers all over the country, a collaborative project that aimed to get students interested in problem solving. This group of pioneering elementary educators agreed to try a new software program—My Make-Believe Castle from Logo Computer Systems, Inc. (LCSI)—with their students and share their observations on a listserv.

This project began with a dozen or so teachers in the Dallas–Fort Worth, Texas, area and an Internet invitation to other teachers to join the curriculum project. Before school was out in May, postings to the listserv came from approximately 100 teachers and math educators from around the country. All of

them have contributed to this article because they continued to relate new stories about how their students were solving problems. Sometimes we tried to summarize the teachers' comments, but in many cases their words were so powerful that we included them verbatim.

Using the Program
After a brief introduction from the teachers, the students explored the program on their own. Teachers then shared their observations about the children's experiences on the listserv. In this way the project was two-layered: It focused on (1) how children learn and (2) how professionals develop through their shared reflections about children's learning. But this article is not about professional development, so we will consider only what our students learned.

What Is My Make-Believe Castle?

My Make-Believe Castle is an adventure program that provides an environment with many options. The castle includes several rooms, including an entryway, a bedroom, and a dungeon. Outside the castle are a forest and underground mazes. The cast of characters includes a dragon, witch, wizard, jester, knight, horse, and two children. These characters can be placed in various scenes and programmed to perform different actions. Icons allow program users (children, in this case) to make the characters fly, spin, dance, slip on banana peels, scurry over ladders, and so on. Icons also allow students to manipulate the characters' emotional reactions. Students can construct their own stories or solve any one of several preprogrammed problems. Although the program is marketed for ages 4 to 7, it is appropriate for children throughout the primary grades. And the manual describes the problems posed by the program as well as many extension activities.

Students enjoyed using the program again and again. They returned to solve more problems and make up more of their own stories. As they used the program over several weeks, they seemed to move in and out of three identifiable learning modes: pointing and clicking, wandering and wondering, and persistent probing. Within each mode, the children learned a lot vicariously by watching and imitating other students. Collaboration seemed invaluable at first, but as children became more familiar with the software and its controlling icons, many of them liked to think about and carry out their own ideas by themselves.

Pointing and Clicking

Children were captured initially by the characters and tools. As they randomly pointed and clicked on various icons, they became familiar with the options available to them. A great deal of excitement and sharing occurred as the children made discovery after discovery.

My early-bird student approached the computer with caution. He sat down and began moving the mouse, discovering on his own what the symbols mean and how he could move to different levels. He was so engrossed that he didn't notice how many of his classmates had gathered around him. He couldn't ignore them for long, though, because they were shouting at him: "Try this." "No, try that!" "What does this do?"

Although a few teachers were anxious for their students to move more quickly, they remained true to the agreement to allow students to establish their own pace. Indeed, some children needed a great deal of practice.

I want them to discover the microphone so badly, but no one has tried it yet. Perhaps they are so focused on the different options that they have discovered and that others have shared with them that they are not seeing undiscovered icons.

Many teachers were eager for the children to "get beyond" pointing and clicking, but the children's absorption in this process suggests that powerful learning was going on. The aspect of surprise was particularly evident during this phase. The children could not yet anticipate what was going to happen when they pointed and clicked. Indeed, some with less computer experience were discovering that their actions caused the antics they saw on screen. Only by observing the results of these actions were the children able to connect their own actions with the consequences. This process of learning what to control and how to control it is a matter of coming to understand the meaning of parameters. Playing with parameters leads to recognizing constraints within a situation; it is an important prerequisite to problem solving.

Wandering and Wondering

The children's natural inquisitiveness led them to wander through the castle and wonder aloud what would happen if they tried various combinations of actions and characters. Once they discovered they could make one character change size, for example, they tried chang-

ing the size of all of the characters. Sometimes a student would focus on an action, such as slipping on a banana peel; every character would then be subject to the banana peel test. At other times characters themselves would become the focus of attention, and the children would run each character through every action icon. A single character would slip on a banana peel, climb a ladder, reverse direction, plunge into water, and so on.

> *Two third graders working with the Castle program for the first time focused only on size and were having a great time with that single variable. They put all the characters in a scene and then kept changing their sizes so that some were very large and others very small. They seemed to find the juxtaposition of sizes quite funny.*

When the children discovered a new tool or action, they tended to concentrate on that tool until they learned all of its capabilities. The children's actions appeared to be repetitive, but they were actually fine-tuning their skills with each new tool. Eventually they began to combine new tools with old ones, which led to increasingly complex interactions.

The point-and-click mode gave students information about the parameters of the Castle program—what they could and could not do. Wandering and wondering allowed them to explore the world of conditionals and its enticing "if ... then" situations. For example, "If a ladder is placed across the stream, then the jester can cross over it instead of falling in." As the children discovered the causal relationships characteristic of "if ... then" situations, they were able to master the conditions needed to make decisions and could thus determine what they wanted to do within each one. Now the children were prepared to plan. The difference between the children who needed to continue exploring and those who were ready for strategic planning was evident.

> *One student had not had as much experience as two veterans who were coaching him. He was very caught up in changing the form of the characters with the magic wand as well as the actions they were performing with the ballet slipper and the top. He really liked seeing the dragon whirl. The coaches, a*

boy and a girl, got quite bored with what he was doing and directed him to go to the woods or to the dungeon.

Although the boy at the controls followed many of the coaches' suggestions, he preferred to lead his own explorations. He was captured by the simple variations and would probably have continued for hours if he had not been interrupted. Meanwhile, the veterans were ready for something more challenging.

Persistent Probing

The first problem the children encounter is in the entry hall of the castle. It's the old dunking-booth challenge. The scene includes a catapult, a bowl of fruit, a chair high up on the wall, a target, and a barrel of water. By putting the witch in the chair, placing a watermelon in the catapult, and then having a character jump on the other end, the child can make the watermelon fly through the air and hit the target, causing the witch to plunge into the water and scowl quite angrily. The catapult problem is not easy to solve. The variables include the weight of the item chosen to put in the catapult, the weight of the character chosen to jump on the other end, the path the character takes toward the catapult, and the location of the jumping icon. The children tried various combinations, engaging in a kind of successive approximation as positions

were adjusted and readjusted. The program provided the immediate feedback, which enabled children to respond with modifications.

Although the software includes several problems, many children preferred to pose their own. Something would spark their interest, and they would begin to wonder what would happen if they tried this or that.

> *One kid was in the dungeon with the jester who kept falling in the water. The kid put the foot at the edge of the concrete walkway so the jester could jump across the water. The jester made it and then bumped into the wall at the other end. When a character hits a wall, it turns back in the other direc-*

tion. This time the jester fell into the water coming from the opposite direction. So the kid put a foot on that side of the walkway. The jester jumped the space over the water but then landed on the first foot and got kicked into the water. The kid never solved the problem of keeping the jester out of the water, but left determined to work on it more.

Variations on Persistent Probing

Two cases in particular demonstrate how differently children might approach the same tasks and challenges.

Today Jennifer went to her favorite place, the maze with the log and swimming hole. She chose the witch to go through the obstacle course. She placed the sneakers on either side of the log. As the witch hit the first sneaker, she cut (with the scissors icon) the sneaker on the other side to see what would happen. This caused the witch to fly around the rest of the course. Jennifer called me over to watch and about eight Castle Kids followed me. After she showed me what she had tried, everyone wanted to see if the dragon would fly with one sneaker. They then tried the wizard, the knight, the horse, and the jester. "Try this" and "I have a good idea" were echoed during this time…. The students wanted to set up their own problems on the course rather than follow the program suggestions.

Juan Carlos, a first grader, was at the computer. I was really surprised that he didn't ask me what certain icons did like he usually did. In fact, he was real quiet and was thinking of how to solve a problem. I asked him what he was up to, and he said that he was just trying something new to hit the bull's eye. Normally, he had relied on others' directives to guide his choices. After some time, he excitedly called out. When I turned around, I saw this big smile on his face. He was so proud that he had devised his own way of hitting the bull's eye. He wanted to tell everyone about it. So, of course, everyone dropped what they were doing and went over to listen and watch.

The difference between Jennifer's and Juan Carlos's problem-solving approaches is revealing. For Jennifer, the problem is dynamic: It shifts and transforms in response to her own actions. Her initial problem was getting the witch to negotiate

the obstacle course. Once she discovered the sneaker's power, her problem became one of checking the sneaker's impact on all of the characters. The preset problem of the obstacle course did not engage Jennifer as much as her own questions about what she could do with the sneaker.

Until they really understood the different dimensions of the castle environment, the children tended to pursue problems that involved the capabilities of the characters, tools, and action icons. Only when they had the parameters firmly in mind did they show persistence in following a plan like Juan Carlos. He spent considerable time working with the catapult and watching his friends do the same. Because he knew the complexity involved and was familiar with the different variables, he was able to imagine and then persist in discovering a new way to hit the target.

Working Together and Working Alone

The collaboration and sharing of information seen in the earlier explorations became even more evident during problem solving. Children became teachers and offered their insights to their classmates.

Ryan asked Taylor how he got to a particular game. The sharing of ideas and the explaining to one another the how-to's, the pointing to the screen, the search for the words to explain to each other—it's amazing to watch and listen!

The children genuinely and gladly acknowledged someone else's expertise when he or she discovered something new. They were eager to learn and thus afforded each other many chances to teach. No one child acted as the leader; leadership instead cycled from one child to another and was a function of what each child had learned. Leadership was thus acknowledged in terms of having learned something new.

Tyler began the day with, "You can learn a lot from us. We can be a teacher, too." The kids had found something I didn't even know existed. They were enthusiastic to tell how they had made the discovery and how to do it when I got my turn.

Once the children began solving the problems built into the program and devising their own, an interesting phenomenon occurred. Children who had previously shared their computer time and did not seem to mind having four or five

coaching spectators began to express an interest in spending time alone. A teacher who had one student working alone with the headset was the first to observe this desire.

I just knew that Patrick would say that he hadn't enjoyed the Castle program as much without the crowd. Just the opposite. He loved it because he got to plan and take his time.

Other children expressed similar feelings. They liked time alone to plan.

I've been giving a lot of thought to how Patrick and several of the other Castle Kids are enjoying their own private, quiet time on the Castle program and how they are able to plan what they want to do and then pause and reflect on the consequences of their actions. They have time to decide what they want to do next, not what someone else wants them to do next. I will continue to give them their private space and personal time. Sometimes I think we get so into cooperative learning that we forget the need for individual planning time.

Extending the Castle Environment

At one point in the program, students must solve a maze. Most of them enjoyed this task so much that they began constructing their own mazes.

Believe it or not, two of my students (Ryan and Brett) made a maze using wooden cubes at the tables. They said it was like the maze in the anthill in the Castle program!

After a few days of watching the maze construction develop, someone decided to draw their own maze on paper. This led us off on a tangent for the rest of the afternoon. The children drew mazes and shared them with their friends to see if they could do them. I tried to draw one and it was hard. I'll be anxious to see what Kenneth comes back to school with. He is always inventing things, and he couldn't stand it that he did not get his finished, so he took it home to figure something out. By the way, his science fair project was a hamster maze that won third place.

Perhaps the best indicator of the Castle program's power can be seen in children's activities and insights as they go beyond the constraints of the computer and flow into other dimensions of the classroom. The measure of a good learning environment is its power to help children see connections and develop ways of thinking that are sensitive to complexity. With many computer programs, children engage until there is nothing new to discover or they have the game figured out. The Castle program offers children an opportunity to pose some of their own problems and then solve them rather than solve only preset problems.

Learning environments such as that created by My Make-Believe Castle encourage probing and experimenting. Children develop a powerful intuition about math and science even before such intuition can be articulated or reflected

upon. Solutions to problems can be achieved only through persistence. Through these challenges, children have opportunities to estimate measurement, note relationships between variables such as size and speed, and test the effects of variables on one another. Also, the interactions seem genuinely collaborative in the way that children share perspectives.

It was exciting watching them problem solve together. They would disagree but in a respectful way. They would predict what would happen next if they chose a certain task or sequence of actions. They laughed out loud when the consequences of their actions were a total surprise. I was amazed at one of my students who has difficulty with self-control and can become very physical. When it was not his turn, he showed respect for whoever was in charge of the mouse by quietly offering suggestions.

Since the kids are constantly making new discoveries and creating their own sets of problems, no one has an I-know-it-all attitude. They seem to know that they are working on a never-ending story. The continued support they give each other in this environment continuously energizes me.

Summary

The collaboration, the group and individual problem solving, the sharing of information, and the immediate feedback were all identified by teachers as important factors in both the software and the project. Although important, these factors may be the consequence of something even more significant. My Make-Believe Castle may be as important a learning environment for teachers as it is for children because it enables teachers to observe how children learn and then change their own teaching accordingly.

Resource

My Make-Believe Castle is available on Macintosh or Windows CD-ROM for $39.95 (home) or $49.95 (school; comes with additional classroom materials) from Logo Computer Systems, Inc., PO Box 162, Highgate, VT 05460.

Note: The curriculum project described in this article was supported by the Exxon Education Foundation. The opinions expressed here do not necessarily reflect the position, policy, or endorsement of the Foundation.

Student-Reviewed
SOFTWARE

Helping Middle School Students Identify Their Own Needs

Critical-thinking skills can serve kids far longer than they're in the classroom. Being an informed consumer, for instance, means being able to assess the value of a particular product and how it might enhance one's life. In this article, Rose Reissman describes how she got her students to assess something sight unseen and how that helps them think critically.

By Rose Reissman

Subject: Writing, technology, critical thinking

Grade Level: 5–8 (Ages 10–14)

Although technology as a classroom tool—particularly software designed for middle school students—would seem inherently student-centered, many educators actually direct their students to use teacher-centered software. These programs certainly serve specific curricular objectives and promote student performance, but they don't nurture students' abilities or their creativity as independent, reflective software users.

I want to promote both reflective and active software use among my middle schoolers, so I collect reviews of newly published software from newspapers and online resources. I group them by age level, intended grade, and level of interest. To help foster students who are independent, informed, and proactively engaged in a technology-centered workplace, I ask that they read the reviews and descriptions of new software products (some are paid advertisements written by the companies themselves) and come up with as many uses and applications for each product as they can. The students do not actually need to sample the product; in many cases, in fact, these new products are neither readily accessible nor affordable within the constraints of our inner-city budget. Still, the assignment challenges each student to work on his or her own file of potential software uses.

In March 1997, for example, Microsoft Corporation introduced Plus! for KIDS—a Windows 95 companion collection of programs targeted to children from 3 to 12 years old. The program costs less than $25, but before

we were able to explore the product, I collected two reviews, one from the peripherals column by L. R. Shannon in *The New York Times* and one from the *New York Post.* I photocopied the reviews for all of the students in my sixth-grade language arts class. The students were challenged to read the reviews to develop their own ideas about whether they would pleasurably and practically use this companion collection of programs.

At first, the students were puzzled by the challenge. If we didn't actually have the software, then why review it? We talked about software they had bought or had been given, and software they were expected to use for school projects but found wanting. What if they could examine these products before they bought or received them from others? Even without actually exploring a program, couldn't they tell by reading its packaging or the accompanying press sheets whether it might be interesting? As we spoke, the students began to see how they might personally benefit by reviewing programs designed for them, even if it only helped them decide what should not be purchased or set aside for their recreational or educational use.

The students were invited to read the software reviews in teams or work individually on their own reviews. After initially hesitating, they were eager to react to the software reviews once they understood their role as reviewing a review. Because the initial Plus! for Kids package was broken into different applications, the students listed their responses application by application. As they worked independently or in teams in writing and keyboarding their reactions to the product, they closely read the reviewer texts and used them as outlines for their own remarks.

The students took approximately 20 minutes or so to go through the reviews and carefully list their comments program by program. After they had finished their individual or team reviews, they were invited to share their reactions with the class. Here are some of their observations.

Microsoft's Plus! for Kids Talk It
(a text-to-speech application in Spanish or English)
This program is really neat, because hearing the words you write out spoken by different voices (one could be a Martian) makes writing and reading fun. Talk It means a story a little child writes can be read aloud to other children. It would also help children act out their story characters. I think that the fact that a child could talk in Spanish is a plus!!

For a child who needs more time for spelling to be able to hear a story he or she tells without worrying about the spelling of the words is terrific.

Microsoft's Plus! for Kids Play It
(turns the computer keyboard into a musical keyboard with musical styles, bands, and sounds)

This lets kids add in their own voices, and sounds to their stories. They are now real media producers!

If a class or student is studying Native Americans, the sounds of buffalo and actual chants can be added into a report. That might even make the other students more interested in listening to the report.

Why not put Talk It and Play It together so if students wanted to record their own favorite books they could do it with their own sound effects and music?

Microsoft's Plus! for Kids Paint It
(a painting and drawing program)
This application has standard tools like a color bucket, airbrush, eraser, and line. It also has a blender to change a drawing in unusual ways, a bomb to destroy the artwork violently, and an oops icon to cancel the last thing done by the user!

I really loved "bombing" the art and playing around with the blender! The kinds of drawings I could create to go with my stories or friends' stories or reports would be really awesome! I also like the *oops* because lots of times you make a mistake or you get upset but you can't go back and cancel it!

This application is similar to MECC's Storyweaver and KIDS Works which I have already tried out. But being able to do it in Spanish means I can really tell stories in my "best true words" without having to translate and "simple" them down to English.

You know, students could use the Paint It feature to create product and campaigns. . . . This feature could really help us create, see, share, and fix up as campaigns that look like and sound like what we see on television. That's really neat!!

One of my problems with art is I see a picture in my head, but when I try to draw it, I can't. With Paint It, what comes up on screen is pretty close to what I see in my head. Wow!

Microsoft's Plus! for Kids
Picture Picker
(clip-art application and typefaces)
You know I would like to use the Ransom font to create a kidnap note like that used in the Mel Gibson movie—*Ransom*. Then other users could develop stories and scenes to go with it, and, of course, all the sounds and music that could go with a kidnap suspense story.

I have a collection of Japanese comic books. This Comic Sans form will let me create my own story in this style.

I think Ransom would help involve students in following kidnap cases in the news. We could use all the different Microsoft's Plus! for Kids programs to create our own news magazine. Then we could show it to other classes.

We took a full period and a half—some 90 minutes—to share the student's software reviews. I made no comments other than those to facilitate conversation about the product's potential uses. Beyond the students' response to the particulars of Plus! for Kids, I was pleased by the way they independently linked their reviews to projects we had already done in class—news stories, recordings and illustrations of favorite literary pieces, personal creative writing, and review writing.

Approximately 30% of my students are Spanish-speaking and have limited English proficiency, which is reflective of this inner-city Brooklyn school. For that reason alone, I was happy that my young software reviewers were so appreciative of the ways in which Talk It

would allow them immediately to tap their native language and realize their writing talents. In reading their reviews aloud—they had been entered on the computer but not yet enhanced with Paint It, Play It, or Picture Picker—I found that the students were most taken with the Plus! program's visual and oral language possibilities. This fact, of course, reinforced for me the need to use technology's spatial and auditory capacities to engage students who were not naturally linguistic learners in literacy activities and collaborative learning.

Finally, the students also reacted rather surprisingly, from my perspective, to Protect It, the program's control feature that allows parents to restrict access to programs, files, settings, and modems. Almost all of my sixth graders favored such parental or teacher supervision, perhaps because many had heard horror stories of children who had been stalked online and then physically attacked or molested by adults. Although few of the students had home access to software programs or the Internet, one who did told of being punished by her father after she ran up a huge telephone bill by using the modem. Another student who spent time in his aunt's office after school told how he got in trouble after inadvertently changing the sound card when he was just nine years old. His aunt had not appreciated his efforts.

The students have overwhelmingly given their approval to our plan to purchase the Plus! for Kids collection. The student software review project, however, won't be used in our classroom just to review specific programs that the school can actually purchase. It will become a regular authentic writing activity and turned

into a Web site or bulletin board feature on which students exercise and hone their critical skills; we hope these will become lifelong technology consumer skills. Such skills can actively engage students at the upper-elementary and secondary levels in evaluating and developing the ways in which new technology products meet or fail to meet their interests and concerns. Such feedback can be sent directly to software publishers or published in technology magazines alongside teachers' or educators' reviews.

If technology is to be used as a classroom tool to integrate curricula and promote students' lifelong learning, then teachers need to shift from using specific technology products to addressing students' identified needs and potential. If we do that, then we will indeed see our students leading and learning through technology.

Note: Microsoft PLUS! for Kids is no longer available from Microsoft (www.microsoft.com/).

Processing Ideas

Move Beyond Word Processing into Critical Thinking

Technology can help students access and process information to generate knowledge and communicate it to others. However, most classroom technology use focuses on access and communication without paying adequate attention to the critical processing component. This article provides a detailed look at how teachers can support students in using basic word-processing technology to influence the way students reflect and respond to a wide variety of print and nonprint texts to build an understanding of these texts.

Students might create a newsletter to share news among themselves.

Students might create a newsletter geared toward their parents to share class news, important dates, and so on.

By Sara Dexter and Susan Watts-Taffe

Subject: Language arts, graphic design, multidisciplinary

Grade Level: 5–9 (Ages 10–14)

Technology: AppleWorks (Apple), Word and Works (Microsoft)

Standards: *NETS•S* 3–6. (Read more about the NETS Project at www.iste.org—select Standards Projects.) *NCTE/IRA* 3–8. (Read the language arts standards at www.ncte.org.) *New Standards: Language Arts* 1–5. (Find out more at www.ncee.org/OurPrograms/nsPage.html.)

Increasingly teachers are finding technology useful for helping students access data, process information, and communicate knowledge. Technology facilitates access to a greater amount of data than traditional research methods; speeds search and retrieval; provides templates or scaffolds on which to organize, select, and formulate ideas; and encourages and simplifies revision of communications for greater precision and effectiveness.

Though each stage of knowledge production has its own distinct characteristics, the stages are also interconnected; learners move among the three as they work. For example, for students to effectively communicate their knowledge, they must convey content clearly to a specific audience. Yet such a message requires more than access to raw data; the data must be processed into useful information. Clearly, if any phase in this process is neglected, the others will be weakened as well.

Despite this interdependency, classroom technology use all too often focuses only on the accessing and communicating phases of students' work. Many classroom teachers have already discovered the benefits of CD-ROMs and the Internet for accessing information, and computer applications are widely used to communicate information through multimedia reports, slideshows, and text documents. For the *processing* of information, however, technology's potential for aiding student learning and achievement is undertapped. This article focuses on the relationship among:

1. The instructional planning for the style and format of the communications students use to demonstrate their knowledge
2. The specific modes of information analysis and synthesis required by such communications
3. The role technology can play in students' processing of their ideas

Thus, it emphasizes the key role teachers play as instructional designers who create assignments that maximize learning and technology use.

Idea Processing and Effective Communication

In the past 10 years, educators in most subject areas have developed national standards that call for student performance to reflect authentic, real-world tasks and require students to think and communicate at new, higher levels. To demonstrate their mastery of these content-area standards, students must often produce original products or performances that reflect their acquisition and processing of the information in question.

Language arts national standards have come to stipulate that students be able to write across the curriculum in a variety of formats, such as persuasive essays, short stories, or research reports. As stated by the National Council of Teachers of English (NCTE, 1996), students should be able to:

> employ a wide range of strategies as they write and [to] use different writing process elements appropriately to communicate with different audiences for a variety of purposes (standard 5).

Although specific content-area standards provide a variety of topics and areas of inquiry that students should be able to write about, the NCTE points out that students also require numerous opportunities to compose communications:

> for different audiences and purposes [so as to] enable students to understand the varying demands of different kinds of writing tasks and to recognize how to adapt tone, style, and content to the particular task at hand (standard 7).

This standard thus reminds us that the form of the written product assigned shapes the thought processing required to produce it.

Idea Processing and Communication Format

The relationship between format and thought can be demonstrated by examining two writing assignments that use a word processor: newsletters and posters. As they show, a writing format can be enhanced by using a word processor. The assignments employ features of word processors that extend beyond producing simple text, functions such as the incorporation of graphics and the formatting and styling of text. Using these functions requires students to carefully examine their content and its expression, thereby encouraging them to extend and refine their thinking. Examples of word-processing programs that include these capabilities are common in classrooms, such as AppleWorks (formerly ClarisWorks), Microsoft Works, and Microsoft Word. (Desktop publishing software can also be used for such activities, but we chose to focus on software that most teachers already have and know how to use.)

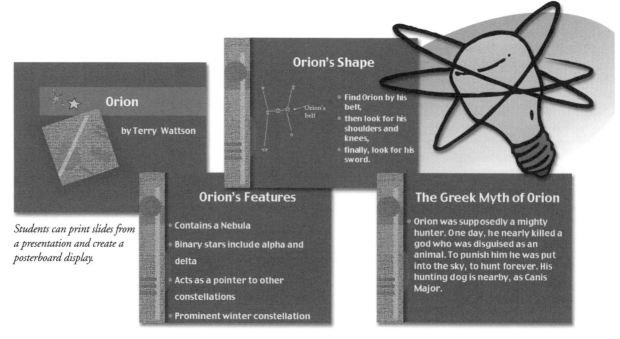

Students can print slides from a presentation and create a posterboard display.

Assignment One: Newsletter. Newsletters have several distinct features. They usually are short, are easy to browse for quick extraction of information, and incorporate graphic design elements. They also serve as a means of building and maintaining a community. Usually written with a specific audience in mind, they tend to reflect and perhaps even advocate a supposedly shared point of view while also presenting content in ways that allow people with varying levels of expertise or interest to find it useful. Teachers can analyze example newsletters with their students to help them understand the challenges of writing for a specified audience and to fit limited space.

First, to make a newsletter easy to browse, writers must "translate" their information into words familiar to their audience. They must select language that is precise and details that are essential to their purposes. Because newsletter articles are brief, writers must summarize information by identifying and selecting the main ideas. Possible topics for inclusion must be narrowed so that page requirements can be met. These needs also dictate that the authors must synthesize the "big picture" and rearrange information into new or more concise categories. For example, Ms. Barrett's fifth-grade class creates one newsletter for parents and another for peers. In the newsletter for parents they include items of interest for that particular audience such as upcoming test dates, brief summaries of the units of study under way, reports of the recent field trip, and progress reports on the fundraiser. To their peers they report movie reviews, recommended books, and the results of a recent opinion poll on everyone's favorite Pokémon™ character.

Newsletter designers must arrange text and graphic elements so that the most important ideas stand out and their relationships to one another are clear. Graphic design elements such as type style, columns, photos, tables, graphs, and bullets help the designer establish a tone appropriate for the content and audience and make the newsletter visually appealing.

Finally, because newsletters are so often intended to maintain community, newsletter writers must analyze the information to be included to determine how it corresponds to the key values, needs, and interests of the audience and then craft the message accordingly.

It is easy to see that when a teacher presents his or her students with an assignment to create a newsletter and reviews with them its salient features, they have to think about their knowledge in new ways to communicate effectively. Thus, using a software program that facilitates newsletter creation can support students' decision making about how best to meet such communication needs. Word-processing software allows authors to try out their ideas and see actual renderings quickly. This not only facilitates the authors' revision process but also allows others to provide specific suggestions for improvement. It also emphasizes and provides practice in the inevitable editing required of final written products.

Assignment Two: Poster. Another style of communication that is easily achieved with robust word-processing software is the poster. A poster is essentially a printed version of the formatting used in programs such as an AppleWorks slideshow presentation, in which presenters usually place just a few words and perhaps a visual on one or a series of slides to accompany an oral presentation. A poster uses these same features but in the end is printed, rather than projected onto a screen. Several 8.5" × 11" pages can be grouped together for presentation, in a manner reminiscent of a booth

at a science fair. Teachers can decide if the poster presentations can stand alone or if they should be complemented by either the oral remarks of the author or a more formal and detailed written report.

In this assignment, the teacher helps

students recognize that the unique features of a poster include the use of short phrases instead of complete sentences and of concise and catchy language to capture a reader's attention and convey major ideas. Posters also usually use bullet points, visuals, and large print so that they can be easily read from a distance. Noting these features allows teachers to talk with their students about how best to craft their communication accordingly.

Because the poster dictates short phrases and bold language, its creators must identify key ideas and eliminate nonessential information. Short phrases also require the most vivid and direct language to convey their message.

A poster also includes graphic-design elements, such as text formatting, borders, and other geometric shapes. These require the designers to analyze the aims and tone of their messages closely and then find compatible design elements to serve as symbolic equivalents. As with the newsletter, the authors must coordinate the visual message with the needs of the presenter and the audience.

Students presented with an assignment to create a poster, reminded of its essential characteristics and allowed to put the features of a word processor to work for them as they craft an appropriate message, will have to carefully consider how best to communicate their knowledge within the given format. As with the newsletter assignment, the word processor can also facilitate the revision and editing process as students respond to teacher or peer feedback and shape the message to the audience.

Instructional Planning

The newsletter and the poster (1) illustrate how the manner in which students process ideas is shaped by the format of the assignment they are given and (2) speak to the importance of instructional planning in the effective use of technology. During instructional planning, teachers need to formulate the focus of inquiry, the mode of analysis, the purpose and audience, and the format appropriate for a given communication that students are asked to produce. This means determining the extent to which students must both analyze and communicate subject matter and effectively use available technology. In other words, using technology effectively in the classroom involves instructional planning that considers how technology might assist students in accessing data, processing information, and communicating their findings and insights.

Because software such as Apple-Works, Works, and Word significantly extends the variety of formats teachers can use to measure student learning—newspapers, posters, graphs, and concept maps, for example—it can also extend the amount and nature of thought demanded of students. As with any assignment, however, students will require sufficient models, teacher demonstration, and guided practice if they are to be successful. Day-to-day assignments in language arts, social studies, math, and science should provide prac-

tice in accessing data, processing information, and communicating learning in a variety of ways and for a variety of purposes. To these ends, a cross-disciplinary approach cannot be over-emphasized.

There are two cautions to keep in mind when planning to use a word processor as an idea processor. First, students need certain software operation skills to be adequately proficient with the design elements required in these assignments. Second, there is a tendency of some students to get wrapped up in the beauty and originality of their product at the expense of its content, which can distract from the desired intellectual tasks of the assignments. Yet teaching the students how to master specific software features can be a worthwhile investment if they are used for multiple assignments, as suggested previously, and if the relationship between the format of a communication and the thinking required to produce it is adequately recognized.

Thoughtful instructional planning will also help keep the focus on the purpose and content of a communication rather than on the "gee whiz" features of the software. Stressing the analytical features of an exemplary model with students and the conceptual criteria by which their work will be graded—perhaps a rubric that students would use to assess their own work and that of their peers—will clearly declare what will be valued in their end products (see the "Self-Assessment Checklist" included with this article.) Finally, having an authentic assignment—real work being produced for a real audience—will also help students focus on what they have to say as well as on how they present it. For example, if students receive assignment guidelines that emphasize factual accuracy and know that their neighbors and other community members will be reading their work, they should know to focus their

attention on the content and its clear expression.

Conclusion

The newsletter and poster examples we elaborate on here are only two examples of using a word processor as an idea processor. As teachers begin to design instruction that integrates technology in ways that support all the dimensions of students' work with ideas, the technological resources at hand will more greatly enhance student thinking and achievement. It is then that we will have realized the true worth of classroom technology.

Resources

For product overview and academic pricing for AppleWorks (formerly ClarisWorks), visit www.apple.com/appleworks.

For product information for Microsoft Works, see www.works.msn.com. For information on Microsoft Word, visit www.microsoft.com/office/word.

Reference

National Council of Teachers of English. (1996). *Standards for the English language arts.* Urbana, IL: Author.

Editor's Commentary

A wonderful resource for analysis of the critical-thinking, idea-processing aspect of word processing is *Working with a Word Processor* by William Zinsser (1986, Harper and Row). In addition, the authors' comments about the applications of critical thinking to newsletters and posters also apply to newspapers created in word-processing software that reflect, report on, and retell language arts stories, novels, and poems. Furthermore, language arts educators and other integrated-language-arts teachers and literacy specialists may also want to consider how word -processing technology reflects and resonates the principles of learning that are the philosophic underpinning of the New Standards put out by the University of Pittsburgh in 1997 (**www.ncee.org/OurPrograms/nsPage.html**). These performance standards include such word-processing-enabled activities as models of student work, celebration with family and community, learning as apprenticeship, performances for authentic audiences, products that meet quality standards, extended projects, active use of knowledge, interpretation of texts, and testing understanding of knowledge by applying and discussing comments.

—Rose Reissman

Self-Assessment Checklist

Name _____

Check off if present	Characteristic of written piece	Provide a specific example of this characteristic from the assignment
	Appropriate for audience, including language use, tone, topic choice	
	Level of detail is appropriate for format and audience	
	Graphic design enhances communication, does not distract the reader	
	Feedback on draft gathered and responded to	

Predicting the Future

Students Create Content for New Millennium Newspapers

Partner students with adults in the community to create multigenerational predictions about the next century.

By Rose Reissman

Subject: Multidisciplinary

Grade Level: 5–10 (Ages 10–16)

Technology: AppleWorks, Power-Point, Storybook Weaver, graphics programs, desktop-publishing programs

Standards: *NETS* 3, 4, & 5. (See http://cnets.iste.org for more information on the NETS Project.) *NCTE/ IRA* 1, 2, 3, 4, 5, 6, 7, 8, 11, & 12. (See www.ncte.org for more information on language arts standards.)

Online Supplement: www.iste.org/L&L

W hy not use newspapers coupled with technology as a vehicle for focusing literacy skills and expecting high standards for authentic student-centered projects?

We can use this type of project to bring in the perspectives of other generations, as students compare their ideas about the millennium with those of their parents or caregivers, older siblings, aunts, uncles, and other adults. Such projects can truly bridge generation gaps and highlight generational differences. During a class discussion, one student put me and my generation of 1960s teens in a glaring middle-aged perspective: "Didn't you used to listen to those vinyl records on stereo? They had some at the flea market last week. How long ago was that?"

To bring the generations a bit closer together, my students and I are devel-

oping Millennium in Newspaper Educator (MINE) projects as part of our "regular" technology-enriched language arts curriculum.

MINE Projects

Multigenerational Essays. Students and their adult partners (who can be parents, caregivers, aunts, uncles, senior citizens, older siblings, or other adults) answer the question "What does the millennium mean to you?" Then they create ready-to-send newspaper writings. The idea grew out of the suggestion made in class that students come up with their own collective and individual visual, verbal, and emotional responses to the millennium. Once the students had generated a diverse range of responses in small groups and as a class, they were asked to share their collective list with parents or caregivers, family members, seniors, and other

INTO THE MILLENNIUM

November 1998   Published By The Davis Family   Volume 1, Issue 1

Point Counterpoint

The tale of two sisters and their thoughts about the next century.

The Best Is Yet To Come
Joan Davis

With advances in technology, including greater access to computers and the Internet in schools, homes and other places in communities, the future continues to look bright. More opportunities are opening up in various fields, more time and energy are being invested in solving problems of food scarcity and diseases.

The Glory Days Have Come and Gone
Sela Davis

Gone are the days when people could walk out of their homes, not lock their door and still be assured that their belongings and home would be safe. A time when community was a reality and not a fantasy. Is there any hope for a return to glory and a better time in the new millennium? If every person looks to him and herself as a part of the solution, there is. However, if people continue not to take responsibility and not to care about problems and issues facing individuals and society unless they are directly affected. The glory days have come and gone.

"Is there any hope for a return to glory and a better time in the new millennium?"

Inside this Issue

Interview with
Grandma Davis 2

The Davis Family's
Hopes For the Future 2

In Our Next Issue!
Find Out What's Being Done
To Fight Off Potential Problems
Caused By The Year 2000 Bug

Figure 1. Student newspaper showing the different perspectives of members of one family on the millennium.

```
To: egq2345@useit.net
From: altoons@newstimes.com
Received on useit.net system UXV3 at 21:48:16 Monday,
November 16, 2015

Dear Mr. Quigley:

I just received your e-mail and sketch and thoroughly
enjoyed your concept. You are right about our differing
styles, but I thought the dialogue between the two
Congresspeople was had just the right bit of wit
regarding Act 3201.  You can look forward to seeing a
credit in the paper for your suggestion.

Congratulations, reader of the week! Thanks for your
time and for taking an interest in my work.

Hoping you,ll keep reading the News Times,
Al Toons

>To: altoons@newstimes.com
>From: egq2345@useit.net
>Received on newstimes server 1 at 21:37:07 Monday,
November 16, 2015
>
>Dear Al Toons:
>Please find attached in this e-mail my suggestion
>for a continuation of your cartoon series begun today
>regardingthe new tax laws passed by Congress. You can
>e-mail me at the above e-mail address with your
>comments. Should you not choose to use my artwork—
>I know your style and mine are a bit different—feel
>free to use my concept.
>
>Sincerely,
>Elmer G. Quigley
```

Figure 2. Sample e-mail correspondence between a cartoonist and a reader in the year 2015.

adults. When they reported back with the adults' responses, one student suggested doing a coauthored, multigenerational editorial similar to a multigenerational reader response diary they did earlier. AppleWorks or any other word processor or desktop-publishing program can provide a professional look for these family perspectives (Figure 1).

The multigenerational editorial essays are being published as part of a weekend shared family literacy program and will be read at a special parents' organization program. Because some students didn't have family members who could serve as partners, many school staff members (including teachers, secretaries, security officers, paraprofessional support workers, and cafeteria professionals) volunteered. This project thus strengthened school community spirit. Furthermore, adult millennium perspectives introduced students to some of the cultural, religious, and social aspects of the millennium, which varied according to the ages and ethnic, social, demographic, and economic backgrounds of the adults. Students shared their desktop-published newspapers online in class to get immediate feedback.

At the end of each essay, we included two special pieces: a section detailing the issues, questions, concerns, and topics for further research generated by each of the pieces for its authors, and a feedback form for readers to either respond, comment, or add their own concerns. The projects were posted on the Web, so responses come from people outside of the school community.

Long Island: Our Future—A "Paperless" Newspaper. As many of the students had already created multimedia projects and used multimedia resources, they envisioned a transition to multimedia news presentations instead of paper newspapers.

For this project, some students re-created front-page stories as Power-Point presentations. Other students used Storybook Weaver to render their multigenerational millennium essays. They even had the participating adults tape their own voices.

Inspired by previews for upcoming movies, shows, art exhibits, and so on, a few students suggested including video clips with the text of arts reviews. The students recorded themselves reading the reviews for their presentations.

We explored online copyright issues for both text and graphics or videos as part of this project. I showed students how to request permission from publishers and producers, and I showed them sample letters granting permission and the parameters given.

Rapid Reader Response. Students thought of many ways the increased importance of the Internet could enhance reader response in newspapers.

First, they envisioned added inter-activity in the syndicated cartoons and editorial cartoons in print currently. They imagined readers responding by e-mail and adding new panels to the cartoons (Figure 2).

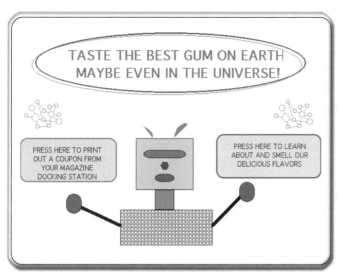

Figure 3. An interactive multimedia ad for chewing gum.

Second, students were certain that they would e-mail the editor, columnist, or reporter responsible for a piece. What they felt would be really neat was getting personalized e-mail back within a few hours! Only a limited number of students expressed any reservations about this possibility eventually working out this way.

Third, students saw how easily print advertisements could already be animated and presented as multimedia presentations complete with voice, music, and multilingual translation capacities (Figure 3). They thought that readers would also be able to immediately access the advertisers' Web sites to purchase goods and services.

Time Capsule Predictions. Many of our students had participated in time-capsule compilations for other projects. (Some students had even had the pleasure of actually unearthing a Presidential Predictions time capsule from the 1992 election to compare their predictions with the 1996 election results.) Based on these experiences, they decided to publish Millen-

nium 2010 special sections. They chose education, fashion, teens, environment, health, sports, and science as their themes. For each theme, students collected 1990s newspapers. They then asked experts in the selected areas what kinds of stories, trends, issues, and concerns might be relevant in the years 2010–2015. Finally, based on their research, they wrote parallel articles, features, and sections.

As in other millennium projects, student-expert letters, e-mail, and actual interviews are often a substantive part of projected millennium publications. What the students found most interesting as they worked collaboratively on their theme issues were the key questions and issues within each selected theme area and some of the surprising (to the parents!) predictions of how trends would play out. Some "surprises" pondered in the millennium theme issues were:

- The extent to which online technology, the Internet, and distance learning would really transform everyday teaching and learning. Was education really going to be that different in the new millennium?
- Would the rights, finances, and viewpoints of teens in 2010–2015 remain similar to those of teens today?
- Would we know by 2015 the outcome and consequences of global warming and environmental preservation?
- Would space exploration, voyages to Mars, and searching for alien life still be topics, concerns, and issues in 2015?
- Which sports would fade from prominence or be dramatically altered?

Resources

AppleWorks is available from Apple Computer and your local software reseller. Find more information at www.apple.com/appleworks.

PowerPoint is available from Microsoft (www.microsoft.com/office/powerpoint) or your local software reseller.

Storybook Weaver is available from The Learning Company directly (www.shoptlc.com) or visit www.learningco.com to find a retail outlet.

THEORY INTO PRACTICE

Constructivist Learning
Background and Theoretic Principles

Learners construct their own meaning. In the 1990s constructivism became popular among educators, although it is based on decades of psychological research, particularly in the field of schema theory (Abelson, 1975; Bransford, 1979; Schank & Abelson, 1977). Constructivism refers to the general principle that learners use their prior knowledge to construct a personally meaningful understanding of new content that is the focus of learning.

The instructional principles engendered by constructivism require that teachers actively engage students in designing their own unique understanding of new content, and that teachers legitimize and even celebrate the design differences from student to student. Brooks and Brooks (1993) describe the underlying principles of constructivism:

> Each of us makes sense of our world by synthesizing new experiences into what we have previously come to understand. Often, we encounter an object, an idea, a relationship, or a phenomenon that doesn't quite make sense to us. When confronted with such initially discrepant data or perceptions, we either interpret what we see to conform to our present set of rules for explaining and ordering our world, or we generate a new set of rules for what we perceive to be occurring. Either way, our perceptions and rules are constantly engaged in a grand dance that shapes our understandings (p. 4).

Principles were developed to guide classroom pedagogy (Brooks & Brooks, 1993). The principles specified the following actions that constructivist teachers should follow (Brandt, 2000):

- Encourage and accept student ideas and initiatives.
- Use raw data and primary sources along with manipulative, interactive, and physical materials.
- Encourage students to engage in dialogue, both with the teacher and with one another.
- Encourage student inquiry by asking thoughtful, open-minded questions and encouraging students to ask each other questions.

- Seek collaboration in students' initial responses.
- Allow wait time after posing questions.
- Provide time for students to construct relationships and create metaphors (pp. 81–82).

Children do not just receive content; in a very real sense, they re-create and reinvent every cognitive system they encounter, including language, literacy, and mathematics (Brooks & Brooks, 1993).

Children's learning always involves constructing ideas and systems. In a very real sense, people have always reinvented whatever they encounter by constantly making and revising mental models of the world. Inventing and constructing are exactly how we learn complex systems like mathematics, language, anthropology, or anything else. For example, when two-year-olds invent and use words like *feets* or *goed*, words that they have never heard from anyone, they are demonstrating constructivism.

Constructivist theory in education comes primarily from the work of John Dewey and Jean Piaget. Working from the idea that learners construct their own knowledge, both Dewey and Piaget contend that the stimulus for learning is some experience of cognitive conflict, or "puzzlement" (Savery & Duffy, 1995). Dewey argued that learning should prepare one for life, not simply for work. He proposed that learning be organized around the interests of the learner and that learning be an active effort by learners interested in resolving particular issues. Piaget proposed that cognitive change and learning take place when a learner's way of thinking—or scheme—leads to perturbation instead of producing what the learner expects. This perturbation (puzzlement) then leads to accommodation (cognitive change) and a sense of equilibrium (Torp & Sage, 1998).

Constructivist learning involves the following (Torp & Sage, 1998):

- Posing learning around learner tasks or problems relevant to students.
- Structuring learning around primary concepts.
- Supporting the learner working in a complex, authentic environment.
- Seeking and valuing students' points of view.
- Assessing student learning in the context of teaching and incorporating self-assessment.
- Supporting and challenging student thinking through cognitive coaching.
- Encouraging collaborative groups for testing student ideas against alternative views.
- Encourage the use of alternatives and primary sources for information.
- Adapting curriculum to address student questions and ideas (p. 31).

References

Abelson, R. (1975). Concepts for representing mundane reality in plans. D. Bobrow & A. Collins (Eds.), *Representation and understanding: Studies in cognitive science*. New York: Academic Press.

Brandt, R. S. (2000). (Ed.). *Education in a new era: ASCD Yearbook 2000*. Alexandria, VA: Association for Supervision of Curriculum Development.

Bransford, J. D. (1979). *Human cognition: Learning, understanding and remembering.* Belmont, CA: Wadsworth Publishing Co.

Brooks, J. G., & Brooks, M. G. (1993). *In search of understanding: The case for constructivist classrooms*. Alexandria, VA: Association for Supervision of Curriculum Development.

Savery, J. R., & Duffy, T. M. (1995). *Problem-based learning: An instructional model constructivist frameworks*. Educational Technology (35, 5:31-35).

Schank, R. C., & Abelson, R. (1977). *Scripts, plans, goals and understanding.* Hillsdale, NJ: Lawrence Erlbaum.

Torp, L., & Sage, S. (1998). *Problems as possibilities: Problem-based learning for K–12 education.* Alexandria, VA: Association for Supervision of Curriculum Development.

Bloom's Taxonomy

By Rose Reissman

In 1956 Benjamin Bloom produced his *Taxonomy of Educational Objectives in the Cognitive Domain,* in which he classified a hierarchy of thinking skills. The following list illustrates the levels in Bloom's thinking hierarchy. Note that the ability to evaluate information requires all of the lower-level skills.

- **Evaluation (Judging)**
  appraise, assess, choose, compare, estimate, evaluate, judge, measure, rate, revise, score, select, value

- **Synthesis (Creating)**
  arrange, assemble, collect, compose, construct, create, design, formulate, manage, organize, plan, propose, set up

- **Analysis (Examining)**
  analyze, appraise, calculate, categorize, compare, contrast, criticize, debate, diagram, differentiate, distinguish, examine, experiment, inspect

- **Application (Solving)**
  apply, demonstrate, dramatize, employ, illustrate, interpret, operate, schedule, shop, sketch, use

- **Comprehension (Understanding)**
  describe, discuss, explain, express, identify, locate, recognize, report, restate, review, tell, translate

- **Knowledge (Memorizing)**
  define, list, name, recall, record, relate, underline

As teachers infuse their curriculum planning, teaching, and learning with the levels of Bloom's Taxonomy, technology can support learners in working through all of the levels of this hierarchy and in concretizing, demonstrating, and disseminating their use of each skill at each level.

Evaluation (Judging). Independent learning and peer evaluation take place when technology is used to carry out projects that are accessible and have measurable outcomes. Tools used can include word processing, desktop publishing, multimedia portfolios, and Web site constructs. Students, teachers, and other audiences (visitors to a Web site, administrators, parents, community members) can use technology tools to design their own rubrics, feedback forms, multigenerational logs, surveys, online focus groups, electronic critiquing circles, criterion-referenced checklists, and other tools for evaluation.

Synthesis (Creating). The descriptors in this skill level match up almost precisely with the features of word-processing and desktop-publishing programs. In addition, multimedia offers video, audio, and sound effects that can immeasurably enhance an audience's appreciation of the material.

Analysis (Examining). The use of word processors and multimedia and graphic arts capacities facilitates data analysis. The results of computer-aided data analysis can easily be printed out or stored on a hard drive. Technology enables collaborative menus to be generated though the use of e-mail, preplanned conferences, listserves, threaded chats, and Web-based projects. These opportunities are limited only by the creative abilities and communication skills of the participants.

Application (Solving). Technology is inherently about the application of student-centered inquiry to teacher-presented problems. Students can address these constructs by applying skills in the following ways: creating their own books and publications, dramatizing their stories in multimedia presentations, employing HTML to create a Web site, illustrating a story with clip art or graphics created in a drawing or a desktop-publishing program, interpreting data using charts or spreadsheets, operating a Web site or a student business, scheduling their own study homework, using a database or chart from a template, shopping online for the best candy discounts for a school-wide community fundraising sale, or sketching a plan for a new auditorium using a CAD program. Technology is the stuff of which application skills are made.

Comprehension (Understanding). Again, each of the comprehension (understanding) descriptors can be realized not only through the use of word processing and desktop publishing but also through the use of telecommunications, e-mail, chat rooms, forums, universal translators, specific translating software, speech-to-text capacities, and multimedia video and audio input capacities. Furthermore, technology offers immediate access to English language learners and a broad sector of special needs learners who do not have full spoken language, visual, or hearing capacities.

Knowledge (Memorizing). Technology skills such as using databases, spreadsheets, font selection, multimedia sound-to-text applications, file merging, and desktop publishing are all directly correlated to the knowledge/memory descriptors. For students who inherently have problems going through the various levels of the taxonomy because they do not effectively store or retain their past work, the database, spreadsheet, and electronic gallery constitute an electronic portal to ascend up what was once the unattainable scaling of Bloom's taxonomy pyramid.

Of course, this realization of knowledge (memorizing) is inherent in maintaining a writing-sample portfolio, which is achieved through the "ordinary" magic of desktop-publishing and word-processing files.

Bloom's Taxonomy continues to offer a powerful unifying overview for reflecting on higher-level thinking skills. It is exciting to see how after being developed in 1956, it forecast (and still aligns so neatly with) the technology of today. The application of technology can support teachers in addressing and infusing the taxonomy into their everyday teaching and learning.

Reference

Bloom, B. (1956). *Taxonomy of educational objectives in the cognitive domain*. New York: Longmans and Green.

CHAPTER 4

Oh, the Places You'll Go

From the Classroom to the World

The Conversation Continues

Mark: When I was in school, I'd often look out the window and daydream when the lessons didn't interest me. I certainly wanted to learn, but I needed to investigate the world, too. Adventuring won out. The four walls of the classroom are too confining for many imaginative and restless young minds. The Internet is a way to satisfy both needs—acquiring literacy skills and exploring a fascinating world.

Rose: I, too, would often daydream when what the teacher was "delivering" and "telling" the class didn't captivate me. Unlike you, I would explore my internal world, imagining what it would be like to talk to a particular writer. I would create stories in my head or pose questions that didn't fit the teacher's set lesson plan.

In the 1950s and 1960s, we were all using basic language arts readers and grade-level social studies textbooks. If you successfully completed the text and its activities, you were "finished" for the year. Had Internet Web sites and the freedom to surf been around at that time, my teachers and I would have had a vast library of resources and an infinite number of dynamic virtual bookshelves to roam.

Mark: When you look into it, Rose, the Internet is making it possible for youngsters to have the security and support of the traditional classroom while having the virtual equivalent of a magic carpet that can whiz them off on field trips to extraordinary natural environments, the world's greatest libraries and museums, the studios of artists and writers living and gone, and the laboratories of famous scientists. The possibilities are endless. How cool is it for kids to collaborate on projects across distances of thousands of miles or just a few blocks? This is the way the world will soon work. Why not have our classrooms lead the way now?

Meet Harriet Tubman
The Story of a Web Site

"I looked at my hands to see if I was the same person, now I was free.
There was such a glory over everything. . . . I felt like I was in Heaven."

—Harriet Tubman on escaping (as cited in McGovern, 1993).

By Patty Taverna
and Terry Hongell

Subject: Language arts, social studies, technology

Grade Level: 2–5 (Ages 7–10)

Technology: Internet/Web, Kid Pix Studio (Mattel), word-processing software (e.g., Microsoft Word), Web authoring and management software (e.g., Microsoft FrontPage)

Standards: *NETS•S* 1, 3, 4, & 5. (Learn more about NETS at www.iste.org—select Standards Projects.) *NCTE/IRA* 1–9, 11, & 12. (Read the language arts standards at www.ncte.org.) *NCSS* 1, 2, 4, 5, & 10. (See the social studies standards at www.ncss.org.) *New Standards: Language Arts* 1–5. (Find out more at www.ncee.org/OurPrograms/nsPage.html.)

Online Supplement: www.iste.org/L&L

With that simple statement, Harriet Tubman reached out and enveloped our second graders in a way they will always remember. Her remarkable life became the subject of a Web site (**www2.lhric.org/pocantico/tubman/tubman.html**) that integrated social studies, language arts, and technology (see Figure 1).

First Steps
In January 1998, our second-grade class at Pocantico Hills School in Sleepy Hollow, New York, began studying historical biographies, with the study continuing through Black History Month in February and Women's History Month in March. An in-depth examination of Harriet Tubman grew from these roots.

The children began by thinking about the kind of person Harriet Tubman was. They discussed and listed character traits and supporting facts. From these charts, students prepared character sketches of Harriet Tubman, enriched by two field trips.

Field Trips
Field trips gave students more in-depth understanding of Harriet Tubman and the issues she faced. First, we visited the planetarium at the Hudson River Museum in nearby Yonkers, New York, to see "Follow the Drinking Gourd." The

Harriet Tubman.

planetarium staff taught our students that the Big Dipper was called the "Drinking Gourd" by slaves escaping the South to freedom in the north. The slaves used this song to pass on information about how to reach the North. For example, the song helped slaves find the North Star so they could keep their bearings. The show taught us how slaves used astronomy and geography on their journey to freedom. We also went to a Theatreworks presentation of "Freedom Train" at Marymount College in Sleepy Hollow. This show

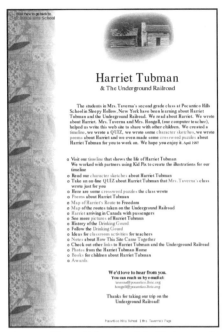

Figure 1. Harriet Tubman and the Underground Railroad Web page.

brought Harriet to life for the children as they watched the actors portray Harriet's childhood with her family, hardships as a slave, and daring escape to freedom.

Web Content

Based on our research, we discussed important dates and events in Harriet's life and, as a group, chose the 10 most important. We took our choices to the computer lab and created a time line. Working in pairs, the students used Kid Pix to illustrate one event per pair. They worked on their illustrations for two 40-minute class periods. Then,

Mrs. Hongell, the computer teacher, created individual Web pages for each pair's event (Figure 2).

We also challenged students to write a multiple-choice quiz about Harriet (Figure 3). We believed this would be a meaningful way to share their knowledge with others and to inspire other children to learn about Harriet. We worked as a group brainstorming, discussing, and researching questions that had one correct answer, as well as two incorrect ones that were related to Harriet's life. The children remembered visiting an Abraham Lincoln site (**www.siec.k12.in.us/~west/proj/lincoln/**) that used this quiz format. They were really challenged by the quiz and anxious to try one of their own. After we put the final polish on the questions, Mrs. Hongell created the quiz using the students' saved files.

We decided that our Web site also needed an authentic constructivist component and that making crossword puzzles would be a great activity. Working in pairs, the children wrote clues in the classroom and then took them to the computer lab to key in and create puzzles on the Puzzlemaker Web site (**www. puzzlemaker.com**). We checked their work for spelling errors and then helped students save their puzzles.

Finally, we were ready to put all the pieces together. We felt the background would really set the tone and therefore was a crucial piece. We chose a quilt be-

cause the station masters used quilts to let the slaves know that the station was safe. We chose bare feet (from Word's clip art collection) as navigational tools because many slaves escaped on bare feet.

Mrs. Hongell created the teacher links and class activity page to make the site useful for other teachers.

With NASA's permission, we used two pages that explained the importance of the Drinking Gourd. To get permission, we e-mailed the authors (the addresses were listed on the pages). We felt the information was too valuable to lose should NASA decide to get rid of the pages in the future.

Navigating the Underground Railroad

With all the pieces assembled, links checked, and files sent to our server, we staged a mock journey on our own Underground Railroad. On the morning of April 8, 1998, the children read a note on the classroom chalkboard saying, "Class Trip Today." "Harriet Tubman" (Mrs. Hongell dressed in dark cape with a hood) arrived at 11:30 and led the children from their classroom to the computer room. The journey was a short one, but along the way, the group looked for signs that we were safe. The children used quilts that we had placed at five different locations as signs that it was safe to go on. As we neared the computer room, an unsus-

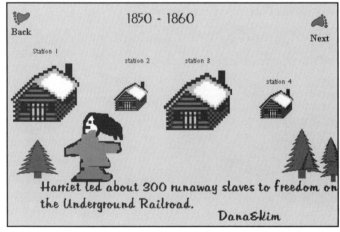

Figure 2. Time line entries.

Who is the most important person that we read about so far in American history?			
Criteria	Harriet Tubman	Thomas Alva Edison	Martin Luther King, Jr.
1 The person is well known	* 1	** 2	*** 3
2 The person helped people who were in need.	*** 6	* 2	** 4
2 The person overcame personal obstacles to do what he or she did.	*** 6	** 4	** 4
1 The person's accomplishments have affected you.	*** 3	** 2	*** 3
Totals	16	10	14
Note: The numbers in each criterion represent the importance the students gave to each criterion. The asterisks represent the extent to which each person possessed each criterion. We weighted the criteria by assigning each an importance score. 0 = the alternative does not possess it at all; 1 = possesses it a little; 3 = possesses it totally; 2 = somewhere between 1 and 3. Quality points are the numbers in the columns under each name, and the totals are at the bottom. The final step in the decision-making process is to ask whether you are comfortable with the decision.			

Figure 4. The matrix students used when choosing the most important person they had studied in American history.

pecting eighth grader became our final guide to freedom. The quilt hanging over the computer room door let the children know they had made it to a safe station. One of the children exclaimed, "We are in Canada!" as we entered the computer room. The children logged on to the computers, went straight to the Internet, and were truly ecstatic as they followed the link from our home page to their site! The children made a few suggestions about changes in wording and checked all the links to make sure they worked properly. During the next few weeks we met several times and made a few minor modifications. One important addition was a journal of sorts designed to help other teachers understand how we created this site.

Making Connections

The biography of Harriet Tubman was only one of several we read during the

year. As the Tubman project drew to a close, we decided to choose the most important person we had read about in American history. We used the following criteria to begin our discussion.

Ideas to think about:

- The person is well known.
- The person helped people who were in need.
- The person overcame personal obstacles to do what he or she did.
- The person's accomplishments have affected you.

We limited our choices to Harriet Tubman, Thomas Edison, and Martin Luther King, Jr., because the students had read biographies of all three.

We used the decision-making process from Dimensions of Learning (Marzano, 1992). This instructional framework teaches that learning has five dimensions: (1) positive attitudes and perceptions, (2) acquiring and inte-

grating knowledge, (3) extending and refining knowledge, (4) using knowledge meaningfully, and (5) productive habits of mind. Because we were working with second graders, we used a simplified method. We asked the children to think in terms of first, second, and third, with three being the most important. We discussed and weighted criteria. After serious discussion and debate, the class chose Harriet Tubman based on the matrix in Figure 4.

As a homework assignment, the children were asked to think about the group's choice and either agree or disagree. Their task was to write at least one supporting statement for their opinion. One student stated, "I think Harriet Tubman was most important because she helped lead slaves to freedom. She saved a lot of slaves. She risked her life for them. That is why Harriet Tubman was important to us." However, we really knew we were suc-

Figure 3. A student-written quiz question.

cessful in stretching the children to think about this period in our country's history when one student offered the following statement during the discussion: "Harriet Tubman was not the most important person in American history because Lincoln would have freed the slaves anyway."

Conclusion

This year we have responded to requests for information by again adding to the site. Two students from the original group, now fifth graders, created a map of Harriet's actual route to freedom (Figure 5). We created a list of books appropriate for young children on the topics of the Underground Railroad and Harriet Tubman. We had a reunion party with the children on March 10, 1999, the anniversary of Harriet Tubman's death. We celebrated our work and our 100,000th visitor to the site. The same magic and closeness we had felt the year before was still there as we discussed the hundreds of e-mails we had responded to and the many awards and accolades we had received.

This learning experience was valuable for the children and for us as well. The children learned a lot in their attempt to make Harriet Tubman a real person for others to study. They learned many technical skills, and several used the Puzzlemaker site for another project. It was gratifying to see two of the children create an original crossword puzzle on their own during recess and computer class the next school year.

Inspired by the enthusiasm and commitment of the students, we have continued our collaboration with the creation of four additional sites—Vietnam: A Children's Guide (**www2.lhric.org/pocantico/vietnam/vietnam.htm**), Charlotte's Web (**www2.lhric.org/pocantico/charlotte/**), John Davison Rockefeller Sr. (**www2.lhric.org/pocantico/rockefeller/jdr.htm**), and Benjamin Franklin: A Man of Many Talents (**www2.lhric.org/pocantico/franklin/franklin.htm**). As teachers everywhere are struggling for meaningful ways to integrate technology into their curriculums, we believe we have found one mixture that really works: interesting and challenging content and authentic tasks with real-world application.

Resources

Kid Pix is available at your local software retailer or on the Web at www.mattel.com/store/main.asp.

Word is available from Microsoft at www.microsoft.com/office/word/, and Front Page is at www.microsoft.com/frontpage/. Both are also available at your favorite software reseller.

References

Marzano, R. J. (1992). *A different kind of classroom: Teaching with Dimensions of Learning.* Alexandria, VA: Association for Supervision and Curriculum Development.

McGovern, A. (1993). *Wanted dead or alive: The true story of Harriet Tubman.* New York: Scholastic.

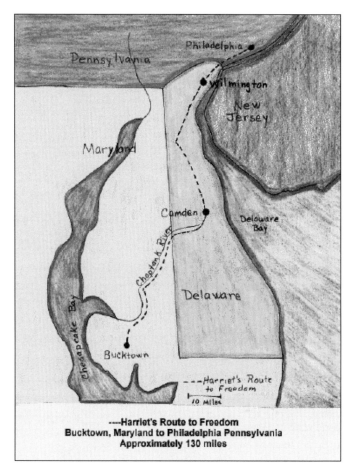

----Harriet's Route to Freedom
Bucktown, Maryland to Philadelphia Pennsylvania
Approximately 130 miles

Figure 5. Harriet Tubman's route to freedom.

THE TWELVE DAYS OF CHRISTMAS

A popular Christmas song can lead to exciting activities across the curriculum.

Have you ever wondered about the origin of "The Twelve Days of Christmas"? I remember thinking about it as a youth, wondering where and why they had such an observance. Then it occurred to me to consider how many gifts were received. Back then the math would have taken quite a bit of time. Today, students can use a spreadsheet to determine the number of gifts enumerated in the

By Ivan W. Baugh

Subject: Math, history, economics, science, language arts, multicultural studies, music

Grade Level: 4–12 (Ages 9–18)

Technology: Internet/Web, spreadsheet

Standards: *NETS* 3, 4, & 5. (Find out more about the NETS project at www.iste.org—select Standards Projects.) *NCTM* 1, 5, 6, 8, & 9. (View the updated math standards online at www.nctm.org.) *NCSS* 1, 5, & 9. (Read the social studies standards at www.ncss.org.) *NCTE/IRA* 1, 3, 7, 8, & 11. (Find the NCTE/IRA standards online at www.ncte.org.)

Online Supplement: www.iste.org/L&L

Christmas song. And they can search the Web for information about the background of the song.

History. Challenge your learners to discover the origin and use of the song. I used the MetaCrawler Internet search engine and found that, according to some sources (e.g., **www.byrum.org/ misc/christmas/origin.html**), the song originated in England during the rise of Protestantism. Beginning in the reign of Elizabeth I, members of the Catholic Church were forbidden to practice their religious faith. Encourage your students to figure out how long this ban lasted. Here are a few Web resources to help with these explorations.

http://www.geocities.com/ alexstevenson.geo/christmas/ 12days.htm

This Web site discusses the origins of the song and provides insights into the period of English history during which it was supposedly written.

http://graceland.gentle.org/xmascel/ 12days.html

www.kencollins.com/Question-17.HTM

These pages describe the hidden meanings of the song. Have some of your students visit the first page and others

visit the second. They can then compare the information they gather.

www.luminarium.org/renlit/eliza.htm

Visit this site to learn about other events during the reign of Queen Elizabeth I.

www.catholic-history.org.uk/

This site discusses the history of Catholics in England. It mostly contains bibliographic citations of primary source documents.

Science. Students could research the differences between doves and turtledoves. Information I found at **http://library.northernlight.com/ BM199812210101119436.html? cb=0&sc=0#doc** indicates they appear on the endangered species list in England. How do French hens differ from other hens? And what are "colly birds"? What do they look like and what sounds did they make? Finding this information provides a challenge to students. According to Rupp (1996), "The four calling birds ... were probably 'colly' birds, from the Old English colly, meaning to blacken, as with soot or coal dust. ... Colly birds were thus European blackbirds" (p. 7).

What are some other winter holidays celebrated throughout the world?

Hanukkah
(or Chanukah)

Kwanzaa

Ramadan

GRAPHIC COURTESY OF MELANET.COM.

Language Arts. Through the years, people have created parodies of the song. Challenge your students to create their personal versions of the song.

Music. An interesting extension of this historical insight involves looking at other uses of music to convey hidden meanings. Researchers will find that music played a significant role in African-American history. For example, African Americans used songs to help children learn to count ("Children Go Where I Send Thee") because they could not attend school. They also used song to send secret messages, for example, "There's a Meeting Here Tonight," which communicated information about a special meeting. Students could find different songs and describe their hidden meanings to the class.

Parents often think that current popular music contains hidden meanings. Have students examine the lyrics of their favorite songs to see if they contain any hidden messages.

Multicultural Studies. Which countries or groups of people also celebrate Christmas? How do their traditions differ from ours? To research Christmas traditions in other countries, visit **www.santaland.com/tradit.html**. Use the World Wide Web to locate schools around the globe that have

e-mail. (Go to **www.mightymedia. com/keypals, http://web66.coled. umn.edu/schools.html,** or **www. epals.com** to find keypals for your students.) Write letters to exchange holiday customs. Conduct a survey to determine the number of different countries where the song is sung. How does the version sung in other countries vary from the one you traditionally sing?

What other winter holidays are celebrated throughout the world? Start by visiting the Diversity Calendar at **www3.kumc.edu/diversity/ december.html** or Christmas.com's Winter holiday WorldView at **http:// christmas.com/worldview**.

Hanukkah (or Chanukah). Have your students research the origin of Hanukkah at **www.ort.org/ort/hanukkah/.** Read personal accounts of Hanukkah celebrations around the world at **www.caryn.com/holiday/holiday-Hworld.html**. What numbers have a significant role in the observance of this holiday?

Kwanzaa. Students can research the history of Kwanzaa on these two Web pages: **www.cnn.com/EVENTS/1996/ kwanzaa/history.html** and **www.**

melanet.com/kwanzaa/whatis.html. Have them compare the information on these pages. Which numbers have special significance in Kwanzaa? Find out more about celebrating Kwanzaa at **www.dc.peachnet.edu/~mhall/ mypage/holidays/winter/Kwanzaa/ kwanzaa.htm**.

Ramadan. Get the background information you need as a teacher at **www. submission.org/teachers.html**. Send your students to **www.holidays.net/ ramadan/**. They can read about the history and the celebration of the Fast of Ramadan. Do particular numbers have any special significance in Ramadan? Students can search the Web to find the starting and ending dates of Ramadan for the past few years. See what they can learn about the lunar calendar and have them search for patterns to predict the starting and ending dates this year.

Find other lesson plans for the winter holidays at **www.4teachers.org/ premier/holidays.shtml, library.hilton. kzn.school.za/Interest/events.htm,** and **http://members.aol.com/Donnpages/ Holidays.html**.

Conclusion
Through these experiences, learners gain new historical insights, develop an appreciation for the many different ways people can and do communicate, and construct personal knowledge as they extend their understandings. Happy holidays to all, and happy learning, too.

Reference
Rupp, R. (1996). 12 days and 184 birds. *Early American Homes, 27*(SPEISS), 4–9.

Students often have a natural interest in doing volunteer work in their communities. Getting them to work creatively to address these needs, however, can be something of a challenge. In this article, Rose Reissman shows how a focused Internet search can show students all the ways in which they can do service learning and volunteer work.

SURF AND SERVE

Student-Navigated and Student-Designed Internet Service Learning Projects

By Rose Reissman

Subject: Service learning

Grade Level: 7–12 (Ages 12–18)

Technology: e-mail, Internet/Web

Standards: *NETS* 5. (See http://cnets.iste.org for more information on the NETS project.)

Online Supplement: www.iste.org/L&L/.

Sometimes the best learning happens when adults move out of the way. When government officials, community leaders, school administrators, board members, educators, and parents work on community-service learning programs, the design of these projects focuses on adult educators and parents. The resulting model might provide exemplary service-learning experiences for students, but they are not necessarily the ones the students would have chosen by themselves. So, how can upper elementary and middle school students be involved from the outset in selecting and designing service-learning experiences and projects that reflect their input, talents, and concerns?

Ironically, the answer presented itself to me at midnight while I was surfing the Web. I typed "volunteer" into the Yahoo! search window. The resulting list included several sites as well as readings of categories the search engine could match with my query. Among them were issues and causes, philanthropy, community service, volunteerism, organizations, and students K–12.

As I began to follow through on the category headings by visiting sites, visions of potential student service-learning projects danced in my head. I was about to start an outline of potential site-inspired projects when it hit me. When all of the national, state, city, and the IRA/NTE standards for language arts called for authentic student learning inspired by their own interests, why was I delivering teacher-centered learning to them? If the students design community and family literature and writing investigations, then why couldn't they use the same search engine to identify sites to surf and communities to serve? Or at the very least, couldn't they generate their own school adaptations of these viable projects?

Through these sites, students also would have the unique opportunity to bounce their ideas off other distanced students and communities that were already conducting their own projects. The only obstacles I could see were time and access. My students could use only two library computers with Internet access, so we couldn't tie up the school's online resources for hours on end. My sixth and seventh graders also had other classes to attend.

Given these constraints, Elizabeth Gil (my colleague and assistant manager for NYC Futurekids Technology Training Programs) and I limited our students' initial surfing by sharing some starting sites. With a prepared list and initial Web searching already done, we could send our students on a site search for a pool of community service-learning project ideas and human resources. Elizabeth did the preliminary Web searching and prepared the descriptions we distributed to the students. (Some of these are shown in the accompanying chart, "Great Starting Web Sites.")

We distributed these potential Internet sources to the students and challenged them to dig into the details of the community service projects. We asked them to investigate, chat with, or query any of the sites suggested or use them as jumping-off points to visit other sites. They were to locate and record any projects in which they might want to participate for this assignment.

Finally, they were encouraged to design their own original project or a service learning project.

The students could work alone or as part of a team with no more than three members. Some of the students had Internet access at home, so they planned to spend time beyond what they had at the library, using the sites Elizabeth initially identified as starting sites.

After a week, the students generated the following 10 community service ideas based on what they found in their searching.

1. Compile a school-based print directory of local organizations that accept volunteers, detailing the kind of service opportunities available. Distribute the directory at community centers, grocery stores, libraries, and PTA meetings.

2. Develop a school-based adaptation of the Kids Care Holiday Project Friendship Boxes and Cool Hats for Kids. Contact the Ben Franklin Elementary School and the Lakewood Middle School for help.

3. Start a Kids Care Club in our school using the Club Link for Kids Care Clubs on the Kids Care Club site.

4. Contact corporate sponsors to support our community service center. Use the Kids Care Club site to identify potential sponsors for our programs.

5. Run a monthly recognition evening at our neighborhood community day care center in which at least one outstanding adult and student volunteer will be designated as "points of light."

6. Create a distinctive graphic certificate using available software. Photograph winners with the digital camera so their pictures can be placed in a school gallery space and displayed on the school or community center gallery page of the school Web site.

7. Create an evolving catalog of community service adult and student winners and present it online.

8. Check the City Cards of America organization to see if students can work with it. Prepare a bulletin board of the organization's activities to share with adults in community centers and service centers through listings on our Web site and through

GREAT STARTING WEB SITES

Web Site	URL	Description
KIDS CARE	www.kidscare.org	• a description of Kids Care • project suggestions • information on Kids Clubs • volunteer events
SERVEnet	www.servenet.org	• post and read about events around the country by state • information about different volunteer organizations with contact information • database with different types of service • extensive listings of volunteer projects
National Service-Learning Cooperative Clearinghouse	www.nicsl.coled.umn.edu	• links to programs around the country • forms for users to specify search criteria (e.g., state, type of activity, area of interest, participant age range) • visit K–12 links at www.nicsl.coled.umn.edu/links/k12.htm
Yahoo!	www.yahoo.com	• Society and Culture • Issues and Causes • Philanthropy • Community Service and Volunteerism • Organizations • Students K–12
Students for Students International	www.s4si.org	• student-run registered charity • uses the talents of young people for humanitarian purposes

print posters. Contact Outreach Director Gail Schecter of Girls, Inc., to have a speaker talk about community service learning activities and perhaps help our class set up a Girls, Inc., site.

9. Develop an event to share for the annual Make a Difference Day on October 25th (**www. usaweekend.com/diffday/ index.html**).

10. Create a school Web site page with information about the National Alliance of Breast Cancer Organizations (**www.nabco.org**).

The students developed projects and outlined additional service learning research possibilities based on these resources. Several of them went even further, using their own time to look up more URLs that included service learning opportunities. The original Internet list that Elizabeth and I had compiled served as a wonderful starting point, a virtual diving board that introduced students to the Internet as a community service learning idea resource. More important, the projects and additional inquiries designed by the students grew from their own authentic interests and thus were owned by them. Through their Web explorations, the students got immediate feedback and acquired more resources for their self-initiated project designs. They also learned to appreciate the national and international significance and effects of community service learning beyond its value as a school or local community learning project.

Often student-centered learning and authentic student-owned projects grow from the desires of well-meaning professional educators to engage their students immediately in worthwhile activities. However, the Internet-driven projects identified, developed, and maintained by students themselves are more meaningful and involving.

So, consider offering your Internet-literate students a compelling initiation to civic surfing and community service. Your students (and their communities) will be the richer for it as learners, caring citizens, and independent thinkers.

Reprinted with permission from Bantam Books, a division of Random House, Inc.

Teach a Novel without the Internet?

Never Again!

Authentic Internet research adds a new dimension to students' experiences of reading a novel.

By Elaine Insinnia, Eileen Skarecki, and Jarnail Tucker

Subject: Language Arts

Grade Level: 7–12 (Ages 12–18)

Technology: Internet/Web

Standards: *NETS•S* 2 & 5. (Read more about the NETS Project at www.iste.org—select Standards Projects.) NCTE/IRA 1, 7, 8, & 10. (See the language arts standards at www.mcte.org.)

Online Supplement: www.iste.org/L&L

Elaine: Have you read the memoir *Night* by Elie Wiesel? With this book, I embarked on an unforgettable journey with my eighth-grade English class. I decided for a change that I would not preread the book. I would experience it firsthand with my students. I joyously savored how fresh it would be to experience the author's memory of events simultaneously with the kids.

Once the reading began, the power of the author's words overtook us. His vivid descriptions haunted us—the ghettos in which Jews were isolated, the deportations, the cattle car journey to the death camps, Doctor Mengele and the "selection," the meager rations, and the many cruelties these innocent people endured.

The eighth graders had some knowledge of the Holocaust but lacked background information. (They would not be studying WWII until the next month—*linear learning!*) So they needed information quickly, while we were still reading the book.

Finding the Background

We had just read of the author's arrival at Auschwitz, the infamous concentration camp where four million Jews died. We had 20 minutes left in the class period, so we flew up to the computer lab and logged on to the Internet.

Using their favorite search engines and key words and phrases such as *Auschwitz*, *Wiesel*, *Holocaust*, and *concentration camps*, the students became immersed in their research. Immediately someone found a photograph of the entrance gate to Auschwitz, the German words incomprehensible, but the phrase "Work is Liberty" fresh in the kids' minds from the reading.

Within minutes the lab's screens revealed photographs of Jewish concentration camp victims; the furnaces; the piles of shoes, eyeglasses, and gold teeth; the camps as they look today; and much more.

The next day, as we read about the author's fight to keep the gold crown in his tooth, and how he finally lost it to a "dentist" who used a rusty spoon to remove it, the kids and I gasped—and we understood.

Several kids made a simultaneous find—Elie Wiesel speaking about his experience and book—with audio and video. Eileen suggested using the LCD projector so everyone could watch Wiesel together. There, on the large screen, was the author, talking about the horrors, his feelings, his outrage.

The following day while reading the book, none of us could erase the image of the author sorrowfully saying, "Hundreds of Jewish children suffered … even more than Jesus Christ." How could we all not remember the narrator losing his faith in God as he watched the lorries carry Jewish children to the edge of the flaming pit and then "the wreaths of smoke" that once were children.

On the Internet again, we had 15 minutes. A girl discovered a map showing the death camp locations. We followed the path of our author and his horrifying journey in the cattle car on the train.

Many found more pictures—kids so starved they appeared to be live skeletons, and Dr. Mengele, the Nazi who made the selections at Auschwitz and performed the horrifying experiments, especially on twins and children. There were interviews with survivors of the camps, pictures of and speeches by Hitler, and a profound photo of an

Six thousand souls waited in this courtyard for 24 hours. In the end, 140 of them were dead. USIMM Photo Archives, July 1941, Franz Amicale Collection.

After liberation, prisoners showed the furnace to liberators. Photo ©1980, 1996 by Alan Jacobs, from a Web page designed by Krysia Jacobs. Visit the Cybrary of the Holocaust at www.remember.org to learn more about the Holocaust and to see more of Alan Jacobs' photos.

American tank liberating the pitiful few left at Auschwitz, just as Elie Wiesel had described.

Extension Activities

As we continued our study of the Holocaust, we discovered other resources and activities.

One student found out that NBC would be airing *Schindler's List* (Spielberg, 1993) over the weekend. All of the students committed to watching it. On Monday morning, they couldn't wait to discuss the movie and how it compared to the book— one corroborating the other.

Then I was truly thrilled by Jarnail's idea: creating a Web page reflecting our experience reading the novel and searching the Web, a page people everywhere could see and react to. (See the online supplement at **www.iste.org/ L&L** for more information about how the Web page was created and a link to it.)

Reactions

One morning I heard Bette Midler singing "From a Distance" (Gold,

1993)— and the image of the "sad-eyed angel" (a 13-year-old gruesomely hanged by the Nazis in the camp) rose in my mind. Finally, remembering the images, the words, and the photographs found on the Internet by the kids, the full force of the book overwhelmed my heart and mind. I shared this with my students, telling them how I had not realized the tremendous effect the book and Internet search would have on me.

They confided in me that they were experiencing the same feelings and shared some further thoughts.

Jarnail: When we first started to read this book, the whole idea of the Holocaust did not really upset or disturb me. Maybe it is because of the fact that my background, too, involves a horror like this: the second Holocaust in India. You see, in my experience studying the pain and suffering that my people went through, I never thought the Holocaust in Europe could be as bad as this. But as the book went along, I could visualize the suffering. At some points it made my stomach

Elaine: I have argued for years that spelling and vocabulary tests are pointless—learning must have meaning to kids if they are going to remember the information. To prove this, I purposefully created an objective test (a pop quiz) related to the Holocaust and the memoir *Night*.

Kids who regularly experienced difficulty spelling and recalling vocabulary meanings were actually my target. There are always those students who will perform well on an objective test.

The results of the test were amazing. WWII dates, the names of the concentration camps spelled correctly, minute details from the book, definitions of words such as crematory, Kapo, Gestapo, ghetto—all perfectly recalled by the great majority of students. Why?

Jarnail: After spending years and years taking useless tests, I totally agree with Ms. Insinnia. Not only do they exclusively test how much we can stuff into our brains the night before, but also we usually forget all of the information in a matter of minutes. The method Elaine used was great because we had no idea that we were in fact studying by using the Internet. We would see words and phrases on the screen again and again, and they would just stick.

So you see, why inform us of tests and give us time to prepare, when we can just study and not even know it and actually remember the information? Of course, there will be those people who never do anything, but the point I'm making is that the Internet is making a difference in the way we learn.

Men's barracks. Photo ©1980, 1996 by Alan Jacobs, from a web page designed by Krysia Jacobs.

feel uneasy, yet I still felt the need to read on, for the whole topic was of interest to me. … Rather than sitting and taking tests, doing dittos, or using any of those old-fashioned teaching styles, Ms. Insinnia expanded our minds and turned up our ability a notch. Before, we were limited to mostly what we could get from books. Now we can get as much information as we want, quickly and easily, from the Internet.

• • •

Paul: I think there is a great value in using the Internet. While we were reading the book, the author used descriptive words to help us visualize the scene or the setting. When we used the Internet, we were able to get a firsthand experience of the real thing. I think this helped us really visualize and understand what was happening.

It's like pointing in the direction of several towns with your finger, but when you put it on paper or, in this case, the Internet, you can have a real understanding of what is happening.

• • •

Courtney: Reading and using the Internet at the same time helped me visualize what exactly was happening. It made the book that much more shocking and effective. It's also more interesting to see what the author didn't include. And we even got to see an interview with Elie Wiesel.

Right now, typing these words, I have to stop to release a breath. While reliving what has happened, the intensity of my feelings, my students' feelings, and our collective outrage has returned. The transformation is com-

plete—a teacher acting as a facilitator, colearner, and guide with her students, collectively experiencing, understanding, and discovering.

Can education get any better than this? After 30 years, I admit that at times I have gone through the motions, looked at early retirement, and been disappointed by the lack of vision in our educational institutions.

Since Eileen, my students, and I have been infusing the Internet into instruction, however, my own liberation and ultimately my students' have renewed my hopes that education will finally leap into the 21st century with everyone—kids and teachers—on the same side.

How the Internet Changes Student Learning
Eileen: Elaine's methodology while using the Internet—allowing students

to research the topic while reading the novel—takes full advantage of the power of the Internet as an instructional tool. I wish every educator could witness what happens in the computer lab during these surfing experiences.

I will paint the picture for you.

Students arrive and sit at a computer station. Elaine briefly explains their task: "Find as much information about the Holocaust and the novel as you can. Take notes either in your notebook or in Word, but do not print." A quiet falls over the room—25 students traversing the Internet, completely engrossed in the task. Elaine walks around encouraging and reacting to their discoveries. (This is very important, as it directly affects the students' behavior.)

After just a few minutes there is a stir of excitement. "Ms. Insinnia, I found the pictures of the camps!"

"Ms. Insinnia, I found the author talking about his book!"

The enthusiasm is contagious: there's almost a one-upmanship evident, kids trying to find better and better information. There is nothing inappropriate; no one is surfing for unrelated information. We have been using the Internet in instruction for five years with a high-speed link to many computers, and we have had very few of incidents of a student finding inappropriate information. They have found information that may not be valid or credible, but we address this issue as it comes up. Most importantly, we supervise the students at all times.

Students are excited about their work; they want to explore further. They are not limited to Elaine's knowledge of the subject or to the information in a textbook, ditto, or the school library. Multisensory opportunities abound; they can see pictures and videos and listen to audio recordings. Students develop increased awareness and sensitivity to the events leading up to the Holocaust and to the varying opinions and interpretations of these events. Elaine's students are actively engaged in learning and are developing a keener understanding of the relevance of the information (see the Assessment sidebar accompanying this article). Perhaps above all, they take responsibility for and ownership of their learning— no one feeds it to them; no one tells them what to read. They find information, decide if it is worthwhile, read it, and remember it. This is a powerful use of a powerful tool.

When Jarnail volunteered to create a Web site with the material and related links he and his fellow students found, he was speaking for eighth graders worldwide. A Web page is a communication tool this generation understands and relates to—it's their world; video, audio, and hyperlinks represent nonlinear learning. Jarnail did not offer to write a paper as a result of his enthusiasm, but rather to create a Web page, an exciting, motivational tool for him. Elaine's job, as educator, is to support Jarnail's enthusiasm, his willingness to do more, to express his new knowledge and creativity. Asking today's student to write a flat, linear term paper is as relevant as asking them to chisel their thoughts onto a cave wall.

Why Give Students Unrestricted Access to the Internet?

Many educators are not taking advantage of the Internet's capabilities. They want to limit the students' search to preapproved Web sites or print the information from the sites and hand it to the kids. Not allowing students to search for the information eliminates their sense of ownership and excitement. It also limits students to the opinions of a select few, much like they have been limited to the opinions of the editors of a textbook.

It is understandable that teachers venture to the Internet with trepidation. They're required to have a specific plan with specific outcomes—they're evaluated on this! But in today's world of rapid change, the teacher's role must be redefined. Teachers must guide their students through this vast amount of information. Is it valid? Is it appropriate?

School administrators must become aware of the power of the Internet and the endless possibilities for instruction. They must encourage teachers to take risks when using this new technology, not to be afraid of failure or the unknown. They must assure teachers that they will not be evaluated if an attempt at using the Internet does not reap the desired outcomes.

Elaine and I have come to realize unequivocally that there is no reason to be afraid. Carefully outlining student expectations, demanding student responsibility, providing adequate supervision, and specifying research topics provide a safe environment for successful surfing.

Recently I've been reading about a "backlash" group of educators who want to revert to old methodologies— "it was good enough for me." These educators don't see the whole picture. Sitting in rows listening to a lecture isn't "good enough" for these kids. Their world demands knowledge of how to handle all the information available to them, how to make sense of it, and how to discover it for themselves.

I also saw a newspaper article about a for-profit group offering an accredited high school diploma on the Internet. This must be our wake-up call, if we are to even stay in the business. Educators of the 'net generation, if they are to remain viable, must step down from the lectern and provide students access to all of the experts by infusing the Internet and all of its splendor into the educational process. Elaine and Jarnail must be our new role models.

References
Gold, J. (1992). From a distance [Recorded by Bette Midler]. On *Experience the divine Bette Midler: Greatest hits* [CD]. New York: Atlantic Records.
Spielberg, S. (Producer & Director). (1993). *Schindler's list* [Film]. Universal City, CA: Universal Studios.

Editor's Note

This project fosters student leadership and citizenship through its focus on Internet research. Beyond the articulated standards at the beginning of the article, it also illustrates the following key learning theories and practices.

- *Emotional Intelligence* (Goleman, l995): self-awareness, handling emotions, motivation/goal setting, empathy, and social relationships
- *Social Decision Making and Problem-Solving Skills* (Elias, l998; Elias & Tobias, 1996; Elias, Tobias, & Friedlander, 1999): taking on new developmental tasks and challenges, behaving ethically and acting responsibly to others, appreciating and respecting others values, developing long-term interpersonal relationships, becoming productive citizens by serving as positive members of their peer groups, and avoiding behaviors that have negative effects
- *New Standards™* (National Center for Education and the Economy, & University of Pittsburgh, 1997): having a tool kit of problem-solving skills and knowing how to ask questions, organizing group work, taking responsibility for one's work, recognizing accomplishments, and fair and credible evaluation
- *Civic Center Principles of Character Education* (Center for Civic Education, 1994): respecting diversity, equity, perseverance, courage, and so on

Interestingly, the Internet is often cast as the villain in terms of involving and engaging students in independent research. This project amply demonstrates that, under expert coaching, the Web has tremendous possibilities for nurturing character, citizenship, and informed proactive global problem solving.

Bravo to the authors. Let us hope that others will "lit out," à la Huckleberry Finn, for this uncharted but rich territory.

References

Center for Civic Education. (1994). *National standards for civics and government.* Calabasas, CA: Author.

Elias, M. J. (1998). *Promoting social and emotional learning: Guidelines for educators.* Alexandria, VA: Association for Supervision and Curriculum Development.

Elias, M. J., & Tobias, S. E. (1996). *Social problem solving: Interventions in the schools.* New York: Guilford Press.

Elias, M. J., Tobias, S. E., & Friedlander, B. S. (1999). *Emotionally intelligent parenting: How to raise a self-disciplined, responsible, socially skilled child.* New York: Harmony Books.

Goleman, D. (1995). *Emotional intelligence.* New York: Bantam Books.

National Center for Education and the Economy, & University of Pittsburgh. (1997). *New Standards™ performance standards.* Pittsburgh, PA: Authors.

WORLD TOUR

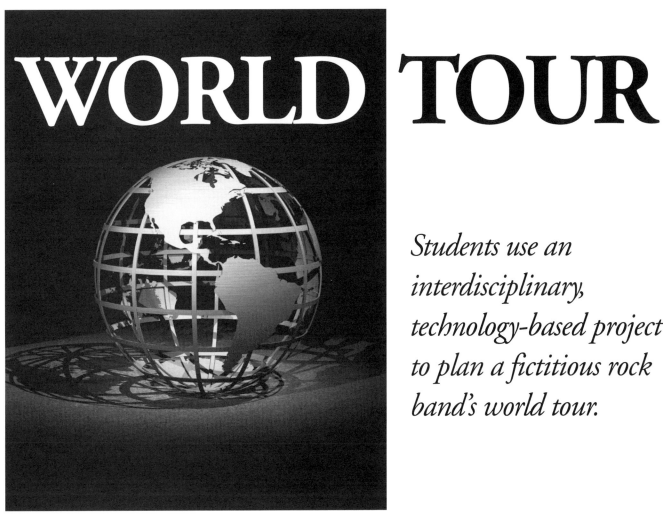

Students use an interdisciplinary, technology-based project to plan a fictitious rock band's world tour.

By Fanny Sosenske

Subject: Mathematics, science, language arts, foreign language, art, geography

Grade Level: 7–9 (Ages 12–14)

Technology: Internet/Web, integrated package (e.g., AppleWorks or Microsoft Works) or word-processing software, spreadsheets, databases, and graphics or desktop-publishing software (e.g., Photoshop [Adobe]); Color It! (MicroFrontier)

Standards: *NETS•S* 3–6. (Learn more about NETS at www.iste.org—select Standards Projects.) *NCTM* 1, 2, 3, 4, 5, 7, & 11. (Read the math standards at www.nctm.org.)

Online Supplement: www.iste.org/L&L

Your band has made it big in your town, and it is time you share your music with the world! This is the premise for World Tour, an interdisciplinary project that is the culmination of a seventh-grade spreadsheet unit. In this project, students plan a world tour for a fictitious rock band. The band seeks a manager to represent it, designs its flyers, and plans all stages of the tour, including calculating all the expenses. Students use spreadsheets, graphic design and word-processing software, and the World Wide Web.

Why World Tour?

Among educators, there is no question that meaningful problems and situations are the best ways to engage students in learning. World Tour has engaged our seventh graders in active-learning and critical-thinking activities in which making connections between different mathematics topics is as important as making connections between disciplines. Seven years ago, I started using a simplified version of World Tour in my math classes. The unit was so successful that each year I expanded it until I wrote the current version with Elizabeth Kratz, the technology teacher. At first, the project was a paper-and-pencil project, and its main objective was to practice arithmetic skills. The first major change in the project was integrating technology. I was already convinced that spreadsheets are powerful tools for teaching mathematics. Spreadsheets, when used to their full capability, have the potential to shift the focus of mathematics education from drill and practice to the development of concepts, relationships, structures, and problem-solving skills.

In addition to the power of spreadsheets in terms of teaching mathematics, I believe that students need experience with all areas that a productivity package provides: word processing, graphics, spreadsheets, databases, and communications. Our seventh graders are already proficient with word processing, so teaching them spreadsheets and graphics was a natural step at this point. In addition, from conversations with the eighth-grade science teacher and a few high school math teachers, the computer teacher and I realized that learning how to use spreadsheets in seventh grade could expand what students can do in future science and math classes.

The final change in World Tour was adding activities from other disciplines. Making connections within and among disciplines can enhance the learning experience. Authentic learning involves interaction between different disciplines and an integration of students' experiences with the environment. World Tour is based on this assumption about learning.

Student Tasks

World Tour is a two- to three-week project. Students work in small groups to take their fictitious rock bands on tour around the world with the objective of maximizing profits. The project is completed during language arts, science, math, foreign language, art, and geography classes. Some pieces are turned in individually, and some are turned in as a group. (See the complete outline at **www.iste.org/L&L.**)

Defining the Band. Students must choose a name for the band, define the background of its members, and design a logo. Students work on this part of the project during language arts and art classes, using a word-processing pro-

gram and a graphic-design program (our students use Photoshop).

After deciding on a name for their band, group members use the Internet to research the educational backgrounds of five musicians of their choice. That information will be used later to define the backgrounds of the members of their own band. Here, students practice research while they connect their fantasy bands with the real world.

The group then writes a letter to a fictitious agent asking him or her to represent the group. The letter has to include the experience and educational backgrounds of the band members, the type of music, and their plans for the world tour. Finally, the group designs a flyer to advertise its tour. The flyer has to include their band's logo, the name of the group, and the places they will be playing.

Planning the Tour Itinerary. This work takes place during geography, math, science, and foreign language classes. Students use spreadsheets, the Web, and a graphic-design program.

We tell each group that it must choose eight cities for the tour. To expand their geography skills, students should choose cities from at least three different continents, with no more than three cities on each continent. Students must research and write a report on two of the cities they will visit. The report has to include the population, country, type of government, weather, language spoken, a cultural fact, and one "extra neat" thing of their choice. Students use an atlas and Color It! to draw their travel paths. Students also are asked to find the distance they will cover in the tours. This information will be put into a spreadsheet that will be used later to calculate airfare.

In science class, students research the weather characteristics of the cities they will visit to decide what time of year their tours will take place.

Finally, students design a flyer to advertise one of the cities they are visiting.

It must be in the language the students are studying that year.

Calculating Airfare. This is done during math class using the Web and a spreadsheet. Students have two choices in terms of airfare; their decisions should be based on minimizing costs. The first choice is to fly on "A Wing and a Prayer" airlines, which charges 25¢ per person for each mile. This includes domestic and foreign flights. The second choice is to find real prices from an Internet-based travel agent. Currently, we are using Internet Travel Network (**www.itn.net**). Students put this information in the spreadsheets they started in the first part of the project.

Calculating Travel Expenses. Students work on this during math class using the Web and a spreadsheet. To calculate travel expenses (food and lodging), students use U.S. government guidelines from the Web (**www.state.gov/www/ perdiems/9704perdiems.html** and **www.policyworks.gov/org/main/mtt/ perdiem/perd97.htm**).

To calculate total expenses, we tell students that they have to stay two days in four of the cities and five days in the other four cities. We emphasize minimizing costs as the criteria for choosing how many days they are staying in which cities. Students put this information on the spreadsheet. The spreadsheet now contains all costs involved in the tour (airfare and travel expenses).

Calculating the Profit. This is done in mathematics class using a spreadsheet program with graphing capability.

To calculate the profit of each concert, students have two choices. They can choose a flat fee for up to four cities, in which case their band will earn $250,000 per concert. For the other cities, the band will receive 30% of the ticket sales. The problem then becomes finding out how many tickets are sold

STADIUM CAPACITY

	Small	Medium	Large
Population	800,000 to 2 million	2 to 4 million	4 to 12 million
Stadium capacity	50,000	69,000	84,000

Figure 1. Stadium capacity versus size of the city.

Figure 2. Percentage of tickets sold versus size of the city and roll of dice.

SUM OF THE DICE

Type of City	Small	Medium	Large
100%	2, 3, 4, 10, 11, 12	5, 10, 12	2, 3, 12
90%	5, 7	4, 8, 9	4, 9
75%	6, 9	3, 7	6, 8, 11
60%	8	6	7, 10
50%		2, 11	5

PROFIT FROM TICKETS

Rate	Size of City	Stadium Capacity	Dice Roll	% of Tickets	Tickets Sold	Ticket Price	Profit
G	S	50,000	4	100%	50,000	$25.00	$375,000.00
F	L					$25.00	$250,000.00
F	M					$25.00	$250,000.00
G	M	69,000	8	90%	62,100	$25.00	$465,750.00
G	L	84,000	4	90%	75,600	$25.00	$567,000.00
G	L	84,000	5	50%	42,000	$25.00	$315,000.00
G	S	50,000	2	100%	50,000	$25.00	$375,000.00
G	S	50,000	4	100%	50,000	$25.00	$375,000.00
Total							$2,972,750.00

Figure 3. Profit on ticket sales.

at each concert. Students briefly learn about probabilities, and then roll dice to determine the percentage of tickets they sell for each venue (Figures 1 and 2). For example, if the band is playing a medium-size city and the dice roll is 8, the stadium will be 90% full.

The profit for each concert can be calculated by finding 30% (the percentage of ticket sales the band receives) of 90% of the stadium capacity (the percentage of tickets sold) multiplied by the price of one ticket (in this case, $25)—0.3 x 0.9 x 69,000 x $25. Students key this information into a spreadsheet and enter a formula to calculate total profit (Figure 3).

Finally, students present their information to the class. Students find the net profit (profit minus expenses), write a short report with their findings, and create a graph that includes the total profit, the airfare cost, the living expenses, and the profit.

Suggestions for Success

The following are some suggestions based on my experience with the World Tour unit.

- Know the importance of keyboarding. Students work better when they can concentrate on their ideas rather than searching for keys to effectively use computer tools. Make sure that at least one person in each group has strong keyboarding skills.
- Have students work in teams. Teamwork encourages higher-level thinking as students share ideas, brainstorm, critique writing, and so on. Students and teachers need previous experience with cooperative learning.
- Allow enough time. "Rushing" students through such a project can lower the quality of their work and their enjoyment of the tasks. They need time to try different approaches, think, and write. A good rule of thumb is to allow twice as much time for the project as teachers think necessary.
- Use projects that are meaningful to the students. World Tour worked really well because of the role that music plays in middle school students' lives.
- Have a good balance of teacher-

directed activities and creative problem-solving activities for students. Though too much "telling" takes away from motivation, complete independence can result in few accomplishments.

• Create a rubric before projects start to let students know exactly how they are being evaluated.

• Start slowly. Do not feel that you have to implement all pieces of World Tour the first year. Given that some of the components of this project (like the mathematics piece) stand alone, you could start by implementing the spreadsheet work and add the rest over time.

• Have fun with your students. The success of this project was due in part to our willingness to laugh with our students and understand their points of view.

Resources

Color It! is available from MicroFrontier, 800.388.8109 or 515.225.9800; sales@microfrontier.com; www.microfrontier.com.

Many different integrated software packages exist. Two common Mac/PC packages are AppleWorks (www.apple.com/appleworks) and Microsoft Works (www.microsoft.com/works).

Photoshop is available from Adobe, 800.49.ADOBE or 206.675.7000; www.adobe.com.

Acknowledgment

Elizabeth Kratz and I created the World Tour project as described in this article. I worked with Elizabeth Bruder and Sarah Milligan to recast it as a WebQuest.

WEB RESOURCES

Rock Musicians' Biographies and Band Web Sites
• www.allmusic.com
• www.ubl.com
• http://rockhall.com/

City Information
• www.worldexecutive.com
• http://usacitylink.com/
• www.lycos.com/travel/

Maps
• www.lib.utexas.edu/Libs/PCL/Map_collection/map_sites/map_sites.html
• www.atlapedia.com/
• www.webcom.com/~bright/petermap.html
• www.indo.com/distance

Travel Sites
• www.itn.net
• www.travelocity.com

Per Diem
• www.state.gov/www/perdiems/9704perdiems.html
• www.policyworks.gov/org/main/met/homepage/mtt/perdiem/perd97.htm

Finding
EDSITEment
in the Humanities

Would you use the Internet in your classroom if you knew you could find reliable humanities resources online? If there were teacher-tested lesson plans that enhanced your curriculum and encouraged analytical thinking and good writing skills? If so, perhaps EDSITEment is for you. In this article, author Candace Katz describes how this Web site is drawing together the best of the Internet's humanities projects in one easy-to-use place.

© 1998, National Endowment for the Humanities.

By Candace Katz

Subject: Language arts, social studies, foreign language

Grade Level: K–12 (Ages 5–18)

Technology: World Wide Web

Online Supplement: www.iste.org/ L&L/. Click on this month's cover and then on the Supplements button.

S upported by the National Endowment for the Humanities (NEH), the Council of the Great City Schools, the National Trust for the Humanities, and MCI WorldCom, EDSITEment (**http://edsitement.neh.gov**) was created to help humanities teachers use the Internet more effectively in their teaching. The portal site now encompasses 49 unrelated individual Web sites with current, accurate, accessible, and rich information in such core humanities subjects as literature and the language arts, history and social studies, government, and foreign languages. EDSITEment's purpose is to guide teachers to the best of more than 66,000 so-called educational sites on the World Wide Web. And for teachers who are hesitant to wade into alien waters, the site includes learning guides to help orient teachers and students in how best to use the Web. These "Tools for Teaching" include information about evaluating sites for accuracy and citing Web sources correctly. Even more important, the guides provide sample lesson plans and activities for using Web sites to enrich classroom learning.

How the Sites Are Chosen

The process of choosing sites for the EDSITEment project mirrors the multitiered national peer-review process used by the NEH in determining and awarding grants. In this case, a call was sent out to humanities teachers at schools and colleges around the country—on Internet mailing lists and by e-mail—to nominate what they considered the best of the humanities Web sites currently available. In two rounds of competition, we received more than 500 submissions; this number was reduced to approximately 150 using the criteria of intellectual quality, design, and impact. Each criterion had its own set of questions.

Intellectual Quality. Does the site provide rich, deep, and multilayered humanities content? Does it provide the student with access to authentic, worthwhile materials with precise references? Is the information accurate, balanced, and updated frequently?

Design. Is the site user-friendly and attractive? Is it easy to find information from different parts of the site? Does the site allow for an active, constructive relationship with the material?

Impact. Can this site serve many different audiences or is it highly specialized? Does the site engage students and encourage them to develop an active interest in and a mastery of the subject area? Is this the best or one of the best sites that you know of in this subject area?

The URLs of the 150 or so selected sites were sent to two nine-member peer-review panels. These scholars and teachers of the humanities rated each site at home over a two-week period, narrowing the list of sites even further with the criteria listed previously. Finally, the sites were further vetted and ultimately endorsed by two blue-ribbon panels of educators, who also met in Washington, D.C. These panels included representatives of such groups as the National Association of Secondary School Principals, the National Parent Teacher Association, the National Council of Teachers of English, the National Council for the Social Studies, and the American Council of Teachers of Foreign Languages.

History, Language Arts, Literature, and EDSITEment

Many of the sites now included in EDSITEment can be used to enrich language arts and literature curricula, and these can be easily accessed by choosing this category within a file folder graphic. Among American literature sites are the American Verse project, an archive of American poetry prior to 1920; Documents of African American Women, a historical collection of letters and memoirs; Mark Twain and His Times, a broad range of materials on Twain; and Nathaniel Hawthorne, a richly documented portrait of the author of *The Scarlet Letter* (see Figures 1 and 2). In ancient, medieval, or foreign literature, sites are devoted to Dante, Chaucer, the ancient Greek world, Francophone literature by contemporary African women writers, Shakespeare, Russian literature, Romantic literature, and Victorian literature. One site, Labyrinth, contains texts, images, and commentaries for studying the Middle Ages; this excellent site is used in an EDSITEment lesson plan that looks at the mythical, literary, and historical views of King Arthur (see Figures 3 and 4).

Of course, other sites that are not primarily about literature can enrich a unit's development or provide additional individual or group assignments. For example, a literary assignment to examine a memoir in the Documents of African American Women site might be enhanced by research at In the Valley of the Shadow, a Civil War history site and another EDSITEment pick. (See the May 1998 issue of *Learning & Leading with Technology* for more information about Civil War resources.)

EDSITEment's own search engine can help here with simple word searches—using key words such as "emancipation"— across all of the sites in EDSITEment, as well as more complex searches for the computer-savvy teacher or student.

Getting Started with Lesson Plans

EDSITEment's lesson plans are meant to be used in a variety of ways and in a variety of classes. First and foremost, they are meant to be complete guides to an exercise that a teacher can follow step-by-step. They are available for downloading from EDSITEment or in print form. (Order online by clicking on "Talk to Us" or by calling 1.800.NEH.1121.) Each is designed to:

- enhance a student's natural curiosity and love of exploration
- encourage students to work in teams, sparking questions and ideas off one another and offering them an experience that is similar to what goes on in the typical modern workplace
- stimulate analytical and synthetic thinking
- create increased sharing of the responsibility for learning among students and teachers
- train students to develop and defend hypotheses with evidence and to comprehend and interpret texts and ideas
- enhance written expression as students seek to communicate with each other and publish their ideas on their own Web pages

Each lesson plan starts with a list of subject areas and grade levels for which it would be most suitable. It then lists the particular goals of the lesson as well as the general skills that the students should develop. These skill areas are pegged to state standards for that particular subject matter. Each lesson plan ends with a section called "Extending the Lesson" that suggests further assignments, often using other

Lesson Plans

EDSITEment sites. Of course, teachers can modify the lessons to their needs or use them simply as stimuli for creating their own activities.

Although each lesson plan is unique, they all share some distinguishing features. Each seeks to engage students in exploring authentic texts and resources on the Internet. Each asks students to compare and contrast materials, develop hypotheses, and reach conclusions. And each asks students to create something for sharing with the class or—if the technology is available—on the Web itself. In one lesson plan, for example, students create an anthology of poetry and visual images, with introductions and critical analysis.

Following Up

Since its launch in October 1997, EDSITEment has reached a large number of classrooms around the country. Through the "Talk to Us" feature, we have received many comments, queries, suggestions, and advice from teachers who have used the site. We hope for more of the same as we attempt to expand and refine the concept, adding new features and ideas and filling gaps in the lists of sites in the ever-changing world of the Internet. The EDSITEment partnership has been extended for two years, through 2000.

In addition, the NEH will feature EDSITEment in Schools for a New Millennium. This newest project supports single schools that are seeking to effect whole-school change by providing intensive professional development for teachers who wish to use digital materials effectively in their humanities teaching.

In the long run, we believe that educational technology can profoundly and positively affect the humanities if it genuinely adds value to teaching and learning. We hope that digital technologies will not speed up teaching and learning in history, literature, language, and social studies. On the contrary, we hope that they will be used to slow

Help students to see Hawthorne in the context of his times, as a contemporary of Henry David Thoreau, Ralph Waldo Emerson, Louisa May Alcott, Frederick Douglass, Elizabeth Cady Stanton, Herman Melville, Margaret Fuller, Walt Whitman, and Abraham Lincoln. To what extent was he engaged by the transforming political and technological forces at work in his society, and to what extent was he (like the narrator of The Scarlet Letter) estranged from his times by an overriding attachment to the American past?

Figure 1. This portion of the lesson plan Hawthorne: Author and Narrator helps students understand life in a different time. © 1998, National Endowment for the Humanities.

Extending the Lesson: To complete this study of Hawthorne's literary and literal lives, have small groups of students each read a Hawthorne short story from different periods in his later life. (Students can find appropriate stories on the Nathaniel Hawthorne website or in the library.) Ask each group to report on the narrative point of view represented in their story, citing passages from the text to support their views. Compare narrators from The Scarlet Letter and a short story. What is the point of view of each narrator? Why did Hawthorne choose these narrators?

Figure 2. Each lesson plan has extension activities. © 1998, National Endowment for the Humanities.

The border between fact and fiction becomes blurred in legend, stories which themselves have a history and in their evolving shape carry the imprint of all the hands that passed them. Through the Internet, students can track the growth of a legend like that of King Arthur, from its emergence in the so-called Dark Ages to its arrival on the silver screen.

Learning Objectives: To examine the historical origins of the Arthurian legend; to investigate how medieval historians and storytellers reflected the concerns of their own times in their treatment of the legend; to gain insight into the use of literature as historical evidence.

Skills: Chronological thinking, historical comprehension, historical analysis and interpretation, historical research, Internet research skills.

Grade Level: 9–12.

Figure 3. EDSITEment lesson plans are categorized by subject area and provide information about state standards and goals and grade level. © 1998, National Endowment for the Humanities.

Use the resources of the Labyrinth website to introduce students to the vast historical period embraced by the King Arthur legend, stretching from the 5th century, when he may have lived, to the 15th century when Sir Thomas Mallory gave the story its most influential form in Le Morte D'Arthur. Click "Arthurian Studies" at the Labyrinth homepage, then on "King Arthur Site" for access to a "Timeline of Arthurian Britain." Have students annotate this timeline by adding non-Arthurian events with which they may be already familiar (e.g., the reign of Charlemagne, the Norman Conquest, the signing of the Magna Carta, the Crusades) to place the evolving story in its historical context.

Have students read some of the key historical records of Arthur available at the "King Arthur Site" and the "Camelot Project," both accessible through the "Arthurian Studies" link at the Labyrinth. In a short extract from De Excidio Britanniae, by the 6th-century British monk Gildas, they will find a picture of the world Arthur is supposed to have inhabited. In a brief extract from Historia Brittonum, by the 9th-century British historian Nennius, they will meet an Arthur already passing into legend. Discuss the character and significance of Arthur as represented in these early accounts. What does he seem to stand for in these narratives? What can we infer about the societies in which these historians lived from the ways they present Arthur and his actions?

Figure 4. Each lesson plan links to authentic documents and informative Web sites. © 1998, National Endowment for the Humanities.

things down, to help students learn to pause, reflect, evaluate, and deepen their understanding. We hope to see digital tools used less for drill and more for exploration. From our combined experiences with humanities teachers over the years, we believe they are looking to technology to enrich their classroom experiences and to encourage students to think critically. We hope that EDSITEment goes some distance in helping teachers accomplish some of the hardest and most important work being done today.

POETIC SURFING
How I Used a Focused Internet Search to Keep Students on the Crest of a Wave

Few educators these days will publicly belittle technology or its usefulness. Most teachers know that media literacy is perhaps the most essential skill that children will have to develop if they are to survive in the workplace of the future. When the topic of productively using the Internet comes up, a common lament is heard: "I know there's tons of current information and great ideas out there, but what do I do with it all?"

When black history began to be celebrated in many areas of the Web last February, I wanted my students to be able to tap the information at various sites, many of which included student-generated work. I had to answer three basic questions as I thought about a classroom project. Do I bookmark all of the best sites and encourage my students to explore them in their allotted weekly computer time? Should I have the students sign up in pairs to examine the sites in the computer lab? Or should I attach a video display system (e.g., the Apple system) to the computer and show the monitor on a television screen so that we could discover

the sites together? The paired lab setting proved to offer the broadest access for the entire class in a one-hour session.

Accessing the information became the critical issue. How could I be certain that all reading and attention levels would benefit from the sites? How could I be certain that the sites would hold the students' interest? How could I ensure that their knowledge of African-American history would be enhanced after they spent time with a set of Web sites? Too often, students are not sure what they are supposed to do with a Web site. If the information is not presented like a video game, then their interest can wane more quickly than on a Friday before vacation.

As with all successful endeavors, planning made the difference between students clicking aimlessly in search of anything related to black history and an hour spent creating written proof of what they had learned.

With these questions in mind, I reviewed a half-dozen sites that had information on black history, assessing their reading levels and text densities. A site

with more than two or three consecutive paragraphs and no graphic images will not hold most fifth graders' attention. But time lines of the lives and activities of Rosa Parks, Ida Wells, and Dr. Martin Luther King provided concise information that everyone could interpret on some level; remarkably, these were produced by third graders across the country.

The sites were compiled into a Web resource file that students could open from their Web browsers; they simply had to click on the sites listed on this page. If creating an HTML resource file sounds intimidating, then simply bookmark the sites on the computers that students will use.

Students needed an open-ended way to record what they learned as they interacted with the information they found. For that reason, I had them create an acrostic poem on black history using just the notes they took while searching the Internet. They were to use an acrostic from the phrase *black history*, with *B* standing for *brave leaders*, *L* for *Langston Hughes*, and so on.

In a computer lab, pairs of students

By Tom Banaszewski

Subject Areas: Language arts, social studies

Grade Level: 4–6 (Ages 9–11)

Technology: Web browser, Internet connection

Children's curiosity can lead them to sites that are interesting but not related to the task at hand. In this article, the author describes how he was able to keep his students on task in learning about black history by having them use a poetic theme and a thoughtfully assembled collection of Web sites.

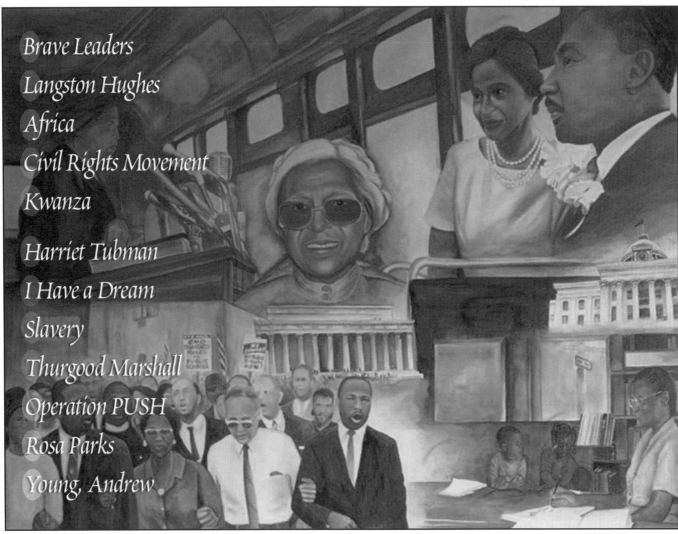

Brave Leaders
Langston Hughes
Africa
Civil Rights Movement
Kwanza
Harriet Tubman
I Have a Dream
Slavery
Thurgood Marshall
Operation PUSH
Rosa Parks
Young, Andrew

The Mentor. *Artist: Anthony Douglas. © 8th Avenue Art, 10326 Alta Loma Dr., Rancho Cucamonga, CA 91701; 800.799.7914; kevin@8thavenueart. com; www.8thavenuegraphics.com. Reprinted with permission.*

composed their poems as they surfed the sites and shared ideas. A focused task was produced by using the combination of buddy system, acrostic poem, and predetermined sites. Balancing the skills of the computer pairs allowed me to move among students and encourage them to be more elaborate in phrasing the language of their poems.

The computer was able to engage the students, and I was able to teach them poetry.

An Example of Collected Web Sites: *Welcome to Room 21's Resource Page of Civil War Web Sites!*	
SITE	URL (http://—)
Read Union Capt. James Grace of the 54th Mass. Unit	extlab1.entnem.ufl.edu/olustee/letters/index.html
A Letter Home	ngeorgia.com/history/cwletter.html
Women of the Civil War	scriptorium.lib.duke.edu/greenhow/
Alice Williamson's Diary	scriptorium.lib.duke.edu/williamson/
A Civil War Diary	uts.cc.utexas.edu/~churchh/civwdiar.html#diary

An Eye on the World

How GlobaLearn Helped My Class Overcome Limited Access and Technical Challenges

Sometimes just getting out on the Internet is tough. For many a teacher and many a classroom, there may be more challenge in just finding the equipment and scheduling the time than in finding the right project.

By Fran Castiello

Not having a computer with Internet access in my classroom is like having my car parked in the neighbor's garage. To get to the car, I usually have to get through or around some obstacles—the garage door might be locked, there might be an angry dog in the driveway, or I may get there too late to run any errands. But when I finally reach my car, I'm gone!

I feel the same way about having my class use the Internet. My fifth-grade classroom is on the second floor of our school. Our computer room is in the basement, and the Power Mac that connects to the Internet is in this room. That makes it a little difficult to integrate the Internet into my day, wouldn't you say? Besides the location, the phone line for the Power Mac is shared by the office and four other teachers who have online access in their rooms. Frustrating? Absolutely.

With technology moving at a snail's pace in our system, I decided to find a way to bring the Internet into my class-room in a different way. So what if we didn't have immediate access? We should still be able to do something on the Internet. So my search began for a way to use that Power Mac without interference and to find a project that would allow us to enjoy the wonders of Web sites, as well as work on corresponding pieces in our classroom—without actually being online.

I carefully studied the schedule for the computer room, made deals with other teachers for their Internet time, and resigned myself to the fact that I would have to do some homework to bring information to the class each day. I also encouraged any student who had Internet access at home to get ready to do some extra work.

Then I needed an Internet project that the students could easily connect with in a short amount of scheduled school time. The students would have to be able to easily pick up where they left off, and, of course, the project would have to offer something that I would be able to work on in class when we were not online. It also had to teach my students things that they did not already know and inspire them to think about things differently. And it had to be fun.

GlobaLearn:
An Ideal Connection Between
the Classroom and the World

I found all of the above criteria in GlobaLearn's Trans-Asia Expedition. GlobaLearn's business is sending explorers out into the world and inviting students to travel along with them by way of the Internet. I found this Web site—http://www.globalearn.org— while browsing through a newsletter and thought the students might like to do a little traveling. I love to travel, and I love geography. Knowing that students in general are weak in world studies and in locating various countries, I thought this might spark their interest. In this particular project, we followed five young explorers as they traveled through parts of Europe and Asia in 146 days. It was wonderful!

The expedition began in Italy and ended in Hong Kong. The online expedition had various ele-

ments that we could check out each day: journals to read, pictures to view, and a large resource section to help the students learn about the different countries. Every day, each GlobaLearn explorer was required to write a journal entry that described and explained the day's happenings. A "Noon Day Photo" also was taken, and all of this information was displayed on the Web site. Whenever we could, we collected the explorers' journal pages, read them at our leisure, and in this way kept up with the journey.

Our Own Class Explorations

Within the class, we formed our own exploration teams, with the five students in each group role-playing the five explorers. Twice a week, one team used our computer time to log on to GlobaLearn. These students read the journals, downloaded the "Noon Day Photo," and prepared an oral summary of the explorers' daily happenings. The summary lasted only five to ten minutes, which was short enough to fit into a busy day yet long enough to maintain everyone's interest in the expedition. As each student team member took on the role of a GlobaLearn explorer and related his or her daily experiences to our class, I could see the history, values, and traditions of this region of the world coming alive in our classroom—social studies at its best.

I found that GlobaLearn truly enhanced our fifth-grade curriculum better than any creative worksheet ever had and probably ever could. And as an enhancement, GlobaLearn took us beyond textbook print and brought us real, up-to-date information on geographic regions that are both similar to and different from our own.

Children Meeting Other Children

One day we switched our attention to the "Host Profiles." In each community that the explorers visited, a child—that is, a student in the local school—was chosen to be profiled. After spending a fair amount of time with him or her, one of the explorers prepared a biographical sketch that was presented in the student's first-person voice. These profiles gave us a glimpse into the students' schedules, families, communities, interests, and views of life. I decided that this was the closer look that my students needed in studying their counterparts around the world. After downloading a profile during our scheduled time, we took the information back to class, where we broke into our collaborative groups. The assignment entailed studying the profile and discussing the similarities and differences between students in class and this foreign child. From the beginning, the reading engaged my students. Just as babies are fascinated with other babies, my fifth graders were fascinated with the very first student.

His name was Arnur, and he lived in the city of Almaty in Kazakhstan. As I walked around the room listening to the students read, I was delighted by their enthusiasm about Arnur. During the reading, my students commented on the similarities and differences between their lives. Their minidiscussions turned into comparisons among themselves as well as between themselves and Arnur. It was wonderful to observe the students' interest, involvement, and seriousness about this exercise. Who says kids don't like to read? After sharing their thoughts, each group of classroom explorers charted its comparisons on large pieces of paper. All group charts were then displayed for a whole-class discussion, with each group eager to share what it had found.

Some of the differences my students found concerned school. Arnur's school had 1,000 students, and we have 500; Arnur went to school for five hours, while we go for six; there is no fourth grade at his school, so students just go from third to fifth. My students were also intrigued by the fact that Arnur was taught to be the same as all of the other children—starting when he was in kindergarten. This is in sharp contrast to how I look on my students as unique individuals who possess different personalities and intelligences. We discussed how boring it might be to try to be the same as someone else. The idea of having to be the "same" really bothered my students.

On the other hand, the list of similarities went on and on. My students found endless bits of life that were basically the same, from the style of Arnur's haircut to the time he did his homework. The most surprising bit of information came when we found out that Winnie-the-Pooh was the name of Arnur's kitten. Winnie-the-Pooh? How did he get to Kazakhstan?

What We All Learned

I realized that this activity had two important outcomes. First, my students were included: They saw themselves on the charts right next to Arnur, the boy from Kazakhstan. They were amazed at the differences but truly shocked by the similarities. They enjoyed studying themselves as well as Arnur. Second, a lot of learning took place during the activity: drawing conclusions, comparing and contrasting, inquiring, predicting, sequencing, collaborating, visualizing, analyzing, reading, speaking, and forming opinions—and all in one easy lesson!

During the 146 days we followed the expedition, information came into our classroom in many different ways. Those students who had Internet access at home brought in information that we did not have a chance to see during our scheduled time, and no one ever complained that it was "extra work." The students used the computers at the local libraries after school and worked on the school's Power Mac during their lunch. I even found myself up until midnight downloading information to bring to school the next day. We compiled all this information in a three-ring binder that students could read in their free time. This project not only brought a steady dialogue of "travel talk" into my classroom, but also gave my students interesting, unusual, and current information about places they never knew existed.

I am so glad I made the effort to find a way to begin Internet exploration—and that I used GlobaLearn as our first Internet project. I can only dream of how much easier it will be when I do have immediate access.

"He who hesitates is lost" is an appropriate expression. If I had hesitated this past year in finding a way to bring the Internet into my classroom, my students would have lost an opportunity to meet some wonderful, courageous, and intelligent explorers, as well as some of the coolest kids on the other side of the planet.

So, even though you may have to borrow the neighbor's car and get around some obstacles to do it, don't hesitate to take it for a spin. Just get the car out of the garage.

WHAT IS GLOBALEARN?

A nonprofit organization, GlobaLearn was incorporated in August 1993 to encourage interactive learning and communication between children in and among classrooms around the world. The company conducts live expeditions worldwide to teach students about geography, history, culture, and other subjects.

Students cannot actually accompany these expeditions because of the cost, but they *can* actively participate by using their classroom computers. GlobaLearn's information technologies and dynamic curriculum materials have allowed the company to build a highly interactive, multifaceted, and flexible learning environment that is ideal for classroom use and free to anyone who wants to follow along.

www.globalearn.org

Life Goes On

Using the Insights and Reflections of Sarah Delany to Help Teens Deal with Loss

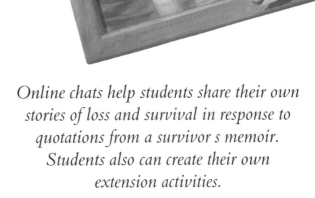

When *Having Our Say* and *The Delany Sisters' Book of Everyday Wisdom* came out in the mid-1990s, my multiethnic inner-city middle schoolers found much common ground and shared concerns in the reflections of these women. Indeed, they used the Delany sisters' quotations as jumping-off points for peer conversations, family discussions, journal writing, multigenerational online chats, and community service/outreach at senior citizen centers. They followed the Delany sisters' burgeoning celebrity over the next few years.

Online chats help students share their own stories of loss and survival in response to quotations from a survivor's memoir. Students also can create their own extension activities.

By Rose Reissman

> **Subject:** Language arts, community service, bereavement
>
> **Grade Level:** 6–8 (Ages 11–14)
>
> **Technology:** Internet/Web, e-mail, word processing, graphics, multimedia authoring
>
> **Standards:** *NETS•S* 3–4. (Find out more about the NETS Project at www.iste.org—select Standards Projects.) *NCTE/IRA* 1–4. (Read the language arts standards at www.ncte.org.)
>
> **Online Supplement:** www.iste.org/L&L

I was not surprised when, in late September 1995, four students from past years contacted me with the news that Bessie (the younger Delany sister) had passed away. "You know, Ms. Reissman," one of my students said, "I wonder what Sadie will do. Will she die too?" I, too, wondered what would happen to this woman who had lived most of her life with her younger sister. Therefore, I was most eager to read *On My Own at 107: Reflections of Life Without Bessie,* which came out in early 1997.

Starting the Project

As I read Sadie's memoir of her first year after Bessie's death, I found my-self jotting down quotations. Surprisingly, I realized that the majority of them were articulate statements and reflections about dealing with the loss of a loved one.

I decided to see how Sadie could connect with my Inwood Manhattan students. I deleted any references to "Sadie" or "Bessie" and any age indicators. I noted at the end of the list that I had taken the quotations from a new memoir book I had just read. My students and a group of students we chatted with online in a Harlem school were challenged to review the quotations and use them to create their own visions of the author. They were told that they could work individually or in teams or invite other online community members to assist. Among the characteristics the students were asked to envision were gender, age, and ethnic, economic, cultural, and religious background. I invited them to scan or create photos and graphics and to use any available software to assist them. I also requested that the students write a reflection or reaction piece providing their personal (or team) responses to the quotations. The students were given a half hour to begin to absorb and react to the material. The classroom became uncharacteristically quiet as students began working. Most students were freely chatting online, writing, drawing, and uploading. Several just printed out the quotations and sat by themselves.

Student Responses

After examining the quotations, we began our classroom discussion with the students' hypotheses and visions of the memoir author's identity.

Although I had not suggested drawing the author of the memoir, many students had used drawing software to sketch the author in addition to or instead of describing the author in writing. The sketches depicted potential memoir authors of varied ages and with various relationships to the individual being mourned in the memoir. They included:

- an old man gazing at his wife's picture on a table by his bed
- a man morphing into a woman
- a small child looking out a window
- a teen sitting up in bed
- a self-portrait of a young girl in our class whose older sister had died of leukemia
- two male teens at a cemetery
- a young child looking at a photo album

Though some of the drawings and animations depicted universal figures without any suggestion of particular ethnic, racial, or cultural features, several of the portraits and pictures included ethnic,

racial, and cultural data that mirrored that of the student artists. For instance, the male teens were at a cemetery with a Roman Catholic name and the surname of the grave they stood at was the same as that of the Dominican Republic student who had drawn that scene. As I viewed their independently developed graphics, I realized that as an unanticipated byproduct of graphics capacity the students had been "freed" to draw what they wouldn't normally have written! The student artists were asked if they wanted to provide any background, ethnicity, racial, or cultural information about the memoir authors in their pictures. Most said they saw the author as any widow, widower, orphan, or mourning sister/brother. But a few insisted that the quotations must have been written by a Latina because they sounded just like someone they knew. (The majority of my students were from Dominican Republic backgrounds.) Students from our Harlem chat partner were certain an African American authored the work.

These contrary but firmly held graphic and linguistic hypotheses provided a perfect segue for an online chat in which students shared the gender, age, ethnic, economic, cultural, and religious characteristics of the memoir author. One student at each school site recorded each individual or team. I made no comments during the student discussion, but asked that each individual or team justify the characterization of the memoir author by referring to specific quotations that revealed or demonstrated the author's identity. Here are a few of their characterizations:

- A widow who was married more than 40 years. She can't even pay her rent. She goes to church everyday. *Supporting quotation:* "For the first time, I don't have you by my side."
- An old woman who has lost her best friend from childhood. My neighbor down the hall wears her best friend's

blouse. *Supporting quotation:* "I started wearing one of your suitcoats. You know, the gray one you loved so much. ... It's like a married couple, you kind of merge into one person after a while."
- A mother whose child died. He or she was a teenager because of the mail she still gets for him. *Supporting quotation:* "I'm still receiving mail for you ... and it always makes me feel a little bad." "Sometimes I wake in the middle of the night calling your name."
- A brother who lost his brother to leukemia. I lost my brother, so I can tell. I felt he left me all alone. *Supporting quotation:* "You were a part of my life since I was two years old ... now you're gone." "If you had really wanted to, you would have kept going. You wouldn't have left me alone."
- A widowed young husband left to raise his wife's babies who are two and three. My uncle. *Supporting quotation:* "If you had really wanted to, you would have kept going. You wouldn't have left me alone."
- A woman who has lost a great grandmother in her 90s. My mommy just lost her abuela who was 97 and still lived in the Dominican Republic. She held me when I was a baby, but I didn't remember her. She just died. Mommy misses her. *Supporting quotation:* "I'm so grateful for each and every day of your life. You used your time well." "There's a lot of sorrow, but there's a lot of happiness too."
- A son or daughter whose mother died. *Supporting quotation:* "It occurs to me that I did get over mama's death."

For the most part, the students who only wrote descriptions seemed to leave out ethnic, cultural, religious, and economic traits. A few, when pressed, said the author was definitely a Christian, probably Roman Catholic Latino (again, these were my Inwood students). But most said that the quota-

tions were about losing persons who were dear and dealing with that loss.

"The author could be anybody and everybody," argued one of the students.

"It doesn't matter who the memoir author actually is, it could be people we know and many students in this room right now," another said.

At the end of the discussion, I told the students about the African-American Delany sisters: their joint "discovery" when they were each more than 100 years old, their two books, the Broadway play based on their writings, and the subsequent death of Bessie at 104. The Harlem students were elated. They had been right! But my Inwood group was initially upset about the identity of the memoir author; not a single student had accurately identified the author as a 107-year-old African-American woman.

Extending the Activity

I asked my students what, if anything, could be done with the quotations and the memoir that inspired them. Was this memoir pertinent for sixth to eighth graders? The students were given a few days to reflect and an opportunity to share their reflections both in class and online with our Harlem neighbors.

When we met again to discuss Sadie's book, the students were eager to have their say. Students at both schools were overwhelmingly in favor of studying *On My Own* in their classes. (Rarely do students ask to study a book.) Beyond that, they came up with multiple social outreach and community service applications. I was impressed and heartened by the breadth and scope of "uses" they identified for Sadie's memoir, including:

- Pick out quotations that relate to your feelings. Write a response or create graphics to illustrate your responses.
- List ways technology can help people survive someone's death and share his or her legacy.
- List advice for survivors to continue and flourish after loss.
- Use Sadie's ideas and statements about loss to help family, friends, seniors, or bereavement society members create stories, memories, and other written tributes to those they've lost.
- Compile the upbeat statements in which Sadie talks about how she will survive to send to those who suffer loss.
- Start a chat group for those who are recovering from loss.
- Set up an art therapy and multimedia online survivor's exhibit for kids who could use graphics to work through their losses.
- Create a Web page for family or friends who had died of AIDS, cancer, and other illnesses or violence.
- Make a memory storybook of happy stories about people we've lost in our lives, so other people can learn how wonderful they were. Use scanners to include actual photos, writings, and memorabilia of the deceased. Then run a multimedia exhibit *Celebrating the Lives of Those We Lost.*

Find more ideas online at **www.iste. org/L&L**.

Conclusion

My students' initial responses to *On My Own* demonstrate the power, poignancy, and pertinence of Sadie's wisdom for this generation. By tapping into technology, middle-school students not only can get immediate comfort and inspiration from Sadie's strategies for dealing with loss, but also can take her techniques of reflection, memoir, and commemorative activities to a new plateau of action and sharing through technology.

Toward the end of her memoir, the prolific Sadie notes, "I think they'll remember us, and our stories long after we're gone" (pp. 124–125). She further asserts: "I believe it's up to each person to make the best of life, to keep trying no matter what. A lot of it is how you look at it. A lot of it is attitude. … Don't worry about me, … child, I've got plans" (p. 149). What wonderful words of wisdom passed on by an elder to a new generation!

References

Delany, S. L., & Delany, A. E. (1993). *Having our say: The Delany sisters' first 100 years.* San Francisco, CA: HarperCollins.

Delany, S. L., & Delany, A. E. (1994). *The Delany sisters' book of everyday wisdom.* San Francisco, CA: HarperCollins.

Delany, S. L., & Hearth, A. H. (1997). *On my own at 107: Reflections on life without Bessie.* San Francisco, CA: HarperCollins.

THEORY INTO PRACTICE

Social and Emotional Learning Applications of Technology

By Maurice Elias

Technology, or at least the way we usually think about it, poses a bit of a paradox for those of us interested in promoting children's emotional intelligence and social-emotional development. We have an image of technology as something individual, something electronic, something isolated. But that is a narrow view. True, we have not found a substitute for interpersonal interaction as a way of developing human sensitivities and interpersonal effectiveness. However, technology can be what it is supposed to be: an aid, something to assist in our work, to make our work more "technically" simple. As we move toward forms of technology that are interactive and interpersonal, we are reducing the paradox.

We can use technology to promote children's well-being in ways that we are only beginning to imagine. My colleagues and I have developed the Student Conflict Manager, a software package for counselors (for more information, e-mail eq@eqparenting.com or visit www.EQparenting.com). The package is a technology-driven literacy instrument to use with children who are reluctant to communicate verbally. The software takes children through a tailored problem-solving process. For example, students grapple with issues of discipline or substance abuse problems or a problem they are trying to solve, such as how to ask for a date, ask their parents for the car, study for their next exam, or find a present for Mother's Day or Father's Day. Technology helps to create a situation in which certain children can feel more comfortable in the presence of adult helpers, and this allows them to progress to the point at which they can engage in actual counseling conversations.

Another innovation we have developed, with the help of Dr. Brian Friedlander, is a way of teaching problem-solving skills interactively. The Interactive Course in Social Problem Solving allows children to learn how faces convey feelings, how to control their upset feelings, and how to identify and better handle upsetting situations. We are actively working on developing animated characters who will lead students through literacy-related problem-solving activities individually, in small groups, or as an entire class. We want to inspire students' imaginations about the books, the characters, and the choices the authors have made, and the choices the students would make if they were authors.

We are also working to connect parents to parents in our Emotionally Intelligent Parenting Circles (**www.EQParenting.com**). We hope groups of parents will share their expertise in parenting and help decrease the need for professional assistance and out-of-home meetings.

Technology offers creative ways to make the teaching and learning tasks easier and more effective. We are seeing this in the work on emotional intelligence and social-emotional learning, and I think we are only at the very beginning. What appears to be "magic" to many is really just the outcome of creativity being married to technical know-how and love of children. The multiple applications of this combination are circumscribed only by the level of creativity and caring in cyberspace literacy communities.

INSIGHTS

Technology-Linked Literacy Communities
Close-Ups of Community Citizenship Technology Tools

By Rose Reissman

Consider the following community citizenship projects:

- Students read online newspapers and surf the Web, identifying pertinent Web sites, spontaneous acts of goodness, ordinary heroes (**www.myhero.com**), and inspirational stories.

- As part of an ongoing community service collaboration with a neighborhood kitchen, students decorate holiday meal baskets and personalize them with custom-made wrappings and gift tags.

- As part of a weekend community service project, junior high school students provide instruction to senior citizens and English language learners on how to use e-mail.

- A survivor of the Holocaust brings in her Cypress Island Refugee Camp photo and ID papers to be scanned and imported into an oral history document. She reviews the document with the recorder of the history, a high school student. The student makes the editorial changes she requests. Together they create a dialogue-reflection piece as they each respond to the recorded history and its scanned images. The project is uploaded to the Web.

- Second graders use graphics programs to design placards celebrating a garden project that took place in a vacant lot.

These are but a few of the ongoing social and emotional learning projects accessible through the linking of technology and literacy. As students work collaboratively and individually they gain self-awareness through interaction with other online students. The online environment of the community allows everyone to read, observe, and react to various individual and group methods for handling emotions. E-mail and other online communications with multigenerational, multicultural audiences immeasurably increases students' capacity for empathy and social skills, in addition to alleviating immediate geographic, scheduling, and social constraints.

The use of telecommunications—particularly e-mail, online forums, and topic-specific, expert Web sites—enhances the models described in Elias and Tobias' (1996) *Social Problem Solving Intervention in Schools*. It fosters a fertile cyberspace frontier for developing cognitive literacy skills—reading, writing, speaking, listening, discussing, viewing, and responding to issues, problems, and concerns.

The projects we have identified provide students with a validating sense of self-worth. For instance, technology-supported, student-recorded oral histories engage students in thinking about how to act ethically and responsively toward others. The very nature of telecommunications encourages exchanges on issues and concerns and promotes the use of multimedia to share culturally reflective presentations, such as family celebrations. It fosters appreciation of diversity and interpersonal relationships.

Booting up a computer and getting online links social decision making and social competence to literacy skill development. Technology provides students with a literal and virtual literacy portfolio for contributing immediately to their communities.

Reference

Elias, M. J. & Tobias, S. E. (1996). *Social problem solving intervention in schools*. New York: Guilford.

INSIGHTS

Questing after Learning

By Mark Gura

When I asked Dan Buettner if he had a background in education, he shrugged his shoulders and explained, "No, I'm just a guy who's addicted to adventure." Background or not, he's a world-class teacher. Dan's classroom is Planet Earth, and when his class is in session, often a million or more youngsters follow his lessons with rapt attention. Most important, Dan wants to team teach with you!

Over dinner Dan explained that by rights he should have been doomed to the normal life of a successful Midwest lawyer. Instead, he and a group of friends decided that setting a world record for long-distance bicycling would be more fun. Their scheme to do a 15,500-mile "trek" from Alaska to Argentina turned out to be more than an action-packed diversion. In reality, it was one of the most fruitful lesson-planning sessions in the history of education.

To finance the project, Dan began to transform his ongoing global adventures into content-generating educational events. Schools would pay a modest fee to have classes participate. The first couple of efforts were "Learning Treks," long-distance adventures during which Dan periodically informed participants of his progress and discoveries. The events continued to evolve into full-blown learning expeditions. Eventually, it became clear that by encouraging students to partner with the expedition team in collaboratively defining research questions and methods for answering them, a very rich learning resource would develop. With the addition of state-of-the-art technology, particularly something new called the World Wide Web, a remarkable level of success for the expeditions, finally dubbed "Quests," was assured.

Here's how it works. Dan and a team composed of scientists, educators, videographers, technologists, and other professionals select a geographic area to study. During the course of an extended journey they attempt to solve a mystery that's central to the area through which they are travelling. By posting material to the Quest Web site, the team reports on its progress to a broad mass of students, who follow the team by visiting the site. The feedback the students give the team directs its inquiries, making for the type of interactive, highly motivation virtual experience that assures student engagement in core content as well as in wonderful activities that build thinking skills.

Since the Quests were taken under the aegis of Classroom Connect, the nation's foremost Internet-based instructional content provider, the production values of the Quest Web sites, teachers guides, videos, and other accompanying material have set a new standard for creativity and quality. They are stunning. Most important, the cost for a class to participate is quite modest.

To date, in addition to the original AmericasTrek and the subsequent SovietTrek and AfricaTrek, there have been several MayaQuests, in which the team traveled throughout Central America, investigating aspects of the mystery of the fall of the Mayan Empire. There was the GalapagosQuest, which investigated environmental issues with the assistance of Jean Michel Cousteau, son of Jacques Cousteau. Currently underway is the AustraliaQuest.

Having your class participate in a Quest is probably the quickest and most effective way to get started in taking advantage of the exciting learning possibilities offered by the Internet. For more information, see Classroom Connect's Web site at **www.classroom.com**.

INSIGHTS

Why Is the Mona Lisa Smiling?

By Steve Feld

Why is the Mona Lisa smiling? Because she has bridged the digital divide with ThinkQuest's contagiously engaging learning. As the ThinkQuest project Why Is the Mona Lisa Smiling? nears the completion of its third year, Mona Lisa's timelessly captivating smile is more expansive than ever. Why? Over a three-year period, through the ongoing efforts of John F. Kennedy (JFK) High School students under the facilitation of coach Steve Feld, the Mona Lisa has digitally bridged and dissolved various divides, including digital, social, cultural, academic, linguistic, and economic.

The student team members who originally created the Why Is the Mona Lisa Smiling? Web site digitally dissolved international divides of geography and culture when they were invited to submit questions about and designs for the Miho Museum, located in Japan (**http://library.thinkquest.org/13681/data/museum/trees.htm**). With the cooperation of social studies and art history teachers, the students accepted the offer to design questions for their Japanese peers.

They also used these digital designs as the catalysts for cross-cultural conversations with their Japanese student peers. This project, inspired by the OvationTV ArtsZone (**www.ovationtv.com/artszone**), actively fostered the involvement of JFK students in a global community of knowledge workers.

The original multidisciplinary thrust—art, social science, and language arts—of the ThinkQuest project facilitated multiple subject integration. With the support of their foreign language instructors, the students and Mr. Feld were pleased to respond to a Millenaire invitation (issued by Deborah Phelan, Millenaire's inspirer) to become knowledge workers in an international translation project. This project focused on having students do multilingual translations of the MikSike Estonian Web site (**http://miksike.com/space/index_esp.html**).

JFK students produced a requested eWorksheet translation of the material (space module). In addition to the translations, they produced illustrations for these pages, which were linked to other images created by the students. Their work was shared through the MikSike Virtual Student Factory, a cyberspace knowledge workers collective located in Estonia.

Not only did the students who designed and maintained the Mona Lisa Web site expand their activities into recruiting student translators, they also initiated outreach to an Estonian student, 13-year-old Sabena Zinovjeva, who volunteered to translate the Mona Lisa Morph page and our scientific inquiry into Russian (**http://library.thinkquest.org/13681/data/rulink2.htm http://library. thinkquest.org/13681/data/rusci.htm**).

Students delighted in being part of a collaborative with an isolated, digitally challenged international partner on a low end of the digital divide. While working with their peers from the lower end of the digital divide, JFK inner-city students expanded their boundaries of learning to include cross-cultural conversations and an understanding of the strata of technology around the world. As they worked with Estonian students in this virtual student factory, they dealt with real issues of gender, geography, and race (**http://library.thinkquest.org/13681/data/nyc/ africa.htm**).

In studying the Mona Lisa, the students naturally became interested in the artist. Their interest lead to a fascination with Leonardo and some of his other works. Of particular interest to the students was Leonardo's famous book, the *Codex*. JFK students examined a videotape produced by ArtsZone and created their own piece, Codex Comes to Kennedy.

Prompted by OvationTV and their own study of Leonardo's notebooks, JFK students compiled, as an expansion to their original ThinkQuest problem construct, their own school-based journals (**http://library.thinkquest.org/13681/ data/museum/codex.htm**).

The *Codex* study led JFK students to become interested in Leonardo's inventions and vision of the future. One of his visions, the Bronze Horse Colossus, was re-created in 1999 by Japanese artist Nina Akuma. The students and Mr. Feld were invited to the Tallix Foundry in Beacon, New York, for the unveiling of the art work, where they documented the event and digitally photographed the horse. The JFK students' photographs grace their Web site (**http://library.thinkquest. org/13681/data/links/flash.htm**).

The Leonardo project was resurrected when OvationTV invited the JFK students to participate in an Arthur C. Clarke project. In classroom discussions, the students immediately linked Clarke's and Leonardo's vision of the future. This insight lead to a wonderful computer graphics drawing in which one student placed Clarke's trademark glasses on the Mona Lisa (**http://library.thinkquest.org/ 13681/data/links/clarke.htm**).

Technology had served as a tool to literally "art"iculate learning. The Mona Lisa had served to engage students in an intensive case study of Leonardo as artist, futurist, scientist, inventor, and writer. Students linked him with a 20th-century futurist as well.

Several students found the My Hero Web site (**www.myhero.com**) on their daily Internet search and wrote about Leonardo for the Web site. Their writings were so rich and detailed that they were given a separate page and awarded Genius t-shirts. The photo of team members wearing their t-shirts was placed on the page as well (**http://library.thinkquest.org/13681/data/links/hero.htm**).

With Leonardo as their hero it was not surprising that when Microsoft issued its challenge for students to design a Web project predicting what art would be like in 2100, the JFK students immediately identified the Mona Lisa as a pivotal master-piece in art—past and present. Their Microsoft project, which required students to deal with issues of copyright and intellectual property, enriched and inspired their development of this new research challenge. The new project is a broad, multidiscipinary expansion of the original ThinkQuest project that had focused on Leonardo and Renaissance.

Because the students and their coach were "graduates" of a previous ThinkQuest experience, they were able to use their scripting, graphic arts, multimedia, and Web design expertise to craft a new Web site that drew on the original Why Is the Mona Lisa Smiling? project. The new site (ArtiFAQ 2100) encompasses a broad study of art history and reflects the students' experiences with the Mona Lisa (**http://library.thinkquest.org/13681/nyc**).

The Mona Lisa smiles as she traverses past, present, and future. Her smile reflects the fact that although she was painted in 1506 she inspired 20th-century students to envision the world in 2100. The Mona Lisa is confident that her smile and mystique will promote Internet learning and empower students to dissolve the boundaries of time and the digital divide.

CHAPTER 5

Beyond the Basics
Products, Performances, and Projects That Keep Building

The Conversation Continues

Rose: Beyond the daily classroom routines, tests, and assignments, teaching and learning is about experiences. What students take away from a class, a book, or a course is not the facts learned or the grades earned but rather the things they produced. The most vivid memories and inspirations for students are the performances they took part in, the publications they authored, and the projects they conceptualized and brought to fruition.

Mark: Yeah! And the computer more than any other tool will help students get a handle on how to create those things, create them well, and have an extraordinary experience in doing so.

Rose: Where students once simply authored a publication and then photocopied it, the magic of desktop publishing now allows them to create a highly professional publication that can be endlessly reproduced and disseminated to their schoolmates, parents, and local community members, as well as the vast cyberspace audience. The yearbook staple of every school can now be taken to another level, with the students' recorded voices, music, video clips, and photographs included.

Mark: Yes, youngsters can create a remarkable variety of easily made products. Most interesting to me, though, is how technology has democratized media. The line between author and reader, artist and viewer, performer and audience is becoming more and more blurred—and that's great! Nothing increases a student's ability to appreciate and learn from products and performances more than personally taking one's turn at creating and producing them.

Memories in living color

Multimedia Yearbooks

By Ken Kwajewski

t raditional yearbooks try to capture the passage of time and store images that can be reviewed in the future and evoke fond memories. The traditional yearbook is certainly worth keeping, but there is also another method of preserving those memories: multimedia yearbooks. This is a great activity for eighth graders, and these yearbooks can be distributed on disk or videotape. All you need is a digital camera, HyperStudio or another multimedia authoring program, and a dash of creativity.

I have helped my students create multimedia yearbooks for the last two years. I use the term "helped" because my eighth-grade students did most of the work. Using HyperStudio, each student designed his or her own yearbook card complete with a digital photo, layout backgrounds, graphics, text, clip art, and original artwork. This is a fantastic method for involving all of your students in a worthwhile project.

Creating the yearbook

You should start this project early in the year. The goal is to create a HyperStudio yearbook stack that has one multimedia card for each student in your middle school graduating class as well as some cards with candid photos. Link all of the cards together, and demonstrate this yearbook to your students at the end of the school year. Then you can save the yearbook to disk or videotape for students to take with them. If you use HyperStudio 3.0 on an AV computer, exporting the final stack to video is a snap.

The students truly enjoyed creating a tribute to their three years at our school. I gave them the flexibility to create HyperStudio cards that reflected their talents and memories of

Multimedia yearbooks make great companion pieces to traditional yearbooks. Allowing students to create their own yearbook entries ensures that their unique personalities will shine through. Students in middle school and up will enjoy creating and viewing these mementos.

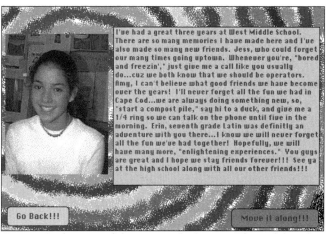

Figure 1. Students created their own yearbook entries. This card shows how a student captured her own personality.

middle school life. I told them to keep the content of the cards in good taste, and I reminded them that other students and parents would view the final product at graduation. This was enough of an incentive to do quality work.

Each student poured some type of creative talent into the

construction of his or her card. Some painted original backgrounds using the tools provided with the software. Many paid tribute to close friends or teachers who had made a special contribution to their middle school careers. Some signed their names or used some type of identifying signature. Others highlighted contributions that they made to the school, accomplishments in sports, extracurricular activities, or special talents. Each took pride in his or her individuality. Figures 1 and 2 show student cards and the different methods each used.

We used a digital camera (Kodak DC40) to take computerized photos of the students. We saved the photos as PICT files, and students pasted their own pictures into the HyperStudio stack. Students also used the digital camera to take pictures on field trips, at assemblies and dances, on dress-up and dress-down days, and of teachers and administrators. Figure 3 shows one of these candid photos. Although the students took the pictures, no one knew which pictures would be integrated into the yearbook until I compiled the final stack.

The final presentation

Right before graduation, I linked all of the student cards and candid photos together using HyperStudio's "magic button"

Figure 3. Candid shots were interspersed with the student cards in the final presentation.

feature. I was able to set the amount of time each card would remain on the screen before fading into the next.

We displayed the yearbook on a large-screen projector to the entire eighth-grade class after the graduation rehearsal. The presentation went well, and each student was proud of his or her contribution to the yearbook. Each student who brought disks or a videotape received a copy of the yearbook. The first multimedia yearbook took six high-density disks, and last year's required 10 disks. The videotape was about 20 minutes long.

The stack was then shown to parents at graduation. Using a large-screen monitor and an Apple Presentation System, the stack was looped to play over and over as parents and students participated in a social gathering after the graduation ceremony. Students were proud to show off the collective production to friends and family.

This activity generated a great deal of excitement throughout the year. It was fun, personal, and creative, and it allowed all students to contribute to a wonderful memory of middle school. I am already starting students on this year's presentation. It does take quite a few hours to create PICT files from the digital photos, link the cards, and copy the yearbook onto disks or videotapes, but the results are worth the effort. Go ahead and try it out at your school.

Resources

Apple Presentation Systems and other Apple products are available at your favorite educational reseller. For more information call 800/800-2775 or 408/996-1010 or visit the Apple Web site at http://www.apple.com/.

HyperStudio is available from Roger Wagner Publishing, Inc., 1050 Pioneer Way, Suite P, El Cajon, CA 92020; 800/HYPERSTUDIO or 619/442-0522; fax 619/442-0525; Web: http://www.hyperstudio.com/.

For more information about the Kodak DC40 and other digital cameras, call Kodak at 716/726-7260 or 800/235-6325 or visit their Web site at http://www.kodak.com/.

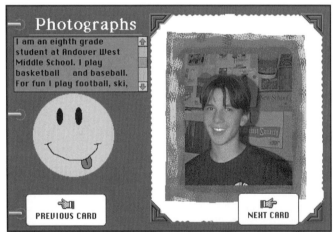

Figure 2. Two more student cards.

Technology-Transformed Dictionary Compilation

Drudgery into Desired Desktop Lexicographer Enchantment

By Rose Reissman

Subject: Language arts

Grade Level: 3–8 (ages 8–13)

Technology: Kid Pix (Brøderbund, a division of The Learning Company)

During my six years as an elementary school teacher, I often have compiled illustrated dictionaries of unit-specific words with my students. The students were proud of the dictionaries they compiled, and individual students often would create their own. Much to my husband's despair (he longed for the clean, uncluttered look in our den and living room), our bookshelves included not only standard resources but also large, profusely illustrated, student-designed dictionaries on large posterboards.

When I started teaching middle school and integrating desktop publishing into my lesson plans, my husband sighed with relief, assuming that my fascination with large posterboard and laminated student lexicography was behind me (and off our bookshelves). Much to his dismay, I suggested that—in addition to their writing portfolios—my first class of multiethnic, inner-city seventh graders should also compile a dictionary as part of our special technology writer's workshop. Furthermore, I specified that this dictionary, due in two months' time, would have at least 200 entries that included sources and dates.

My students were also dismayed and reacted with predictable anxiety and a flood questions until I calmed them down by explaining that 200 "writing" words could easily be found in the Sunday newspapers, from online publications, or from other sources, including adult writers and writing teachers. They could design the dictionary alphabetically using a binder, with several loose-leaf rings holding together large cards, or using a computer printout of words arranged by online or print sources. The words could be copied, photocopied, cut, or pasted into collages. They could be scanned, enhanced with sound effects, and recorded from multimedia resources. They also could be underscored with music using special format design programs such as Kid Pix. In fact, these writers' dictionaries could evolve as shape books or even be done as cubes or in technology-accessible card formats.

All of these design options motivated my nervous novice lexicographers. They began transforming what appeared to be a dull, boring assignment into a multimedia production opportunity. To monitor their progress and foster a community of readers, language lovers, and nascent lexicographers, I built in 10 to 15 minutes per week for students to talk about their dictionaries by using printouts or a large projection screen. Students shared their reflections on the selected words and sources they had collected. They also commented, critiqued, and talked about one another's approaches to the dictionaries. Some students used recorded music, special sound effects, and quick movies to "promote" their work. (I hadn't suggested this multimedia marketing of the project, but I was delighted with it.)

When the final "evolving" Writers' Dictionaries were presented, we set aside two tables at the front of our classroom to exhibit the students' work. Three monitors also were available for in-depth previews of hyperstack, slide-show, and multimedia productions. The displays came in many shapes and forms, including loose-leaf binders, ring-held index cards, laminated big books, posterboard, desktop-published photocopies, and file folder bindings.

As the students gave their short presentations about how their dictionaries had evolved, I passed around a yellow legal pad to let them reflect on their lexicographical endeavors. The students not only showed off their compilations to their peers, but also got a chance to step back and explore what they had derived from their research.

Here are a few of their reflections:

I think my dictionary became a writer's word source. All of the words I found can make my own report on story writing sound better. Also, talking online to actual adult writers and professors of writing from SUNY and Fordham made me understand how real writers value words.

As I was doing the project, I found that I was searching for unforgettable, unusual words. So I created a databank of them to insert in my writings. The sources were really neat. Lots of them were from computer and science magazines. Without a database I'd probably lose them when I need to access them for my own work. Now I know I have them!!

As I went through the online magazines and Scholastic Network activities you suggested, I got ideas for story writing from the words.

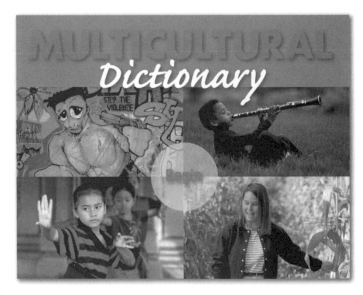

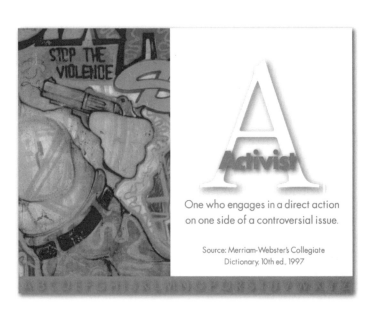

One who engages in a direct action on one side of a controversial issue.

Source: Merriam-Webster's Collegiate Dictionary, 10th ed., 1997

Even though you didn't say to, I did several letters in alphabetical order a week. I felt like I was really creating a dictionary or at least starting up a model for one.

When I was looking through the magazines to cut out words, I began capturing words like "drawing" and "bold" I wouldn't have cut out before because I didn't think of them as going with writing. I felt that I was really the owner of my words. As an owner, the words were mine to use.

Working on this project was easier than I thought. It was fun to do! It helped me think about my writing. It was hard to get started, but once I did, the project was easy. Basically, because you're using First Class, you just need to chat with two or three writers and go through a paper a week. The project does itself.

When we were given this assignment, I thought it would be easy. As I began to put my dictionary together, I thought this was really hard. I found myself taking lots of time to get just the "right" words for each letter of my dictionary.

I ended up enjoying the process of putting together the dictionary. It helped me find, identify, and compile words I wanted to put into my writing. I now have a good-looking resume I can use myself. Since I baby-sit a six year old, I wound up doing a "sixtionary" of writing words for six year olds to use in their stories and pictures. I used KID PIX to do it and he loves it!! Julio, the kid I baby-sit, wanted to draw along with his words.

My students presented their dictionaries in three periods over three days. One student later word processed our handwritten lexicographical reflections for classroom sharing. At the end of the project, I asked the students if they felt they could use their dictionaries or if this was just a "school project." More than a third indicated that they just felt compiling the dictionary was an assignment, but more expressed at least one personal writing or "teaching" use for their dictionaries. Among the uses were:

- a topic and story-starter digest
- basic words for crossword puzzles (one student gave a printout of his words to an aunt who enjoyed crossword puzzles, and she loved it!)
- words built for a writer's online magnet game (students had purchased a commercial magnet poetry product and wanted to try it as a telecommunications poetry project between two classes)
- specific periodical dictionaries for words frequently used in *The New York Times* and *The Daily News*
- sharing with younger children to help them define words, guess where words were found, or create their own dictionaries in Kid Pix
- exchanging and commenting on another classmate's dictionary or modeling a telecommunications project with a class from Canada or Mexico to see what would develop
- continuing to build their dictionaries with favorite words from fiction and nonfiction reading

- creating a cyberspace dictionary using only cyberspace-related words
- using recipe books to develop cooking dictionaries (This grew from a culinary arts project funded by a federal magnet grant.)

In *Just Teach Me, Mrs. K,* Mary Knogress (1995) writes about dictionaries written by middle school students. The efforts of my own inner-city students suggest that targeted technology-driven lexicography can serve as a catalyst for actively and authentically engaging students in an immediately validating, authentic literacy compilation.

Among the most wonderful aspects of middle school writers' dictionaries that technology makes possible are their potential scope and flexibility. Outside sources, a broad spectrum of writing, and adult mentor professionals also aligned with individual students' experiences and interests to meet the general goals of the project.

Isn't connecting language with authentic concerns what writing is all about? Technology can transform dictionary compilation drudgery into desired desktop lexicographer enchantment.

Reference
Knogress, M. M. (1995). *Just teach me, Mrs. K.* Portsmouth, NH: Heinmann.

Resource
Kid Pix, Brøderbund, a division of The Learning Company, PO Box 6125, Novato, CA 94948-6125; 415.382.4400 or 800.825.4420; fax 415.382.4419; www.learningco.com.

Electronic Versus Paper

Do Children Learn from Stories on the Computer?

Many educators believe that children should be read to from a very young age. But does the reading have to be done by an adult to be effective? While working with young students, Melanie Fernandez began studying their reactions to and learning from electronic storybooks. The electronic books held students' attention, and students retained more information from the electronic versions of the stories.

By Melanie Fernandez

Subject: Reading

Grade Level: Prekindergarten through Grade 2 (Ages 3–7)

Technology: Electronic storybooks

Standards: *NETS* 1. (See http://cnets.iste.org for more information on the NETS project.)

I have always been impressed with the quality of the Living Books published and developed by Random House and Brøderbund. The stories chosen for this series are familiar ones that most children enjoy. With the added components of voice, animation, and interactivity, the Living Books are a delightful way for children to enjoy stories.

Reading stories to children has long been considered to be a predictor of their later success in reading. When stories are read to young children, preschoolers begin to understand simple story elements. They see that stories have a beginning, a middle, and an end. They are exposed to sentence structure and new vocabulary. They are engaged in many schema-building activities that will enable them to learn more quickly. Unfortunately, many children begin their formal schooling experience without the benefit of storybook reading in their homes. They come to us "story deficient," positioning them—in the continuum of emergent literacy—behind those children who have been read to by their caregivers since infancy.

Background
While I was completing my doctoral work, my responsibilities included supervising elementary education interns in a rural professional development school. As I observed the interns and the children with whom they were working, it was obvious that many of

these students could be characterized as "story deficient." Because the county where the school was located did not test children in kindergarten through second grade, no standardized test scores were available to examine. However, I could see that these children needed a great deal of experience with storybooks of all sorts before they could begin to become successful readers. Stories were being read to them but not nearly in the volume that was needed. I thought that the electronic storybook might serve to provide some of the elements derived from a traditional reading experience. I wanted to compare the literacy event—the single storybook experience—to see if the computer alternative could be beneficial. This school had a wealth of technology, so all of the children were computer literate to some degree.

Researching Electronic Storybooks
I asked all the kindergarten teachers if they were interested in having their students participate in my research. If their teachers agreed, all of these children then were invited to join in the study. I was warned that my permission slips might not be returned in great numbers, because similar communications often did not make their way back to school. I felt fortunate to receive 50 positive replies. I chose the first 40 children (20 boys and 20 girls).

The Study
I chose the stories Little Monster at School by Mercer Mayer and The Berenstain Bears Get in a Fight by Jan and Stan Berenstain. These stories had

comparable readability and interest levels. Each child was read one of the stories and received the other from the computer. After each story, the student was asked to respond to a number of questions about various story elements. The stories and treatments were counterbalanced.

Two PTA mothers helped with this study. One served as the "escort." She walked children to and from the conference room in the media center where the readings took place. Each child was told he or she would be asked to talk about the story after hearing it. I read individually to each child. Because all of the children knew how to point and click a mouse, minimal introduction was needed for the computer story. The second PTA mom was in charge of the data collection. She asked each student to retell the story and the retellings were audio taped for later analysis. Students were also given a pictorial multiple-choice test about each story's elements and were asked to draw events in the beginning, middle, and end of the story. That was followed by open-ended questions about why they liked the story and whether they had any experiences similar to the characters' in the story. This instrument was examined with qualitative methods. Finally, children were asked which story they preferred.

Results

The qualitative data showed that boys responded more often to the electronic versions of the stories. Yet, they showed by their preferences that the human-read story was their first choice. At first, this finding proved puzzling. Why would boys find the electronic stories more worthy of response yet choose a human-read story as their favorite? Could it be that the electronic story, with all of its movement and zany antics, incited more reaction and stimulated thought while the nurturing element of the human-read story fulfilled a more important need for 5- and 6-

year-olds? Without further study, we can only theorize why the children in this study responded this way.

The statistically significant differences concerning mode of story delivery (either computer- or human-read) from the quantitative analysis appeared in only three of eight comparisons. One significance was found—because of the small sample size—using a p value of .10. The number and strength of the statistical differences were not profound.

However, the evidence of few significant findings is good news. During the time I was developing this study, I saw children experiencing electronic stories. These students appeared to randomly click on items on the screen, diverting their attention from the text more and more with each animated action. In fact, during the story retelling exercise, one child told me that he didn't remember anything about the electronic story. Thus, I expected that the human-read story experience would far surpass the electronic story delivery, which I had hoped would be at least half as effective in terms of literacy learning as the human-read story. As it turned out, the electronic story experience was essentially equivalent to the human-read experience with regard to the literacy learning. With all but three of the comparisons showing no significant difference for mode of story delivery, teachers and parents can be assured that electronic stories are indeed beneficial. Further, teachers can use electronic stories to expose children to a greater number of stories and enhance the possibility for improved literacy. Also, the value of electronic books in terms of children's exposure to repeated readings cannot be ignored.

The potential for electronic stories, however, has yet to be adequately explored. Storybook reading by adults to children within our society is commonplace. Our culture and language are rich with positive references to reading

stories from books in the traditional sense. Therefore, this form of story delivery can be expected to affect children's performance when comparing assessments of human-read and computer-read experiences.

Conclusion

It has been seen from this study that the electronic storybook is one tool that can yield similar, if not in some cases the same, outcomes as those generated by the human-read story. This is not to say that the human reader can be replaced totally by an electronic version of a story. The mediation by the adult reader in terms of discussion and expansion of the text remains a pivotal element of reading aloud. Furthermore, the human contact, the physical and emotional closeness, offered by a human reader cannot be replicated by a computer. But, as seen by this research, the electronic story does provide some of the elements derived from a traditional book-reading experience. Time spent with electronic stories can give children some building blocks to aid their acquisition of literacy.

Electronic texts have extraordinary potential for children. The software is very well done, in that the stories chosen for this medium are, for the most part, written by well-known children's authors. The illustrations are copied directly into electronic format to maintain the beauty of the original art. Software designers then animate the stories and add all sorts of opportunities for interaction with the program by the child. Pleasant voices of both children and adults are used to read the stories. Words on the screen can be accessed repeatedly through a click of the mouse. The computer becomes a tireless storyteller. Children can see, hear, and interact with a story over and over again without the least hint of complaint from the reader.

So, do children learn from stories on the computer? Yes!

QUILTING OUR HISTORY
An Integrated Schoolwide Project

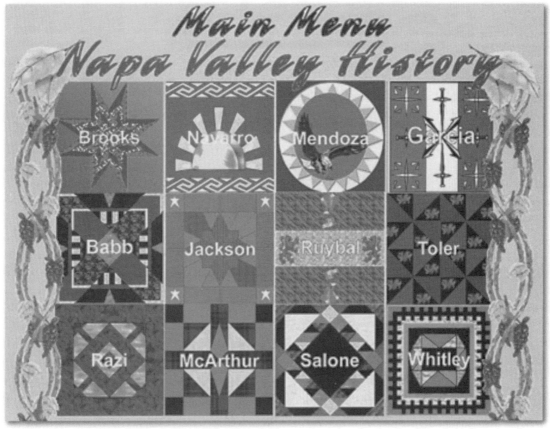

CD-ROM users are able to click on the "Napa Valley History" title to navigate through cultural and historical information about the valley, or they can click a quilt square to learn about a featured family.

Students at a California high school learned real-world technology skills and workplace etiquette when they worked together to create a multimedia CD-ROM that described local history. Although they worked in compartmentalized teams in this whole-school project, the students still created a coherent product.

By Cassandra Van Buren and Deborah Aufdenspring

Subject: Social studies, language arts

Grade Level: 9–12 (Ages 14–18)

Software/Hardware: Director, xRes, Sound Forge XP, Extreme 3D (Macromedia); Photoshop (Adobe); Word, PowerPoint, Bookshelf (Microsoft)

We didn't exactly hold a quilting bee, but like such an event, five of us—all teachers from New Technology High School (NTHS) in Napa, California—stitched together a whole curriculum from pieces of individual curricula. We relied on research findings that told us curricular integration led to meaningful learning experiences (Dressel, 1958; Shoemaker, 1989), and we believed our own experiences from integrating courses at our site. As a result, we created two "quilts." One was simply metaphoric, but it usually held a coherent form and pattern, although the pieces sometimes didn't fall where we thought they would; still, these unplanned design moments often brought the most meaningful teaching. The second quilt was the virtual and high-technology result of our own and our students' efforts.

Project Goals

New Technology High School integrates classes in U.S. history, American literature, and multimedia design. Our design for the schoolwide project, however, had even more goals. The most ambitious of these? To include all subject areas and get schoolwide participation. We also wanted the project to simulate a high-tech company and how it would produce a multimedia CD-ROM; collateral print material would cover the same information. As the students created these products, they would develop the attitudes needed for effective workplace relations and an understanding of interdependent teams, cooperation, and effective communication.

Finally, the project was to be a midyear assessment of students' mastery of several of the school's self-selected goals. We would assess the students' competencies with various computer applications, most notably Microsoft Word, Microsoft PowerPoint, Adobe Photoshop, and Macromedia Director. We also would assess the students' mastery of concepts in literature, writing, U.S. history, algebra, geometry, and multimedia design. Most important, though, we would assess the students' abilities to cooperate with each other and integrate the content from various courses.

This last area, cooperation and integrating course content, brought some of our most rewarding results. All students relied on their research skills as well as the computer applications. Students who did historical research used language skills as they wrote, edited, and continued to rewrite their research results. Our editors stretched to accom-

Student Jesus Chavez used Photoshop to create this background to the information on family history.

modate formatting and stylistic demands, design requirements, and historical research. And the design team learned that content was essential to meaningful multimedia. These threads, these cross-connections, constantly went back and forth among the students' work groups.

To make the project more manageable and to show students how cooperation would make the project easier, we divided the students into several groups: Geometric Design, Artistic Design, Interface Design, History, Genealogy, Artifacts, Publishing, and Video Documentation.

Our original plan called for geometry to be used in the design of our virtual quilt squares. In reality, more math was required in the programming, and members of the Interface Design team were often hunched over their calculators determining the on-screen coordinates for navigation buttons and artwork.

In addition to math, our project design sought to incorporate the history, geography, economics, literature, art, politics, and government of the greater Napa Valley area. These components would be stitched together with the family histories of some of our students.

Getting Started with Students

Once we determined the project's components, we explained the project to students and sent a letter home to their parents that provided pedagogical justification for the project. We also requested the parents' signed permission to include a student's family history in the event the family was selected for inclusion. Finally, the letter explained the greatly modified schedule that such a project requires. The teachers suspended their regular classes for more than two weeks during the spring semester, voluntarily giving up their prep periods during the project. The students would remain primarily with one teacher (or a pair of teachers) throughout a school day from 8 A.M. to 2 P.M.

The Daily Life of the Quilt

This change in routine meant that students had to develop new strategies to communicate with each other, thus avoiding the chaos that would result if students ran around the building to talk face-to-face. Teams and individuals e-mailed one another to exchange information and to schedule meetings and collaborative work sessions as needed, both with their own and other groups. The groups scheduled and made formal presentations when these seemed to be the most effective ways to communicate information to other groups. Interface Design, for example, used its presentations to explain file-formatting guidelines; this way the students could field questions quickly and prevent misunderstandings that might slow the project.

We required students to write each day in their own electronic journals, that is, their "e-journals." This was particularly good for tracking the progress of individuals and teams. The students then mailed these entries each day to their quilt teacher and teammates, a practice that encouraged daily goal setting and an ongoing critique of their progress. Teachers read the e-journals to watch for group miscommunication, misdirected work, and other issues that would require staff intervention. When appropriate, we were able to adjust the project based on student comments. The e-journals also served us well in planning for the next integrated project.

What the Teams Did

Students spent most of their time working closely with one another in their teams. Video Documentation students moved around the building to record the project with video cameras and digital still cameras. They wrote interview questions and questioned students and staff members as they worked, thus providing background and context for the visual images.

Geometric Design students worked closely with Genealogy teams to create quilt squares that would represent the featured families. Using Adobe Photoshop, the Geometric Design students created squares that incorporated the colors, shapes, or patterns associated with the cultures of individual families. When a family provided a crest, for example, the Geometric Design team worked with its design and colors to create an aesthetically pleasing square.

Historians went to the Napa City–County Library and Napa Historical Society to conduct research and gather needed resources. They used library materials, the Internet, and personal interviews to gather information about local history and current events in the Napa Valley. The students chose to investigate the histories of the Berryessa Valley and Napa River, local artists and writers, and the modern Napa economy. They conducted both in-person and e-mail interviews with the school's business partners and community members. The students then wrote about their research and included information from their interviews along with citations and bibliographies. The articles were then reviewed by their teachers and community members who juried the CD-ROM produced near the end of the project.

Publishing students edited and formatted the written material that was created as the other teams finished. These students checked for consistency in writing style and formatting as well as errors in spelling, grammar, and punctuation.

The Genealogy teams were led by students whose families had agreed to be featured in the project. The teams researched the families' histories and collected photos and memorabilia that would be included in written histories, family trees, and illustrations.

As teachers, we felt that traditional displays with tangible artifacts were needed to remind students, the community, and ourselves that our digital work cannot be divorced from the physical world in which we live. So we had Artifacts students create hallway displays to decorate the school. The Artifacts team worked with the Genealogy and History teams and took field trips to collect material that represented the greater Napa area's history. The team's displays featured Robert Louis Stevenson, one of Napa Valley's best known literary figures; the histories of local wineries; and the history of the Wappo, Native Americans of the Napa region.

Artistic Design students used Photoshop to design the visual elements of the interactive CD-ROM, creating all of the artwork, other than the quilt squares, so that the CD interface had a unified, professional appearance. Artistic Design students sacrificed their own personal tastes and artistic styles to create a harmonious design; it was their first commercial art experience. Although some students felt limited by the requirement for overall consistency, they learned that such limits were necessary if they wanted to achieve an integrated look.

Interface Design students worked intensively at the project's beginning and end. They designed the layout and navigation of the final product and developed file-format guidelines so that the other teams could send files with the correct formatting and styles. As text and image files arrived from the other teams, Interface Design students also wrote code to create interactivity with Director.

Challenges

As our school created the quilt, we encountered difficulties that we could not fix during the project. The long and intensive contact between students and one or two teachers all day was difficult for some students. Student satisfaction with the project schedule and organization depended heavily on job assignment. The History and Genealogy students were in the largest and least exclusive groups, and they sometimes expressed their lack of motivation in counterproductive ways. History groups were encouraged with daily rewards for team cooperation, individual effort, and best research of the day.

The conflicts and tensions that arose among groups presented teachers with opportunities to teach students about effective communication strategies and diplomacy. When conflicts between students developed, their first impulse was to blame each other and complain to their teacher. We used these situations to teach them to resolve conflicts in other ways than going directly to their "supervisor" for intervention. We discussed diplomacy, emphasized problem solving, and modeled clarifying behaviors.

When a team of Interface Design students visited the History group to communicate their file-format guidelines in a large-group presentation, they used computer programming jargon and a rapid-fire delivery that confused most of the History students. The puzzled and frustrated Historians sat in silence as the Interface group plowed through its presentation. Noticing the perplexed looks on her students' faces, History teacher Deborah Aufdenspring modeled clarification techniques for her students to show them how to let the Interface group know diplomatically that they were not communicating very well. "I'm sorry, but I don't understand exactly what formats we should use. Could you slow down and explain it to us using different words?" In this way, her students could see how they might ensure clear communication without the presenters becoming defensive. The Historians were then able to ask their own clarifying questions, and the Interface Design students used this constructive criticism to improve their presentations for the remaining work groups.

The Genealogy and Interface Design teams also were challenged when the latter team discovered that the software that Genealogy had been using to create family trees was incompatible with Director. The Interface students had to tell the Genealogy group to re-create the family trees using a compatible software application. The Genealogy students reacted badly to the news by blaming the Interface Design team and complaining to Genealogy teacher Carole Toy. She consulted with Cassandra Van Buren, the Interface Design teacher, and the two teachers decided to use the opportunity to teach students to focus on identifying the problem and finding solutions rather than on pointing fingers and complaining. The students were asked to work out their conflicts directly and diplomatically with each other before they approached a supervisor.

In these and many other situations, the students experienced what adults face in their everyday working lives. Happily, we witnessed both individual and group triumphs in the midst of both problems and chaos. Teachers and students alike reveled in their successes. Latina student Rosa Corona, for example, worked as part of a History team researching Napa Valley farm workers, and she reported immense personal and intellectual satisfaction in connecting with the farm workers in her own community. What she learned about their history during the project informed her work later in the year when she did an integrated project (history, English, and multimedia) that expanded on her work in the schoolwide project.

Successes

Students who researched the history of flooding in the Berryessa Valley developed their own model of integration as they worked on the project. Although we had planned for interdisciplinary integration, these students carried integration on their own to a more complex level, developing a networked approach that led them to seek experts and informants who could increase their knowledge in several areas. Artistic and Interface Design students were thrilled to work so closely with like-minded peers, and a camaraderie was thus born from similar interests and skills. Similarly, we as teachers worked in our own areas of interest and expertise and loved working with students who held the same interests. We enjoyed and appreciated the deeper relationships we were thus able to build with students.

The community judging aspect of the project was highly successful. It brought the school and community—including Napa Historical Society members, district administrators, parents, business partners, and Napa Valley College staff members—closer together. Having community members evaluate their work profoundly affected the students. The sometimes harsh criticism reminded them that the "real world" beyond school and graduation also will judge them. They learned to accept and incorporate criticism with a realistic understanding of what quality work means to their community. They also were able to separate good criticism from bad, such as when some judges incorrectly criticized grammar and punctuation.

The students' journals best reflect what they learned:

Unfortunately, our group chose not to improve our final essay, so we didn't get very good comments. I will use the opinions of the community members for my future projects, though. I will set them up like requirements for a project.

and

Today the judges came and judged our reports. Ms. A went over our report with us after the judges had made their comments about our paper. I think the judges were too hard on us, but, as Ms. A. said, this is how it is in the real world. I understood this a lot better after she said that. I was kind of disappointed with the judges' comments. One of them said that our report had a lot of writing errors. I didn't see any writing errors in our entire report.

What We Learned

An educational system has constraints that make it hard to duplicate a work environment. Businesses hire just the number of employees they need for a given team and presumably people who choose to work in a given area. Public schools neither select their students nor provide them with "jobs" about which students will necessarily be enthusiastic. The members of the two smaller teams, Artistic Design and Interface Design, felt the most job satisfaction and enjoyed the most rewards. In the Bridge Project, we designed heterogeneous teams to work on all facets of the project. This didn't simulate most high-tech companies, but it did provide more students with experiences in various facets of the project and thus brought more satisfaction.

Even with the constraints of their assignments, by the end of last year's project the students were excited about the project and grateful for what they had learned. Their daily journals reflect this excitement:

> Today my group planned out that we are going to talk in the mornings to make sure that we all know what we are doing the next day. I also made sure that they knew what they were going to do toady [sic]. I got a lot accomplished today. My group made up interview questions and did research on the Internet. On Tuesday we will put together our outline. I believe everyone worked really hard and I think that this was the first day that we all worked together and actually got things accomplished. I had lots of fun working with my group today.

and

> One of the things I didn't like at first was that I was the leader of my group, and I thought I didn't have the ability to be leader. Now I think it was a good experience.

Not all students were pleased, however:

> I hated the fact that I got stuck in the history part of this project I didn't learn really learn any new skills, I already knew how to write a essay before this project. Students should have decided what kind of CD-ROM to make, I think the only reason we did the history and families of Napa is to impress the community. I was cheated out of learning.

Nonetheless, one student spoke for many others:

> I think it was a great experience. We all pulled together to make it work. I liked it. We really enjoyed what we did. Lots of community people liked it, too, and that's what we wanted. I wish we could work on the quilt project forever.

We teachers, too, have been enthusiastic about such projects. The benefits we saw followed those described by Perkins (1991) and Shoemaker (1989) who discussed knowledge in constructivist and holistic language. Similarly, Cole, Gay, and Sharp (1971) and Lave (1988) discuss knowledge not in terms of individual reasoning or sets of particular skills, but in terms of the complex interactions between individuals working together on a common task, the tools they use to accomplish that task, and the attitudes they bring to and take away from it.

We believe these interactions are fostered in the course of an integrated project like this, and as teachers we came away buoyed by the many "teachable moments" that we found in the course of the project. Other schools can certainly create projects like this, modifying the details to fit their own environments and histories. The theme that ties together the curricula, the hardware and software used, and the resulting product all can be adapted.

Like the theme, the tools, and the product, the experiences with an integrated project will vary from site to site. But two things are unlikely to be any different: There will be chaos, and there will be genuine experiential learning.

References

Cole, M., Gay J., & Sharp, D. (1971). *The cultural context of learning and thinking.* New York: Basic Books.

Dressel, P. (1958). The meaning and significance of integration. In N. B. Henry (Ed.), *The integration of educational experiences,* 57th yearbook of the National Society for the Study of Education. Chicago: University of Chicago Press.

Fogarty, R., & Stoehr, J. (1991). *Integrating curricula with multiple intelligences: Teams, themes and threads.* Palatine, IL: Skylight Publishing.

Lave, J. (1988). *Cognition in practice: Mind mathematics and culture in everyday life.* New York: Cambridge Press.

Perkins, D. N. (1991). Educating for insight. *Educational Leadership, 49*(2), 4–8.

Shoemaker, B. (1989). *Integrative education: A curriculum for the twenty-first century.* Oregon School Study Council Report, 33(2).

Resources

Macromedia Director Studio 6.0 for Windows and Macintosh (includes Macromedia Director, xRes, Sound Forge XP, and Extreme 3D); $679 (academic price); Macromedia, Inc., 600 Townsend St., San Francisco, CA 94103; 800.326.2128; www.macromedia.com

Adobe Photoshop 4.0 for Windows and Macintosh; $259 (academic price); Adobe Systems Incorporated, 345 Park Avenue, San Jose, CA 95110-2704 USA; 408.536.6000; www.adobe.com

Microsoft Office Professional 97 with Bookshelf for Windows 32-bit; $199 (academic price); Microsoft, Inc., One Microsoft Way, Redmond, WA 98052-6399; 800.426.9400; www.microsoft.com/office

Great Aunt Sophie's
American Journey

Using Modern Technology to Celebrate Our Ordinary Heroes

By Rose Reissman

I have always been interested in oral history. As a child and young woman, I listened to my Great Aunt Sophie's stories for hours on end. I have shared this love of oral history with my students by inviting various guest speakers of different ethnic backgrounds to talk to my classes about a wide variety of topics. These include middle and secondary school experiences when the speakers were young or lived in other countries; World War II; the Vietnam War; the assassinations of John F. Kennedy, Martin Luther King, Robert Kennedy, and Malcolm X; Olympic games; and dating in the 1950s and 1960s.

Many students are captivated by these exchanges and often take them beyond the classroom, creating oral histories and scrapbooks incorporating photographs and other memorabilia. But some students are not engaged by these conversations. Because I wanted these students to experience the same sense of connection that I had when I talked with Aunt Sophie, I asked myself, how can I create a link between these students and their elders?

In the early 1980s, I realized that some easily accessible technology could be used to engage these students. I encouraged them to record oral histories of ordinary community heroes; they were to use computer graphics and scan photos from family albums. Students

who had spatial or kinesthetic learning styles or who were not native English speakers had not previously participated in class projects that had not used this technology; now they became involved and enhanced our desktop-published tales with graphics that provided a global view of community heroes. Some of our histories were even recorded in the heroes' native languages courtesy of Spanish and Chinese word-processing programs. I guided the students by example, and Aunt Sophie's life was realized in a series of graphic scenes that depicted her working in a sweatshop, racing after her sons to force them to go to school, and attending night school.

A New Spin on the Project

One day, as I watched students furtively exchange baseball and football trading cards, I got an idea. I would use this pop culture phenomenon to build community and intergenerational respect.

I bought a pack of commercial trading cards. Then my mother and I went to work on a trading card to celebrate her beloved Aunt Sophie. No high-paid football heroes or hockey stars for us. No baseball Hall of Famers on our trading cards. Mother and I took stock in ordinary heroes. Enter "Trading Card 818—Sophie Gromer—Ordinary Hero." On one side of the card, we superimposed Aunt Sophie's photo on a large menorah cut from a Hanukkah card to signify her Jewish background.

Books, Jerusalem monuments, and Jewish charity-collection boxes represented her commitment to lifelong literacy, Zionism, and charity. The back of the card contained Ordinary Hero Sophie's biographical statistics—not her batting average, win–loss record, or percentage of passes completed, but a chronicle of her lifelong dedication to education, parental involvement, reading, art, family history, and charity. To me and my mother, Sophie was a most accomplished hero.

As I proudly laminated our Ordinary Heroes card, I wondered about my students' reaction to "Sophie" as my hero choice. Would they dismiss Aunt Sophie's unique qualities and depth of character? Could they appreciate a serious-looking, unglamorous septuagenarian who cared deeply for her family, faith, and community? Would this proud Polish woman appeal to students in the 1990s?

Introducing Aunt Sophie to My Students

As the period began, I proudly introduced Aunt Sophie, sharing various images of my beloved great aunt. I looked around to see how students were reacting. I was touched to see many of them nodding in empathy and recognition.

I asked if any of them had known or been told of an "Aunt Sophie" in their own families. They were unusually quiet at first, but several smiled faintly. Then came a stream of sharing about

Aunt Sophie's "peers": Grandpa Giuseppe, Father Ramon, Nana, Aunt Lucy, Cousin Esmeralda, Aunt Heather, Lady Linda, and Deidre. I encouraged students to go to the computers as their memories poured out and sketch plans for their own trading cards. I gave them a trading card template and suggested that they try to get photos, drawings, or memorabilia associated with their heroes.

Finishing Up

After the students completed and shared their Ordinary Heroes trading cards, they began looking for ways to share them with a larger audience. For example, they could post them on the Web so that other teachers, students, and community members could learn to recognize and celebrate other ordinary heroes around the cards. Or they might display them on their own home pages to celebrate "family values" with family members from a myriad of ethnic and cultural backgrounds.

Thank you, Aunt Sophie. May you and your peers—no matter your culture or generation—serve to connect, teach, and guide those who come after you.

Great Aunt Sophie

As a child growing up in the 1950s, I felt quite connected to my Great Aunt Sophie Gromer, a Polish-born immigrant who was then in her 70s. Aunt Sophie had come to the United States in her teens and worked in a factory as a seamstress. When she was in her 20s, she married a man 25 years her senior.

Sophie's husband had a business when she married him, but he soon lost it. She was responsible for raising her three sons solely on her own wages. Because her husband had no savings or disability insurance, Sophie had to skimp and save. When I was about six years old, she told me stories about how she wore her shoes until they literally peeled off. She told how she went to night school at age 30 to get her high school diploma. She proudly kept the diploma on display.

Among the cherished mementos of her youth was a letter from her sons' public school principal, Mr. Laffer, who commended her for her PTA work. She told me also about how she chased her oldest son into school when she found out he had played hooky.

Sophie was a charitable woman, but not usually with herself. She never, for example, bought herself a new dress. A portion of her income from long, hard hours of work as a seamstress went to those who were unable to earn their own living.

She treasured a book of pressed flowers from the land now known as Israel (but then called Palestine); the book was given to her in the 1930s by the principal of her sons' public school.

With her heavily accented English, Aunt Sophie was a master storyteller and quite theatrical. Her native Yiddish was replete with metaphors. I loved listening to her when I was a child and would often spend an afternoon interviewing her about Poland, her stepmother Mima, and an unsolved murder she remembered. As I jotted down her recollections, I would tell her, "Aunt Sophie, I will make you famous."

The years passed. My interviewing, writing, and caring and curiosity about others evolved into a mission to teach children, teens, young adults, new teachers, and graduate students. My passion for recording stories from others' lives revealed itself through my love of oral history, a component I infused into my interdisciplinary teaching at all grade levels.

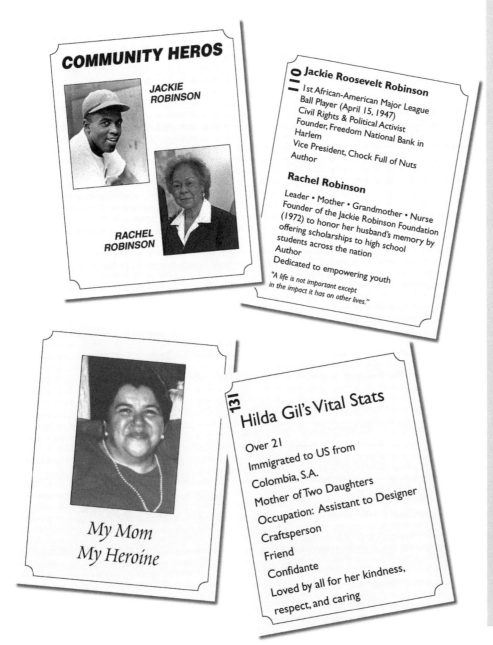

COMMUNITY HEROS

JACKIE ROBINSON

RACHEL ROBINSON

110 Jackie Roosevelt Robinson

1st African-American Major League Ball Player (April 15, 1947)
Civil Rights & Political Activist
Founder, Freedom National Bank in Harlem
Vice President, Chock Full of Nuts
Author

Rachel Robinson

Leader • Mother • Grandmother • Nurse
Founder of the Jackie Robinson Foundation (1972) to honor her husband's memory by offering scholarships to high school students across the nation
Author
Dedicated to empowering youth

"A life is not important except in the impact it has on other lives."

My Mom
My Heroine

131 Hilda Gil's Vital Stats

Over 21
Immigrated to US from Colombia, S.A.
Mother of Two Daughters
Occupation: Assistant to Designer
Craftsperson
Friend
Confidante
Loved by all for her kindness, respect, and caring

It's My Turn!
Motivating Young Readers

How useful are CD-ROM storybooks, poetry collections, and writing programs for teaching young students in the emergent literacy stage?

By Jacqueline N. Glasgow

"Pick me!" "It's my turn!" "Give me the mouse!" "No, it's my turn!" These are the voices of children gathered around my multimedia computer excited and ready to begin a new story. As a result of participating in a language-centered curriculum, these children are well on their way to becoming independent readers. Using modern technology, they are immersed both in oral and written language experiences in a rich context that utilizes multisensory modes of learning. They spend a lot of time in the motivating, low-risk environment of a learning center that is relatively free from anxiety and criticism. The center is equipped with multimedia computers and computerized storybooks, poetry collections, and composing (writing) programs that encourage young readers and writers at any stage of language development.

CD-ROMs for Reading and Writing

Many recently published computer programs are multisensory and multidimensional, with readable text, vivid characters, brilliant graphics, lively music, realistic sounds, and interesting animated movement. Because CD-ROMs have such a large storage capacity, they have become the most popular medium for storing multimedia programs. Because each CD-ROM can store the equivalent of 500,000 pages of text, whole collections of literature can be stored on one disc.

Some very good CD-ROM programs exist that stimulate language development. These programs can be organized in the following four reading-stage categories:

1. Storybook reading and writing programs for children at the emergent literacy stage.
2. Reading and writing programs for beginning students.
3. Reading and writing programs that build fluency.
4. Programs that encourage reading and writing for pleasure.

Here, I discuss the first category—programs for emerging readers. The sidebar entitled "How Multimedia Stimulates Learners" accompanying this article discusses some of the current theories about reading and how multimedia programs can support them.

The Emergent Literacy Stage

Emergent literacy refers to a child's growing discoveries about print and the process of learning to associate pleasure with books (Gillet & Temple, 1994). Margaret Meek (1988) has pointed out that as children explore a variety of texts, they learn how books work. Elizabeth Sulzby (1985), who has studied hundreds of preschool children in relation to their reading of storybooks, has discerned clear patterns of evolution in the strategies they use in such activities. She suggests that the best way to encourage the emergence of literacy is to give young students exposure to good books at the appropriate level and then encourage them to read these books on their own. M. W. Aulls (1982) has provided a framework for decisions related to reading instruction that bridges the gap between children's knowledge of language and their level of "acquaintance with print." He suggests that the first instructional goal is to motivate children to want to learn to read.

Multimedia Storybooks and Young Readers

Multimedia storybooks such as Just Grandma and Me, Ruff's Bone, and Winnie the Pooh and the Honey Tree are multimedia software packages that invite children to read books and interact with the characters. For example, Dr. Seuss's ABC storybook provides young children with silly rhymes and unusual vocabulary as they learn the alphabet in a multimedia setting. This type of CD-ROM storybook helps children explore literature within a rich context of text, narration, graphics, and music (see Figure 1). When they are provided with a rich selection of literature, young readers begin to see that literature is enjoyable and can help them understand the world.

CD-ROM storybooks offer multisensory modes of learning through the integration of print, images, sound, motion, and color. Does this mean we can do without written words? No,

words are the glue that holds together multimedia presentations. What multimedia does is reduce our reliance on text. Instead of using a thousand words to describe an object or idea, multimedia applications use just a few words to introduce a video or still picture showing that object or idea in action. When using multimedia presentations, the learner becomes "an active interpreter and manipulator of environmental stimuli" (Biehler & Snowman, 1990, p. 377) and is able to learn in a rich and stimulating environment in which numerous patterns of thought can emerge by connecting and relating concepts. The importance of providing the learner with a multitude of experiences is emphasized by Bruner (1969), who tells us that "stimulus heterogeneity at an early age is a crucial ingredient in intellectual growth" (Sprinthall & Sprinthall, 1990, p. 79). For children learning to read within an enhanced multimedia environment, reading becomes enjoyable and engaging, even for the most reluctant student. Multimedia allows young learners to manipulate the program at their own rates and feel in control of their interactions.

In keeping with whole-language philosophy, CD-ROM storybooks empower children by providing them with the opportunity to work independently, explore, discover, learn, and make choices about their reading material. They allow young readers to construct meaning from text enlivened by animation, sound, and graphics. Children receive quick responses to their actions, and the responses do not require high-level reading skills.

In most of the stories, the text is highlighted as it is read. This feature helps readers at the emergent literacy stage visually track the words from left to right and top to bottom. On some programs, such as Aesop's Fables, children can even control the rate at which the words are read by adjusting the delay between words on the Speech Control menu. They can then study paragraphs, sentences, and individual words as they click on the text they want to hear or have repeated.

In the Living Books programs, such as Arthur's Teacher Trouble and Arthur's Birthday, discovery is important in the Let Me Play mode. For example, children can click on the "hot

Figure 1. A page from a Dr. Suess's ABC storybook CD-ROM.

spots" (invisible buttons hidden within the pictures), setting off a sequence of animations that make the picture come to life. Characters talk, bulletin boards come to life, fruits and vegetables dance and sing, and fish jump out of the water. For instance, Figure 2 shows a screen from Arthur's Teacher Trouble where students can click several different hot spots to see animations, hear sounds, and experience other multimedia events. These interactive stories are ideal for students who are reluctant to confront print media; the programs provide more comprehension clues and a larger context for the story. As they "play on the page," young readers learn to understand words by seeing them again and again in a variety of contexts, which enables them to figure out the meanings for themselves.

Other Considerations

A potential problem with programs like Living Books is that children may become more engrossed in the dramatic effects of the animations, sounds, and graphics than in the story or text. The question becomes: Does this initial excitement lead to further engagement in the text or does the student ultimately avoid the text and waste time as a result of "playing" on the page? More research in this area is needed, but in my

experience with teaching preschool children, I have found that after children begin their initial exploration of a book, I am able to guide them toward the text and sustain their interest in the story.

The storybook Sitting on the Farm is perhaps the most technically advanced CD-ROM program for children at the emergent literacy stage. In this story, a little girl's peaceful picnic lunch turns into a messy party when her fun-loving animal friends arrive one by one to join her. As shown in Figure 3, the Main Menu screen offers students four interactive learning modes: (1) listening to the narration while reading the story, (2) reading the story independently and clicking on objects to discover new vocabulary, (3) singing the story and recording their own voices, and (4) writing and illustrating stories of their own. In the Write-Along mode, children can fill in the blanks of the pattern story, write a story with illustrations, and print their productions. Language development is fostered as children fully engage in this pattern story through experiences in listening, reading, writing, viewing, and singing.

CD-ROM Storybooks as Teaching Tools

CD-ROM storybooks can play an im-

portant role in supporting and sustaining change in literacy teaching and learning. They can serve as powerful tools for teachers and schools committed to a holistic approach to language arts instruction. Immersing children in interactive storybooks on CD-ROM encourages young readers at all stages of language development. By providing them with a rich learning environment that includes motion, sound, and illustrations, teachers can encourage students to explore fundamental concepts of text. These multimedia environments also help teachers organize student activities and scaffold the cognitive and social processes involved in students' literacy practice. And for students, these technologies represent powerful tools for composition, communication, and access to vast amounts of information.

References

Aulls, M. W. (1982). *Developing readers in today's elementary school.* Boston: Allyn & Bacon.

Biehler, R., & Snowman, J. (1990). *A guide to the development and use of the Myers-Briggs Type Indicator.* Palo Alto, CA: Consulting Psychologists Press.

Bruner, J. (1969). Cognitive consequences of early sensory deprivation. In R. Sprinthal & N. Sprithal (Eds.), *Educational psychology: Selected readings* (pp. 34–36). New York: Van Nostrand-Reinhold.

Figure 2. A screen from Arthur's Teacher Trouble. Most objects in the picture include hot spots for animations, sounds, and other multimedia features.

Figure 3. The Main Menu screen for Sitting on the Farm. The buttons show the four interactive learning modes.

How Multimedia Stimulates Learners

Teaching children to read through interactive storybooks is consistent with the learning theories of Lev Vygotsky and Jean Piaget, who maintain that children must be active participants in their own learning. As children explore these environments, they interpret and give meaning to the events they experience. According to Vygotsky and Piaget, children need to interact with their immediate surroundings and manipulate objects; these actions are critical to language development. Multimedia programs now use speech technology that offers high-quality narration using a variety of adult's and children's voices. Sounds are clear, energetic, and natural. In most CD-ROM books, children can choose either to read the text at their own pace or to activate a voice that reads the story or selected text to them. The text is usually highlighted as it is being read, allowing the listener to coordinate the processing of visual and auditory information. Because the learners turn the pages, they can explore the connections between the sounds of the words as they are being read and their graphic representations. Therefore, the multimedia learning environment is an extremely rich method of instruction that enables children to formulate numerous and meaningful relationships with the material they are reading.

Children who successfully explore concepts about print during the early stages of literacy development lay a foundation that later helps them profit from reading and writing instruction. Those who do not acquire foundational concepts about print may never attain high-level reading skills. One study has shown that almost 90% of the first graders who were behind their peers in reading skills were still in the lowest skill-level group four years later—and by then, the distance between them and the average reader in their age group was immense (Juel, 1988). Interactive storybooks on CD-ROM make valuable resources for early intervention strategies for these children. The current technology allows learners of different backgrounds and varying intellectual and emotional strengths to enter a learning environment in which many of their individual needs can be addressed.

When children read or listen to storybooks on CD-ROM, they are involved in the same complex process described by Jim Trelease (1989) in The New Read-Aloud Handbook:

> Simultaneously, the student-listener's imagination is being stimulated, her/his attention span is stretched, listening comprehension is improved, emotional development is nurtured, the reading [and] writing connection is established, and, where they exist, negative reading attitudes are reshaped to positive attitudes. (pp. 202–203)

Student-listeners are engaged in multisensory modes of learning that they can manipulate at their own pace, which gives them positive reading role models, good sentence and story grammar, and a rich vocabulary. For these reasons, the use of talking storybooks creates a pleasurable experience for young readers.

References

Juel, C. (1988). Learning to read and write: A longitudinal study of 54 children from first through fourth grade. *Journal of Educational Psychology, 80,* 437–447.

Trelease, J. (1989). *The new read-aloud handbook.* New York: Penguin.

Gillet, J. W., & Temple, C. (1994). *Understanding reading problems: Assessment and instruction* (4th ed.). New York: Harper Collins College Publishers.

Meek, M. (1988). *How texts teach what readers learn.* London: Thimble Press.

Sprinthall, N., & Sprinthall, R. (1990). *Educational psychology: Selected readings* (pp. 34–36). New York: McGraw-Hill.

Sulzby, E. (1985). Children's emergent reading of favorite storybooks: A developmental study. *Reading Research Quarterly, 20,* 458–481.

INSIGHTS

Web Authoring Is Good Writing

By Mark Gura

Web-authoring software is potentially a very important tool for the promotion of student writing. While most consider it to be an item suited for advanced "techies" and associate it with the likes of e-commerce, it deserves a place on the desktop of classroom computers as part of the suite of essential applications that support learning and literacy.

Joel Heffner, one of the staff developers assigned to my office, likes to point out the strong motivational power of the Web by suggesting that teachers try to envision the comparative response they might get to the following two questions posed to their classes: "Who wants to write a composition?" or "Who wants to create a Web site?" While the skills employed to create these two forms of writing can be essentially identical, the former question would generally draw a very limited response, while hands would fly up for the latter.

The computer that the browser runs on need not be online for it to activate exciting, Web-based learning products for students. Because browsers are ubiquitously found on the hard drives of computers everywhere, student-produced Web sites can be published and disseminated on disk without relying on phone connections or Internet service. Student work can be taken home on a disk or distributed elsewhere outside the school with the confidence that almost any computer will have a browser to open it.

Web-authoring software is easy to come by. Netscape Communicator, for instance, includes Composer, its own Web-authoring feature. Remarkably, it can be downloaded for free anywhere an Internet connection is available. There are numerous other sources of low-cost Web-authoring software as well. Thus, on close examination, the combined availability of Web-authoring software and a browser is a highly practical reality for classroom work.

Web sites have not only become one of the most important forms of written communication, but they are also especially strong at promoting certain types of skills and thinking. Few forms of communication can compete with the Web site in demonstrating the need for succinctness and precision of language. More important, because the Web site is a hyperlinked medium in which readers may jump from segment to segment following the logic of content rather than of format, it demands that its authors deal effectively with the order and flow of ideas. For teachers struggling with ways to impress upon students the value and importance of planning and outlining in their writing, generating a Web site can be a very effective activity.

In identifying effective forms for authentic writing assignments, the Web site has to come in first. While it is possible to make the leap of imagining a word-processed or desktop-published item as being reproduced and distributed, it is virtually impossible to tell the difference between a Web site that is running solely on a stand-alone computer and one that is being transmitted worldwide across the Web. This is instant, authentic publishing. When it comes to motivation, well, the Web is what's happening, baby. If you ask your students, "Who wants to create a Web site?," I think you'd better be prepared to let them—or face the consequences!

CHAPTER 6

Inquiring Minds
Student-Centered Inquiry

The Conversation Concludes

Rose: Walt Whitman said, "Who is the best student? He who outdistances the teacher!" Technology and Web site design in particular provide students who have initially surfed the Web and sampled the productions, performances, and portfolios compiled by the cyberspace community with the tools to outdistance their teachers with their own original Web sites. These in turn await inevitable outdistancing by their own peers! I can almost envision Walt Whitman, who loved to look to the future, applauding technology's capacity to empower students to continually outdistance their teachers.

Mark: I hope teachers will learn to appreciate being outdistanced. I think this is one of the many and profound ways technology is changing teaching and learning. As youngsters become more empowered by technology, we will need stronger and more confident teachers who will in turn be able to challenge and empower youngsters even further. The only limits in sight are the ones we impose on ourselves. Let's get out of our own way and see how far we can go!

Come Dream with Us
America Dreams

Graphic Design by DUOH!

Technology-infused projects can do much more than just teach subject-area content. They can develop students' skills in ways that can be measured. As the author of this article shows, a social studies project can help students learn to research, analyze, and think critically, all while they learn U.S. history.

By Leni Donlan

Subject: Social studies

Grade Level: 5–10 (Ages 10–16)

Technology: presentation software, Internet connection

Standards: *NETS* 4, 5, and 6. (See http://cnets.iste.org for more information on the NETS project.) *NCSS* Thematic Strands 1, 2, 4, 5, and 10. (See www.ncss.org for more information on its social studies standards.)

Online Supplement: www.iste.org/ L&L/

Appreciative murmurs can be heard as the dramatic images of the Photographers Web site are displayed on the screen. The classroom audience watches and listens intently as the students who created this project explain what photographs tell us about America's past and its people's dreams. The students click through a dramatic gallery of digitized photographs from the American Memory Collections (**http://memory.loc.gov**), explaining each image's significance, origin, and story. These students are sharing their group project and requesting feedback as they prepare to submit their project to the America Dreams ... Through the Decades Web site (**www.internet-catalyst.org/projects/ amproject/splash.html**). Each student group will present its work for peer review—the culmination of two weeks of intensive online study.

The Lesson

America Dreams is structured as a WebQuest. WebQuests begin with a problem, challenge, or compelling reason to engage in the learning activity. Then they define team collaborative roles and tasks, provide links to sites that provide necessary research sources, result in a product that reflects the learning that has occurred, and include a self-evaluation process for students.

In this WebQuest, students are asked to investigate the historical American dream and compare it to contemporary American dreams to answer the following questions.

What is the Dream? Is it the same for all Americans? Is it a myth? How has the Dream changed over time? Some see their dreams wither and die while others see their dreams fulfilled. Why? Everyone has dreams of a personally fulfilled life . . . what is your dream? (**www.internet-catalyst.org/projects/amproject/student.html**)

Teacher Guidelines

Through the online lesson, teachers are guided in how to use the American Memory Collections themselves as well as how to teach their students to use the site (Figure 1). Specific links are provided to the helpful teaching pages provided by the staff of the Library of Congress.

The assignment of team identities provides a structure for engaging and organizing the class for collaborative learning. Figure 2 shows the team identities as described to the students. Teachers are given guidance so that they can lead students through the research-to-knowledge-acquisition process—that is, analysis, comparison, synthesis, evaluation, and, finally, application of their learning as they develop projects to share within their classroom and then online with the world.

Implementing the Lesson

Teachers set the stage for engagement through directed lessons and discussions that help clarify what is meant by the term *American dream* and what influences have colored and changed the dream for different groups within the United States. Students are asked to articulate and record their own dreams for their own and the country's future (Figure 3). When understanding is evident, the teacher introduces the American Memory Collections and research techniques (Figure 4).

Student Guidelines

Identity selection is a guided process for students (see Figure 5), and each identity is designed to help the students understand that we learn about our nation's past through evidence. Such evidence can be found in the arts, laws and policies, significant natural and hu-

man-caused historical events, and the oral and written reports left by previous generations. Selected links to the American Memory collections are provided for each team identity.

Students are also provided with directions for assuming "roles" within their teams to ensure that tasks are completed on time and that all students actively participate in the learning process.

American Memory Resources

The resources of the National Digital Library, of which the American Memory Collections are only a small part, are mind-boggling. The collections and exhibits span our nation's past (from the distant to the present). The awe inspired by using these primary and secondary resources can only be understood by experiencing them. They allow teachers and students to "touch the past." The American Memory Collections include carefully digitized documents, photographs and prints, sound recordings, maps, and motion pictures. The collections can be searched by keywords, collections, topics, library divisions, collection type, and so on.

Using selected links from the American Memory Collections (now 40 strong, and growing), students begin gathering information about the country and nation in a designated decade (the use of decades helps the project more readily fit existing curricula in upper-elementary through high school). Students analyze the information they collect and determine how it illustrates the aspirations of an earlier generation and how it will contribute to an effective "documentary" Web site to share their own point of view (Figure 6). They also compare the historical viewpoint about the dream to today's dream.

Lesson Goals

Kathleen Ferentz and I worked as true collaborators in designing this

WebQuest. In the past few years, we have created and conducted several online projects and have developed a style of online teaching that works for us, our students, and other classes. We believe that teachers need to engage both hearts and minds to ensure that children will really take something of value from the lessons we teach. In America Dreams, we designed a lesson that would enable students to:

- become "historians" by (1) carefully observing and using graphical and other evidence plus their prior knowledge to forge a meaningful interpretation of what they observe, (2) developing an analytical outlook by weighing and measuring what is seen and heard, (3) developing personal hypothesis based on observation and prior knowledge, and (4) delving deeper to see if their theories fit the evidence

- become researchers able not only to use the American Memory Collections but also to transfer their skills into other research projects

- develop an appreciation for history and understand that what has occurred in the past affects the present and the future

- begin to realize that they can affect the outcome of their lives by realizing their own dreams and developing plans to fulfill them

- attach personal meaning to their learning—it is through this sense of "being there" that real meaning takes place

- become part of a classroom community of learners, capable of learning and sharing their knowledge with one another

- effectively use technology within a learning experience that could not occur without the technology but that is much more than just "technology for technology's sake"

Big Picture

The lesson is an effective use of technology as a unique tool for learning,

Phase One of Implementation
Building Background Knowledge and Skills

1. Anticipatory Set—develop the concept of the traditional "American Dream" with your students. This could involve interviews, readings, class discussions, and guest speakers.
2. Teach students how to use the **American Memory** collection. You might try out one of the roles and make a sample product to show students.
3. If using primary source documents is new, read **primary source documents**. Develop a few practice lessons with students before you launch this WebQuest. You will find **student lessons and teaching suggestions** for your use.
4. As you learn to use the **American Memory collection, teach your students basic search skills**. Again, student lessons and teacher guides are available to help here. Time spent reading through the **Learning Page** will be time well spent.
5. Use the **student page** as a guideline for developing your thesis on the American Dream.

Phase Two of Implementation
Researching Online and gathering primary resources

1. Introduce students to the **Student Page**.
2. As a class, define the scope of your desired outcomes for this project. For example, do you want to gather material from a specific decade? from a specific collection? or by theme, such as immigration?
3. Decide how much time students will have to research and gather materials as well as their skill level using technology.
4. Form student teams of four. Teams can select a **ROLE** from the list (photographer, lawyer, poet, politician, producer, comedian, musician). Each student will be assigned a group task and work as part of this **team** to bring the project to completion. Remind students, that while they have specific **group tasks**, all team members pitch in and help.
5. Read the assessment questions (e.g., **photographer**) with your students. Choose just the ones that will provide a focus for the project. Students can use these questions to guide their research and determine how to think about the design of an authentic product from their research.
6. Write an action plan (e.g., **photographer**) with students for the project or encourage teams to develop their own. This aspect of the project will require your students to apply their team planning skills to ensure completion of a quality product by the set deadline.
7. While you might only have time to visit the suggested collections and links for each role, encourage your students to develop their own links in these collections and to expand their links to other Internet sources.
8. Begin independent team exploration. Students can keep a daily research log on paper or computer and collect primary source evidence to build their final project on disk. Allow several days for exploration and research.

Phase Three of Implementation
Creating the Learning Product

1. Students can produce any number of products to demonstrate their interpretation of the materials as a final exhibit for the Library of Congress—a Web page posted at your school site, a multimedia stack, a video documentary, an oral presentation, or even photos of your classroom turned into a museum composed of print documents, multimedia, and realia.
2. Directions for simple Web page building and necessary tools are available in many locations on the Internet. Try visiting **Web66** or the **PacBell Knowledge Network** for ideas.
3. The **Constructivist Project Design Guide** maintained by Columbia University's Institute for Learning Technologies is a treasure trove of additional ideas for teachers.
4. Refining and putting together a final learning product that will permit students to defend their ideas about the American Dream is the outcome of this project. Allow plenty of time for this vital phase. Have students keep a log or journal of what transpires during this phase of the project. This can provide useful insight in the evaluation process.
5. Require that **proper citation** and bibliographical material be used with all collected print material, photos, sound, video, et cetera.

Figure 1. Teacher instructions make it easy to use this lesson in your classroom (www.internet-catalyst.org/projects/amproject/teach.html).

Roles	Description
	Photographer With your artful eye you capture the images of the American Dream.
	Lawyer Your passion for controversy and debate will guide your vision of the American Dream.
	**Poet** Using your poetic grasp of language you seek out the heart and soul of the American Dream.
	Politician With a finger on the pulse of the American people you trace significant political events that shape the American Dream.
	Producer Lights, camera, action! You produce the movie, American Dream.
	Comedian You find the irony in the American Dream.
	Musician With your ear for melody you play the music of the American Dream.
	Newspaper Reporter On the newsbeat you report and chronicle the events which shape the American Dream.

Figure 2. Students can choose to act as photographers, lawyers, poets, politicians, producers, comedians, musicians, or reporters as they complete this activity.

The Process
Define your project

1. Before you jump into your roles, your group needs to define the American Dream. Find out what it means to each member of your group. Brainstorm and share your ideas.
2. Next, decide: Will you investigate one decade or compare how the American Dream evolved over the decades? Will you just compare the past to today?
3. Complete the exercises below to learn about searching the collection.

*Figure 3. Students start by figuring out what the American dream is. Step-by-step instructions guide them through the project (**www.internet-catalyst.org/projects/amproject/student.html**).*

Learn to use the American Memory Collection

First, earn your permit to search and become a Historical Detective. Your mission is to use clues to complete the Scavenger Hunt.

Next, apply your newly acquired detective skills to solve the monthly puzzle. When you hit the Jackpot page you are ready to start this project.

Figure 4. Students learn how to do online research before testing their knowledge by solving a puzzle. After learning and using their research skills, they are ready to begin the project in earnest.

Choose your role
Now you are ready. Here are your team assignments.

1. Divide into groups of four.
2. As a group, choose one of the roles to create your project.
3. Read your task and set up your group management system.
4. Discuss the assessment questions and create your action plan.
5. Search the collection and gather your evidence.
6. Create your learning product. Compare your dream to history.

Figure 5. Students are given assignments to complete.

Conclusion
You've finished, you've presented. Has this activity influenced your view of the American Dream? How? Now that you've completed the project, what new considerations can you offer? Is the American Dream a reality? What can the dreams of others teach you? How will your personal dream become part of America's future? So...what is the American Dream?

Figure 6. Concluding questions help students finalize their projects.

and it allows students to learn from resources that would be unavailable to them without online access. Using primary and secondary online resources to support a classroom-based, collaborative, student-centered learning project provides an outstanding learning opportunity for students. The project is designed for all students—urban or rural, at-risk or gifted, from all socioeconomic levels, all ethnic origins, and of every age. The American dream has been passed down through the generations as something that most Americans want to achieve. But what is it? Students often find that it is both universally the same and specifically different for various groups within the United States. (Visit **www.internet-catalyst.org/cgi-bin/show_wall.pl** for students' reactions to the project.) Students recognize that there is a healthy diversity of individual dreams that are embraced by the American dream. Through our lesson, they see how these diverse dreams and aspirations have shaped American culture in the past, and how their own dreams will shape the American dream in the 21st century.

Reference
Dodge, B. (1995). *Some thoughts about WebQuests* [Online document]. Available: http://edweb.sdsu.edu/courses/edtec596/about_webquests.html.

Web Resources
The following resources can help you and your students start doing online research.

The WebQuest Page: http://edWeb.sdsu.edu/Webquest/Webquest.html

The Library of Congress: http://www.loc.gov/

Learning Page, American Memory Collections: http://lcWeb2.loc.gov/ammem/ndlpedu/index.html

Analysis of Primary Sources: http://lcWeb2.loc.gov/ammem/ndlpedu/lessons/psources/analyze.html

Become a Historical Detective: http://lcWeb2.loc.gov/ammem/ndlpedu/detectiv.html

Internet Resources for Educators: http://lcWeb2.loc.gov/ammem/ndlpedu/websites.html

Citing Electronic Resources: http://lcWeb2.loc.gov/ammem/ndlpedu/cite.html

Constructivist Project Design Guide: www.ilt.columbia.edu/k12/livetext/curricula/general/webcurr.html

Partners in Communication

Technology & Writing

E-mail projects can be useful for students at all levels, but teachers must plan carefully so that the projects increase students' knowledge base. Diane Horban's seventh-grade students learned to discuss reading and writing by working with local high school students on a collaborative e-mail project. The two sets of students discussed issues from their language arts classes, and they were able to meet at the end of the year to discuss their common experience.

By Diane Horban

Technology and communication— what possibilities! As a seventh-grade language arts teacher at Northbrook Junior High School in Northbrook, Illinois, I spend much of my time looking for activities that will help my students find information and communicate with others, all with an eye toward increasing their knowledge base. E-mail projects have long seemed like the perfect activity to fulfill these goals using technology. But e-mail penpals should do more than write to each other. I want my students to share their reading and writing experiences with their penpals.

But who could my students e-mail? This was a question I thought about for quite awhile in 1996. To get my idea off the ground, I contacted Jenny Jordan, an English teacher at Glenbrook North High School. Jenny was in charge of the writing lab, and I thought she would know which students would be good candidates for this project. To my delight, Jenny was enthusiastic about the project and wanted to use her own students. In this way began an e-mail project that lasted the entire 1996–97 school year.

Getting Started

Before we could start such a project, we had to get some issues worked out. We met to discuss our goals and determine the technology support needed to launch our project. We kept our goals simple to start. We wanted to teach our students that reading (and discussing reading) can be fun.

With the help of our district's technology coordinator, my seventh-grade students began using Eudora on the six Apple computers in my classroom. After a few botched attempts to start the project, Jenny's students got access to Eudora as well. Now we had compatibility between systems and we knew how file attachments would be handled by our respective computers. We were ready to turn our students loose on e-mail.

More Than Just Penpals

Each of our students had one penpal to correspond with for the entire school year. They quickly cultivated active dis-

cussions on books and writing. Reading topics included reactions to plot, authors' writing styles, and suggestions for future readings based on genre choice. Writing topics included information about how best to begin an essay, what to do when ideas don't come, and how to use better vocabulary. Even though the goal was to foster something more than simple penpal exchanges, personal exchanges naturally arose. What a wonderful opportunity for my students to find out firsthand what their next level of education might entail while fostering an e-mail writing relationship. Some of the students' correspondence accompanies this article.

Projects

In the spring, Jenny suggested that our students read the same story and respond. This fit right in with the response journals that my students were writing. We selected "The House Guest" by Paul Darcey Boles. The story reflects Northern Ireland's multicultural heritage. It describes a young girl from war-torn Belfast who visits the United States. The students corresponded about their

thoughts and feelings related to the plot and the larger issues of war and its effects. Their insights were remarkable. (A sample lesson plan is provided at the end of this article.)

As a culminating activity, my students took a field trip to the high school to meet their writing partners. For an hour and a half, various activities allowed all of the students to interact socially and discuss literary issues. Groups of six to eight students met to read and discuss poetry. After the discussion, writing partners met and collaboratively wrote poetry on computers in the high school's writing lab. My students went home with copies of the poem to add to their portfolios. A proud addition to a fine collection of work for the year.

Planning for the Next Group of Students

We continued our "technology conversations" with our incoming students in the 1997–98 school year. The sample letters I collected from our first year are proof that communicating about individual reading and writing situations improved the students' ability to make choices about what to read and how to write.

Overall, using e-mail has been invaluable for my students, giving them the opportunity to communicate with people who would not otherwise be accessible. They were able to tap into the knowledge base of high school students; they, in turn, offered their own valuable suggestions about reading and writing. In this age of technology, communication is one of the greatest links offered. Don't overlook e-mail as an invaluable resource.

Resource

Eudora 1.5.1 is shareware. It is available from Qualcomm Inc., 6455 Lusk Boulevard, San Diego, CA 92121-2779; http://www.eudora.com.

Student Correspondence

E-mail projects can fulfill many needs in your classroom, but how can you ensure that students keep their writing on-task?

My students wrote all of their letters during class time. They first wrote them in a word-processing program. Then I conferred with each student to monitor the focus of the letters as well as the use of technology. They made any necessary changes at the computer. Finally, they were able to send the letters to their electronic penpals.

The best way to keep students on-task, however, is to ensure that they are interested in the project. My students were interested in using technology, so they never strayed far from the task at hand.

These letters show a sample interaction between one of my students and one of Jenny's students. Although most of the discussion is about reading and writing, you'll see that Chantel and Aly spent some time discussing personal topics. Don't discourage these types of interactions; they help the students feel comfortable with each other. Just try to keep them a minor part of the e-mail messages.

Dear GBN Partner,

I am very fortunate that I am having the chance to gain your knowledge on techniques and to share my own. It's nice that we will be able to experiment with the reading and writing that we are experiencing right now. When I graduate to high school, your feedback will influence me. I will gladly give you my opinion or thought on your pieces, if you desire. Do you think that you can benefit from a middle school student?

I enjoy reading, as well as writing. What's your favorite genre? I crave mysteries. I am currently reading a engaging mystery called Missing Since Monday. The author is Ann M. Martin. Are you familiar with this author? Reading this book, I predict that the ending will be horribly exciting. Do you have a recommendation for a book that you have read or are reading? I am always looking for a delightful book.

When writing, I always plan ahead and organize my ideas. In my opinion, the best way to begin drafting is to look at all the different angles a concept has to offer. A writing concept is a factual explanation. An example of a concept is disappointment, greed, and curiosity. Concepts allow you to show your belief on a particular situation. Have you ever had a time when you were stuck on a concept? I suspect everyone has a time when they have a difficult time generating ideas. Speaking of concepts, I am always open to topics that have worked well for you.

I am getting in the habit of using upgraded words in my writing pieces. This is one risk that I am taking to develop into an enhanced writer. In my Language Arts class we have identified such words. We have created note cards; therefore, it reminds me to constantly use them. They are practical when I need an upgrade for "good."

I will be eager to hear from you in the next couple of weeks. In the future, this learning experience will be to both of our advantages. Don't think of me as a pen pal however, we will be exchanging letters. I hope to develop a long term reading and writing relationship.

Booker looker, Chantel

Dear Chantel,

I am really excited about being your book buddy. I think this will a fun experience for both of us, and I'm looking forward to getting to know you better. I guess I should tell you a little bit about myself first. I am a junior at GBN. I graduated from Wood Oaks Jr. High School three years ago, so I don't know much about your teachers or classes. You'll have to fill me in about Northbrook Jr. High School. I'd like to hear more about you, like: Do you have any hobbies? or Are you involved in any after school activities. If you're wondering about me, I love to dance. I am on pom poms and I used to be a gymnast.

I was really excited to hear that you liked the book Missing Since Monday. That book was one of my favorites when I was in jr. high! I love mysteries. Agatha Christie was my favorite author. The book All Around The Town was my all time favorite book! I have read it about twenty times! Ann M. Martin is a great author also. I used to love The Babysitters Club series.

English is my best subject, so writing has always come pretty easy for me. When I write, I like to make an outline of ideas before I actually start my essays. Then I go back and write my topic sentences and thesis statement. After that, I write the paper, and lastly, I edit my paper. I'm glad you're so organized with your writing, because it will help you when you get to high school.

Do you like English? Do you have a fun class? Are you a good writer? What types of concepts are you studying in English right now? I'd love to hear all about your classes and look forward to hearing about your after school activities. I can't wait to read some of your essays and hear more about what books you like. Write back soon.

Your writing pal, Aly

———————————

Dear Aly,

I was elated to hear that we enjoy the same books. I am looking forward to hear more strategies in writing. I can't wait to read some of your pieces. I am hoping to send you some of mine in the near future.

I am interested in reading that book you recommended. Can you recall the author of All Around Town? I have just begun the book Go Ask Alice by Anonymous. Are you familiar with this title? From this point, I am fully enjoying this book. It is about one girl's harsh life. I am

trying to break away from reading mysteries and attempting realistic fiction.

In your last letter, you mentioned outlines and a thesis statement. We are making outlines, but I have never experimented with a thesis statement. Could you explain it to me in your next letter? I would like to try this method when I draft.

On another note, I have completed a piece on dreams. I am going to try to publish it in some kind of newsletter. Have you ever been published or attempted to be? If you have, I'd like to read or chat about it.

You probably want to know a little about myself. I love Language Arts because you can never stop getting more advanced in writing. Since the start of this school year, I cannot believe the progress I've made. I enjoy playing tennis in the summer. In the fall, I was on Northbrook Junior High's soccer team.

I will be happy to tell you more about my school in the next letter. I hope that I will have a chance in getting my writing out of this classroom. I am sure that we will benefit from this learning experience. Write back soon.

Your writing pal, Chantel

———————————

Hi Chantel,

I'm sorry it has taken me so long to write back to you, but these past few weeks have been crazy! I have had a lot of things to do; a term paper, finals, etc. So, how's school been lately? Are you reading anything new? It's cool that we like the same books. Go Ask Alice is a great book—I loved it. I cried the first time I read it. I liked it so much that I read it a second time! Have you done anything new in English? Right now I'm reading a really boring book for my English class. It's called There Eyes Are Watching God.

Besides school, what else do you like to do? What movies are your favorites? What books are your favorites? I want to hear about everything.

Well, I hope we get to meet each other. I hope that we will have a field trip to visit you guys soon. I have to go to my next class because I'm really late. I can't wait to hear from you. Write back soon.

Your Book Buddy, Aly

Sample Lesson Plan

Objectives
- To read a short story and share analytical comments with remote partners.
- To share opinions about reading material with an outside, interested source—an authentic audience.

Materials
- "The House Guest" by Paul Darcey Boles

  (Choose a reading selection that will be of interest to varied reading levels and age groups. This could range from prose to poetry. Selection could be based on traditional or contemporary authors. I chose "The House Guest" because of its various themes that could be expanded: war, conflict in Northern Ireland, trust, animal rights, exchange programs, compassion and love, responsibility, etc.)

Procedure
- Read "The House Guest."
- Discuss the story as a class, in small groups, or both.
- Write a letter in which you discuss your reactions to "The House Guest," inferences, the author's writing style, and what you want or need an author to do to make a story worthwhile. Discuss your letter with the teacher before you send it.

  (I sent a copy of the story as an e-mail attachment to Jenny. We agreed on a date by which the reading and in-class discussion of the story had to be done. I scheduled class time to discuss the story in Lit Circles—that is, small groups—to further understanding. We then discussed the story as a whole class to share and gain additional insight. Then my students wrote letters to their high school reading partners.)

Dear Jennie,

I understand the delay. Now I am the guilty one. School has been so busy lately that I have not been able to write. Lately I have been very busy with reading and writing. I am very interested in what you have been doing in language arts too.

Since I last wrote, I have tried to read many books. I began Time Bomb by Jonathan Kellerman. It is about a psychologist who is investigating a shooting by performing a "physiological autopsy" in the sniper. It was mildly interesting, but when the pace did not pick up, I dropped it. After that I read The Chamber by John Grisham for a L.A. project. I will talk about that a little later. Two books that I read and finished over spring break are The Old Man and the Sea by Ernest Hemingway and Invasion by Robin Cook. The Old Man and the Sea was a very simple book, but enjoyable. It is nothing but a personal narrative of a fisherman and his battle with a giant fish. It is his story over a few days. At the end I tried to find a deeper meaning but I could not. I think it had no themes, it was just meant to entertain you. Have you ever read a book like that? How did you feel?

I read Invasion because I am a fan of Robin Cook and I heard that a T.V. movie of it is coming out soon. I was truly disappointed. The book was an action/suspense novel about an alien invasion. This was totally uncharacteristic of Robin Cook. First of all, the plot was cliched, with an alien invasion, and a small group of heroes finds who their weakness and bring back peace and world order. That has been so overused. Robin Cook is usually very original. Second, confusing medical terminology was used. Normally, Robin Cook explains and makes sure that you understand all medical things so that you can enjoy the book. He did not this time. I could go on and on about why Invasion is not at all up to par to Robin Cook books, but I will move on. Did you see

the movie? It is much different, and I feel 'better' than the book.

"House Guest," and the related projects we did relating to it were very interesting. I found the character of Bridgie to be full of points to discuss. The rest of the story was just a platform to display the power of Bridgie's message. I found it very interesting how the time in Ireland had conditioned her. For example, when loud noises occurred, Bridgie would hide. Her time living with terrorism and bombs caused this. At dinner, when she ate quickly and did not take second helpings unless they were offered showed that she was trained to be polite and not try to offend anybody. This is so different from the way we are growing up. This story was a testament against war and terrorism in general. It was not about Bridgie or Project Children. It was about war. How do you feel about that story? What were your reactions?

Your books sounds very interesting. What sort of smaller themes have you noticed in the "coming of age" books? I have read some books like that but didn't really like theme because I couldn't relate to them. Do you feel the same way? I think the reason I like realistic fiction is because I can relate to it, and I dislike books that I cannot relate with. Do you feel this way too?

I agree with your opinions on English class. I feel that the difference between English and language arts is in grammar content. English classes focus on grammar and structured writing, while language arts focuses less on grammar and teaches creativity and reading skills. I hope I never have an "English" class.

As you can see, we have been very busy in L.A. I hope we can both start sending responses a little sooner. Your books sound very interesting. I wish you luck in your books, something that I have not had.

Awaiting a good book,
Kevin

ThinkQuest

Using Problem Solving as a Springboard for Student Web Site Authoring

By Rose Reissman

A few years ago, my students and I received a notice inviting us to a meeting of an organization called ThinkQuest. At that time, my students and I were just beginning to explore Web sites and become familiar with the richness of the Web as a tool for inquiry and a wonderfully fascinating shopping mall of knowledge. Although John F. Kennedy High School was not completely wired at that time, we did have a single Internet connection and 15 old computers. To make a long story short, I took two "explorer" students who were interested in the Internet to the ThinkQuest meeting held at City College campus in the Bronx. There, my students and I first learned about the work of ThinkQuest. The ThinkQuest organization sponsors competitions for students in grades 4 to 12. The goal of the competition is to have the students identify a problem they wish to solve or investigate using the Internet and document their inquiry. The process is facilitated by a coach through the construction of a Web site. In addition to working collaboratively with a team on a school site, these students must partner with international or distanced peers to both pursue their inquiry and develop a Web site product.

Computers and the Internet must have been used in producing the Web site product, which students can find ideas for by browsing through the ThinkQuest library selections (particularly language arts and mathematics) at **http://library.advanced.org**. The site must addresses the following ThinkQuest Internet Style of Learning criteria:

- Active participation by the site's visitors and peer collaborators
- Sharing of data, ideas, and materials on the site, which fosters a cyberspace "learning community"

■ Inclusion of quizzes, interactive chat activities, and participatory opportunities that foster an Internet Style of Learning and inspire all site visitors and creators to further explore Internet resources

ThinkQuest's mission is to inspire student participants, under the coaching of teacher facilitators, to become involved in new distanced peer, international peer, and multigenerational relationships that enhance their geographic communities and broaden their awareness and appreciation of the global cyberspace community. Students are encouraged to develop a problem construct that (1) has broad appeal, (2) has the potential for attracting a broad range of multigenerational and school-age users, (3) involves more than a single language, and (4) yields a site that is capable of working on a variety of browsers.

The monetary and academic prizes in this competition include cash awards for the participating schools and coaches and college scholarships for the students. More important, the student teams become part of a vibrant cyberspace network of 21st-century think-tank problem solvers. They also become connected, not only through cyberspace conversations and exchanges but also through joint Web site creation, maintenance, and upgrading. The Web site product created by international teams documents and demonstrates the students' actual global workplace experiences and real-life workplace networking skills acquired through working on a Web site. The project enhances problem-based content knowledge and academic multidisciplinary literacy skills. The multidisciplinary literacy skills, habits, and attitudes nurtured and supported by ThinkQuest Web site construction include conducting Internet research, taking notes, writing narrative accounts, authoring functional and informational documents, responding to literature, writing business letters, improving critical reading capacities using electronic texts, reading nonfiction, and authoring procedural accounts. The ThinkQuest projects offer improvement in a plethora of literacy skills and attitudes, all concretized in a dynamic cyberspace site.

Visit the ThinkQuest site at **www.thinkquest.org** to view the library of current ThinkQuest projects and projects from the last three years. If your quest is to give your students Web-authoring experiences that are global, authentic, captivating, compelling, and content-rich, you've found your site! Be challenged by the ThinkQuest challenge, and provide your own challenges for the growing international student and teacher literacy community.

APPENDIX I

Voices

As Mark and I were reviewing the *L&L* articles detailing successful practices and projects in the classroom, we also had the opportunity to hear from colleagues about their own classrooms. These colleagues would stop us at workshops, on-site visits, and conferences to share a new piece of software, technology-supported literacy strategy for a special population, or a Web site they found particularly useful in their teaching. As we worked on compiling this compendium of literacy resources, we decided it would be wonderful to enhance the articles with tips and ideas from a burgeoning number of technology-using classroom teachers. Indeed, we hope that the following short reflections and suggestions add value to this book. We hope these voices will inspire other classroom teachers, resource specialists, and librarians to share their new ideas with new teachers and teachers new to technology. As you read these voices, add your own voice to the growing group of teachers using technology to improve their teaching and student learning.

—Rose Reissman

PressWriter

PressWriter is a useful piece of software that creates a window of opportunity for many writers in elementary, middle, and high school. The program contains a choice of six desktop-publishing options: newsletters, brochures, letters and résumés, reports, flyers, and booklets. Within each category is an array of ready-made templates and layouts providing many options for conveying messages more effectively. The final product is visually appealing and professional looking.

PressWriter allows teachers to produce attractive, visually stimulating documents for classroom use. The software package contains a Teacher's Guide with lesson plans and student activities. Documents can also be created to inform parents of class activities and invite them to upcoming events in the school or community.

For students, PressWriter is inviting to both the proficient writer and the reluctant writer. The templates (quick-start layouts) offer guiding remarks to ensure that the writing content flows appropriately. For example, a newsletter sample guides the writer in furnishing the necessary information and provides a format that is likely to appear in most newsletters. Because the samples are predesigned and can be modified easily, students do not have to dedicate their time to designing layouts. Instead, more time is spent on the writing process.

The software's capabilities are not limited to classroom applications; there are wider applications for school and personal use. For example, users can create documents such as flyers, menus, and announcements, or they can create personal documents, such as résumés and letters.

Anna Mendez, Teacher
New York City Board of Education

Science, Computers, Internet

A computer, by virtue of the Internet, is the key that unlocks the door to the international science community. It affords students an opportunity to explore the collective information gathered by scientists from around the world and serves as a tool for recording, manipulating, storing, and sharing data.

Scientific inquiry involves research, investigation, and verification of results to demonstrate the validity of one's work. With the Internet, students can easily be engaged in scientific inquiry because it offers them the chance to explore and research almost all that the world has to offer on any given topic. Students can read and view the enormous amount of scientific information gathered by other people who dared to observe, experiment, record, and explain the world around them. Indeed, civilization has thrived and expanded as a direct result of our quest to understand the world around us.

Using a computer and Internet access, students are able to reach beyond the classroom and communicate with peers and scientists throughout the world. They can even participate in a research project and contribute to the collective wealth of information available. The link between what is studied in the classroom and what occurs in the real world may be just a mouse click away.

The Web site **www.Lightspan.com** is an excellent source for Web-based science projects. At this site, K–12 students can gain access to myriad curriculum-based science projects that stimulate, enrich, and expand the learning experience. All teachers can use this site to engage students in inquiry-based, hands-on scientific investigation.

Teachers who want their students to interact with the international educational community of students may do so by logging on to **www.epals.com**. This Web site affords teachers and students a unique opportunity to establish a dialogue with other teachers and students in all parts of the world. Furthermore, it will automatically translate e-mail messages from one language to another, allowing students who speak different languages to communicate with one another. Classes can use this site to participate in cooperative scientific investigations, such as partnering with other classes from different parts of the world to observe and record the temperature and weather conditions in their respective countries and then share that data using e-mail or a Web site.

David Erdil, Teacher
New York City Board of Education

Palm Digital Assistants

The newest versions of the Palm digital assistants, usually thought of as being tools for busy business executives, are about the same size as a Gameboy and can be used to record class notes, create electronic flashcards, beam homework assignments from the teacher to student, and much more. These devices can be connected to computers, both in school and at home. In light of the fact that there are more than 100 million Gameboys in the pockets of youngsters, using a pocket-sized device such as a Palm doesn't seem to be far fetched. Kids enjoy working with these miniature electronic devices, which are very easy to use. The future of educational technology probably will be in your pocket.

Joel Heffner, Teacher
New York City Board of Education

Computer-Supported Mathematics
A Prime Approach to Fostering Literacy

As a computers-in-mathematics turnkey teacher, I encourage my middle school mathematics colleagues to let students solve word problems on the computer using spreadsheets. This way, students can incorporate reading into their math exercises. I recommend that teachers use *Math with Computers,* by Barksdale, Steffe, and Harman (Computer Literacy Press, 1988), for their word problems. Lesson 6, "Story Problems to Perplex Your Brain," and Lesson 9, "Story Problems to Shape Your Mind," are especially useful. I present a workshop entitled "Using Computers in the Mathematics Classroom" in which I give pairs of teachers samples of several different word problems taken from *Math with Computers.* Teachers have to solve any two of the problems using AppleWorks' spreadsheet component. In this way they have to try the activities that their students will be doing. Here is an example of a story problem I use.

Activity 78: Pond Fractions
The critters that live in a nearby pond are facing a crisis. See if you can solve their problem in a spreadsheet. Organize your spreadsheet in an attractive way.

The Problem:
Last year the following numbers of animals were living in the pond swamp:
Alligators   60   Frogs   80
Muskrats   200   Snakes 64
However, over the period of a year, four-fifths of the alligators were trapped and removed. Trappers also removed nine-tenths of the muskrats. Only one-eighth of the snakes remain from last year. And seven-eighths of the frogs are no longer there; however, the remaining alligators and snakes are much fatter. Use your spreadsheet to determine how many of each animal are left in the swamp.

Formatting and Saving:
Format the number value to display without decimals. (You don't want to even think about fractions of frogs!) (p. 154)

Among other things, this problem encourages students to read fractions as words. Also, to solve the problem correctly students have to explain their answers using word processing. (Students can make a text box within the spreadsheet document itself.) In terms of classroom management, I suggest that teachers have some of the students work on word problems on computers while others work on them at their desks. Students can compare their answers and methods.

Charles Bender, Teacher
New York City Board of Education

Note from the Publisher: *ISTE has published an excellent resource for teachers who want to incorporate spreadsheets into their math curriculum. It is titled* Spreadsheet Magic—40 Lessons Using Spreadsheets to Teach Curriculum in K–8 Classrooms, *by Pam Lewis.*

Teaching Keyboarding

Should keyboarding be taught as a subject? This question evokes passionate responses from educators who are getting used to the idea of having computers in the classroom.

Some educators are convinced that writing is not writing unless a pen and paper are involved and therefore don't see the value of keyboarding. Others feel that students using the two-finger hunt-and-peck method have mastered sufficient keyboarding skills. They need not struggle with the tedium of learning touch-typing. Dealing with the work of slow and inaccurate typists is frustrating to everyone. Most teachers consider themselves lucky to have students who have so fully integrated the skill that it has become second nature to their writing process.

Learning keyboarding is like learning to ride a bike. At first, we have to deal with balancing, steering, and pedaling all at once. It's hard, and we frequently doubt our ability. Then suddenly the day comes when the skill is mastered and we no longer need to concentrate on what we are doing. We ride like the wind—we're free! It's the same thing with keyboarding. As skills increase, the process becomes internalized. Ultimately, the writer relies more and more on the word processor and hates the thought of being asked to use a pen or pencil.

Our computer-savvy students often don't want to use a pen or pencil, especially when taking standardized writing tests. A recent study revealed that students who used a word processor (without the aid of editing tools such as spell checking or grammar checking) to complete their standardized tests scored significantly higher than when they wrote their responses with a pen and paper. The greater their keyboarding ability, the greater the discrepancy in their scores.

Many educators are against teaching keyboarding, arguing that it's boring and depends on using rote memorization. However, as more and more teachers integrate the use of technology into instruction, keyboarding skills become more relevant. In classrooms with computers that must be shared, it is imperative that students finish their assignments quickly.

If students are consistently encouraged to type correctly, they will soon internalize the process. Their speed and accuracy will increase a little each time they use the keyboard. Research has shown that students who use a word processor write better and longer and are more receptive to revising their work. As our society becomes more dependent on the computer, good keyboarding skills will be essential to achieving success.

Teresa Bader, Teacher
New York City Board of Education

Note from the Publisher: *The International Society for Technology in Education (ISTE) publishes an excellent keyboarding program for teachers. Entitled* Keyboard Success, *it includes a Teacher's Guide, a Student Flip Book, and a Keyboard Wall Chart.*

Technology and Literacy Acquisition

As many educators know, using the tools that technology affords us only enhances what we already do in order to help our students learn. When I work with children in grades K–3, I try to reinforce basic skills. Whether the children practice counting and then type the numbers, or are typing their names, I am impressed by what they know and how quickly they grasp keyboarding skills.

Students also help each other. Working in two's, they take turns and teach each other how to accomplish a piece of the task at hand. With some groups of students, I focus on labeling. Using a program such as ClarisWorks (now AppleWorks), I teach first graders how to use drawing tools and create shapes. After this is done, we label the shapes. Depending on the time available, the children can choose a color for their shape and also include the descriptive word in the labeling. In other cases, we go into the graphics library, chose a category, and label the images found in the clip art library. In yet another activity, students create words using "sound flashcards." After students compile a list of words, we type them into the computer and draw or find a corresponding graphic. In all of these cases, students practice a variety of skills, including keyboarding and graphics skills. They also reinforce the basics that their classroom teachers have taught them. By using a combination of writing and pictures, students are also given a chance to see images of the words they are learning, thereby having more concrete examples.

Elizabeth Gill, Teacher
New York City Board of Education

Tales of a Fourth-Grade Web Page

As a teacher integration specialist, I am able to work with teachers to integrate technology into their curriculum. Recently, students in a fourth-grade class expressed their desire to prepare new incoming students. The teacher and I decided to use Microsoft Publisher to create Web pages for this purpose.

To begin the project, we devised a graphic organizer for the students' notes. The students were then divided into groups for handling different subject areas, including book reviews, science, social studies, and math. The students took the roles of editor, illustrator, fact checker, layout specialist, and typist.

The groups agreed on a layout from Publisher's Web Page Wizard. This made it simpler for students to decide on Web page elements, including the placement of buttons, headlines, and links. They found the spell checker invaluable. By clicking the right mouse button on misspelled words, they were offered a list of suggestions to fix mistakes.

To edit their work, students saved their information on disks. To finish their pages, they visited other sites and noticed that too much text made the pages boring. They returned to Publisher to select clip art. They also linked to other sites by copying and pasting site logos and adding hyperlinks.

As the pages were posted, the teacher informed the students that she would allow her incoming students to read the pages to introduce them to the school year.

You can visit the site at **http://www.sachem.edu/schools/hiawatha/ Readaboutit/index.html**

Stephanie Wilbur, Teacher
Allentown, Pennsylvania

The Internet

The Internet has a great deal to offer any enthusiast in search of authentic information. The site **findlaw.com** offers many educational opportunities in that it enables the user to access U.S. Supreme Court data.

Students in my American Government class identified this site as the most valuable tool they used in completing their projects, which were based on U.S. Supreme Court interpretations of Constitutional law and Constitutional amendments.

Source material at this site includes:
- Identification of the violation and parties
- Lower court rulings
- Original testimony
- Names of sitting judges
- The name of the judge authoring the majority opinion, the basis for that decision, and the concurring judges
- The names of judges endorsing the dissenting opinion and the basis for their decisions

This site offers fertile turf from which to launch projects that will catapult students into "real law" situations.

Charlene J. Campbell,
Technology Staff Developer,
North Port High School
North Port, New York

APPENDIX 2

Transforming Student Test Takers into Student Test Makers

How to Alleviate the Anxiety of Standardized Tests

Modeled on the Lucy Calkins Readers and Writers' Approach to Standardized Tests

Students have always feared tests. They fear standardized tests the most. However, in today's teaching world, tests are a reality. As state and local governments begin to demand more accountability, the use of standardized tests is on the rise. Students need strategies to mediate the anxiety that comes with these standardized tests. The following model is one way students can gain a sense of empowerment over the test-taking process.

Seated at computer monitor in pairs or teams of three, students use online resources to select newspaper items or to excerpt key passages from independently selected literature sources. Using the computer as a notebook, students identify news features, articles, stories, items, and listings (classified ads, television listings, daily calendars) that they find interesting. Based on their familiarity with the style and format of standardized reading and writing tests, they select key excerpts and enter them into word-processing files. (This approach can be used for standardized tests in general reading, social studies, science, and history.)

Note to the Teacher: You may need to model the initial technology-assisted test design sequence with your students or make modifications to the following steps to address various strengths and learning styles. The steps can also be adapted for training sessions for family literacy, parents, schools, and volunteers to enable community members to work at home with students to prepare items from the family library bookshelf or daily print newspapers. In addition, a corps of technology-empowered student test designers can be trained to work with younger peers at risk of not attaining district- or state-mandated testing achievement goals or in need of special cross-age tutoring assistance.

Step 1: Distribute examples of standardized tests or other commercially developed test preparation materials.

Step 2: Tell students that rather than practicing for standardized reading and mathematics tests by using boring and worry-producing "stuff" created by test publishers, they're going to build up their test-taking skills by creating their own sample reading and math questions. Once they develop their questions, they'll try them out on each other throughout the year.

In addition, they will be contributing to a desktop-published, class-specific test sampler that will be field tested on their peers in other parallel classes in school. In this way, they will hone their test-taking skills in specific subjects by working together to make a product that will not only help them, their peers, and distanced peers but will also be used as a model for the following year's classes to help those students prepare for the tests. Raise the possibility that those who excel at this type of test design could obtain jobs in the adult world as test-question designers and, at the very least, might want to be part of a student corps of test-taking trainers who would work with younger peers and at-risk students in an after-school enrichment or reading program.

Step 3: Challenge students to take one of the tests and go through the practice materials for a sample test to identify the types of test questions and kinds of answers or responses that are required. Distribute the NICEST TAPS Student Test Designer Worksheet 1 at the end of this appendix.

Students might also be asked to maintain an online log of ideas and models or versions of various test questions as they work with the material. Making this log a dual-entry journal would be a wonderful, authentic, multigenerational response to literature-writing dialogue as well!

Step 4: Talk with students about the types of questions and the answers or responses required. Depending on the time allotted to this project, you may want to discuss in some detail the following subjects: responses, options, selection of a different number of genres, length of reading passages, mathematics problems, prompts, short responses, and extended responses.

If students have access to either e-mail or an online expert (even a colleague at another school), the discussion can become a threaded conversation between students assuming the role of test designers and a consulting expert. Another technology-enabled possibility would be to set up a time for students to e-mail or otherwise confer with one of your colleagues who has written or developed questions for city, state, and national examinations. Since veteran teacher educators are now routinely invited to submit questions for local and statewide examinations, technology should facilitate an authentic exchange that enhances the students' self-concept.

Step 5: Ask your students what inexpensive and readily available written and online textual material other than books might be used by a test designer to develop these tests. Elicit an answer such as newspapers.

Redirect the students to their NICEST TAPS Student Test Designer Worksheet. Distribute copies of the daily newspaper and direct students to online newspaper resources.

Divide the students into pairs or teams of three. Depending on your teaching style and the needs of the class, you may want to model this student-centered inquiry for 5 minutes or more as a whole-class investigation or spend 20 to 30 minutes or more on it as a complete lesson.

Step 6: Give student teams 20 minutes or more to identify news items that will work well as texts from which to generate test questions. Distribute scissors, glue sticks, markers, blank paper, and a large manila envelope or file folder.

Ask them to label the envelope or file folder with the day's date, the team members' names, and the newspaper used.

Tell the students to clip all the good text items for test questions they find and place them in the envelope or file folder. Remind them to look first at the index of the newspaper and go through all the sections and features, not just the front and back pages, to identify those that will work best as texts for test questions.

Distribute the NICEST TAPS TEST Student Test Designer Worksheet 2.

Step 7: Have the students share their finding on the news texts for test questions.

Have one student in the class record each team's findings. These should be shared with the whole class. They should be stored in a class file and printed out for posting as well. Post them with the date so that they can later serve as a pre-assessment of the students' initial news text identification skills.

Step 8: Have students select at least two news items from their online news sources. Request that they use these as texts to generate at least one or more of the test questions. Caution them to include questions that require responses, choices, or options that are just as difficult as those in the exam. Have them print out the news items they used. Ask them to also maintain individual files of the material they selected. Have them maintain separate files of the correct answers to their design questions.

Step 9: When the students have completed this task, review the questions and responses for conformity in format, correctness of suggested responses, and clarity. Support the students in making whatever changes they need to make. Use the computer to make the review of their work seem more like a professional editor-to-author exchange than a teacher correcting their work. This will enhance the students' sense of professionalism.

Step 10: Have the students exchange the questions generated from their model news texts. Allow them to review one another's designs and try out their test-taking skills. Encourage them to visit one another's monitors to field test the questions, or print out their test design questions and share them with another team in class.

Step 11: Have students reference one another's correct answer files or give them printouts of the correct answers.

Step 12: Compile all teacher-reviewed, peer-field-tested questions generated from newspaper items into one binder, or photocopy the material into one packet. You might also desktop publish all of the student-designed questions in one booklet to be distributed and the answers in a separate booklet kept as a key. Questions can also be posted online as part of e-mail exchanges, or on the class, school, or district Web site.

Voila! You now have the makings of an authentic, high-interest project that is practical, proactive, and promotes lifelong literacy.

The Benefits of Using Technology

- Telecommunications offers student test designers immediate access to expert input and advice from adult test designers.
- Use of e-mail and chat forums, student Web sites, and the Internet allows students to field test their model questions with a distance, multisector audience.
- Tapping into the flexibility of technology takes students away from the traditional test-taking environment of school desks and chairs and places them in front of computer monitors and screens. This environment reduces tension as students confer with teachers and peers about the formats of their questions and answers.
- Use of basic word-processing and desktop-publishing technology allows the teacher and students to create a publishable, readily reproducible, professional-looking booklet that can serve as a concrete product of student efforts, a model for parents, and be quickly reproduced and distributed schoolwide.
- Use of technology promotes civic literacy in that students access news Web sites.

Alleviate student and family test-taking anxiety with a hefty dose of news-centered, problem-mediating test design expertise. Add a note of proactive citizenship and reality to test texts so that in preparing for tests, students and families gain meaningful, highly skilled literacy engagement. Make tests count for concrete community involvement and achievement. That's the nicest result of all.

NICEST TAPS
Student Test Designer
Worksheet 1

Name:

Name:

Name:

Exam Title:

Subject:

Question Types (description):	Answers/Options

NICEST TAPS
Student Test Designer
Worksheet 2

Name:

Name:

Name:

Newspaper used:

Question type:	News link: (news item, feature, section, column, comic, graphic, classified ad).

ISTE National Educational Technology Standards (NETS)

The National Educational Technology Standards for students are divided into six broad categories. Standards within each category are to be introduced, reinforced, and mastered by students. These categories provide a framework for linking performance indicators, listed by grade level, to the standards. Teachers can use these standards and profiles as guidelines for planning technology-based activities in which students achieve success in learning, communication, and life skills.

1. Basic operations and concepts
- Students demonstrate a sound understanding of the nature and operation of technology systems.
- Students are proficient in the use of technology.

2. Social, ethical, and human issues
- Students understand the ethical, cultural, and societal issues related to technology.
- Students practice responsible use of technology systems, information, and software.
- Students develop positive attitudes toward technology uses that support lifelong learning, collaboration, personal pursuits, and productivity.

3. Technology productivity tools
- Students use technology tools to enhance learning, increase productivity, and promote creativity.
- Students use productivity tools to collaborate in constructing technology-enhanced models, preparing publications, and producing other creative works.

4. Technology communications tools
- Students use telecommunications to collaborate, publish, and interact with peers, experts, and other audiences.
- Students use a variety of media and formats to communicate information and ideas effectively to multiple audiences.

5. Technology research tools

- Students use technology to locate, evaluate, and collect information from a variety of sources.
- Students use technology tools to process data and report results.
- Students evaluate and select new information resources and technological innovations based on the appropriateness to specific tasks.

6. Technology problem-solving and decision-making tools

- Students use technology resources for solving problems and making informed decisions.
- Students employ technology in the development of strategies for solving problems in the real world.

About the Authors

Rose Reissman (rreissman@yahoo.com), language arts editor for *Learning & Leading with Technology*, is also president of the Association for Computer Educators in New York, New York; R&D consultant for FutureKids Technology Literacy Training Center; president of the New York City Association of Teachers of English; and educational consultant for the Museum of the City of New York. She has developed media and technology courses for the reading and writing master's program and teaches a graduate-level course at Manhattanville College.

Mark Gura (aztec2step@aol.com) has been involved in public-school education for 30 years. Originally a fine arts teacher, he has taught virtually all subject areas during the course of his career. For the past decade, he has been a leader in the use of computers for instruction. He is the director of the Office of Instructional Technology for the New York City Board of Education.

The following authors wrote the articles featured in this collection:

Deborah Aufdenspring (deborah@aufdenspring.com) is chair of the Social Studies Department at the Minnesota Business Academy in St. Paul, Minnesota.

Tom Banaszewski (tbanaszewski@sch.ci.lexington.ma.us) is a multimedia author and educator at the Maria Hastings School in Lexington, Massachusetts.

Ivan W. Baugh (iwbaugh@home.com) serves as adjunct professor of education at Bellarmine College in Louisville, Kentucky. He teaches undergraduate and graduate technology in education classes and collaborates with his colleagues to encourage technology integration.

Donna Bearden (dbearden@dallasisd.org) is the executive director of special projects and evaluations in the Dallas Public School District, Dallas, Texas.

Janet M. Beyersdorfer (jbeyers@aol.com) is an instructional technology specialist at Riley Elementary School in Arlington Heights, Illinois.

Marilyn Catchings (mcatch1@tiger.lsu.edu) and **S. Kim MacGregor**
(kdmacg@lsu.vm.sncc.lsu.edu) teach at Louisiana State University, College of
Education, in Baton Rouge, Louisiana.

Fran Castiello(franc@optonline.net) is a seventh-grade teacher at Derby High
School in Derby, Connecticut.

Sara Dexter (sdexter@tc.umn.edu) is a research associate in the Center for
Applied Research and Educational Improvement at the University of Minnesota in
Minneapolis.

Leni Donlan (donlan@internet-catalyst.org) is an educational resource specialist
at the Library of Congress in Washington, D.C.

Maurice Elias (HPUSYme@aol.com), professor of psychology at Rutgers
University, is a member of the Leadership Team of the Collaborative for the
Advancement of Social/Emotional Learning and a nationally recognized expert on
child and parental problem solving.

Steve Feld (sjfeld@erols.com) is the computer graphics instructor and
Webmaster at John F. Kennedy High School in The Bronx, New York. His team
won an award in the Microsoft Challenge, and he designed an educational Web
site entitled "Why Is the Mona Lisa Smiling?"

Melanie Fernandez (m.fernand@verison.net) is an adjunct professor of education at the University of South Florida in Tampa.

Scott Fredrickson (frederickson@unk.edu) is a professor of instructional
technology at the College of Education, University of Nebraska at Kearney.

Jacqueline Glasgow (lyceum@trumball.kent.edu) is with Kent State University,
Trumbull Campus, Warren, Ohio.

Jeanie Hemmer (jlhemmer@teacher.esc4.com) is a technology-mentor teacher
with the Cypress-Fairbanks Independent School District in Houston, Texas.

Bob Hodges (hodgesb@msn.com) is an elementary school teacher at Apollo
Elementary School in Issaquah near Seattle, Washington. Bob also teaches educational technology seminars to teachers and provides inservice training on task
computing (see *Learning & Leading with Technology,* vol. 25, no. 2) and electronic
books.

Diane Horban (dmhorban@earthlink.net) is a gifted/enrichment resource
teacher for grades 4–6 at Glen Grove School in Glenview, Illinois.

Terry Hongell (hongell@pocantico.lhric.org) is a computer teacher at
Pocantico Hills School in Sleepy Hollow, New York.

Elaine Insinnia (elaine@columbia.bhs.k12.nj.us) is a middle school English teacher in Berkeley Heights, New Jersey, and coauthor of *Educators Take Charge: Teaching in the Internet Revolution—The Liberation, Transformation, and Metamorphosis of Two Teachers* (ISTE, 1998).

Candace Katz (ckatz@neh.gov) has served at the National Endowment for the Humanities for 16 years and is director of the Division of Education Programs. Before joining the NEH, she was an assistant professor of English at Northeastern University in Boston and an attorney at the U.S. Department of Health and Human Services.

Ken Kwajewski (kentheq@aol.com) is a teacher and media/technology director at West Middle School in Andover, Massachusetts.

Kim MacGregor (smacgre@lsu.edu) is an associate professor of educational technology and research at the Department of Educational Leadership and Research at Louisiana State University in Baton Rouge.

Kathleen Martin (martink@u.washington.edu) is the director of the education program at the University of Washington in Seattle.

Eileen Skarecki (esp@columbia.bhs.k12.nj.us) is the K–12 technology coordinator for the district of Berkeley Heights, New Jersey, and coauthor of *Educators Take Charge: Teaching in the Internet Revolution—The Liberation, Transformation, and Metamorphosis of Two Teachers* (ISTE, 1998).

Fanny Sosenke (fsosenke@parktudor.pvt.k12.in.us) teaches seventh-grade math at Park Tudor School in Indianapolis, Indiana. She also teaches education classes at Indiana University–Purdue University at Indianapolis, and works as a mathematics consultant, giving workshops and presentations on math reform in the United States and Uruguay, her country of origin.

Patty Taverna (taverna@ pocantico.lhric.org) teaches second grade at Pocantico Hills School in Sleepy Hollow, New York.

Jarnail Singh Tucker (JarnailSingh1184@aol.com) is a sophomore attending Watchung Hills Regional High School in Warren, New Jersey. He has enjoyed writing prose as well as poetry for more than six years and plans to pursue freelance writing alongside a career as a financial consultant.

Cassandra Van Buren (cvb@trinity.edu) is an assistant professor in the Department of Communications at Trinity University in San Antonio, Texas.

Susan Watts-Taffe (smwatts@tc.umn.edu) is an associate professor in the Department of Curriculum and Instruction at the University of Minnesota, where she teaches courses and conducts research in literacy education. She has published in a variety of areas related to literacy, including vocabulary development, students experiencing difficulty, and cultural and linguistic diversity, with an eye toward helping teachers to grow as effective instructional decision-makers.